WHICH PATH
TO PERSIA?

Which Path to Persia?

Options for a
New American Strategy toward Iran

Kenneth M. Pollack
Daniel L. Byman
Martin Indyk

Suzanne Maloney
Michael E. O'Hanlon
Bruce Riedel

BROOKINGS INSTITUTION PRESS
Washington, D.C.

Copyright © 2009
THE BROOKINGS INSTITUTION
1775 Massachusetts Avenue, N.W., Washington, D.C. 20036
www.brookings.edu

A SABAN CENTER AT THE BROOKINGS INSTITUTION BOOK
Originally released as Analysis Paper 20, May 2009

Library of Congress Cataloging-in-Publication data
Which path to Persia? : options for a new American strategy toward Iran /
Kenneth M. Pollack ... [et al.].
    p.   cm.
Includes bibliographical references and index.
Summary: "Presents policy options available to the U.S. in crafting a new
strategy toward Iran. Considers four solutions: diplomacy, military, regime
change, and containment, pointing out that none is ideal and all involve
heavy costs, significant risks, and potentially painful trade-offs. Addresses
how these could be combined, producing an integrated strategy"
—Provided by publisher.
   ISBN 978-0-8157-0341-9 (pbk. : alk. paper) 1. United States—Foreign
relations—Iran. 2. Iran—Foreign relations—United States. I. Pollack,
Kenneth M. (Kenneth Michael), 1966– II. Title.
   JZ1480.A57I72 2009
   327.73055—dc22   2009020912

1 3 5 7 9 8 6 4 2

Printed on acid-free paper

Typeset in Minion

Composition by Peter Lindeman
Arlington, Virginia

Printed by R. R. Donnelley
Harrisonburg, Virginia

Contents

PREFACE

Which Path to Persia? Options for a New American Strategy toward Iran is a product of the Saban Center for Middle East Policy at the Brookings Institution. The essays were written by Saban Center scholars Daniel Byman, Martin Indyk, Suzanne Maloney, Michael E. O'Hanlon, Kenneth M. Pollack, and Bruce Riedel. Kenneth Pollack also served as the overall editor.

None of the ideas expressed in this volume should be construed as representing the views of any of the individual authors. The collection is a collaborative effort, and the authors attempted to present each of the options as objectively as possible, without introducing their own subjective opinions. The aim was to highlight the challenges of all the options and to let the reader decide which might be the best to go forward.

The authors are deeply grateful for financial assistance from the Smith Richardson Foundation, the Crown Family Foundation, and others in the drafting and publication of this study.

All statements of fact, opinion, or analysis expressed are those of the authors and do not reflect the official positions or views of the CIA or any other U.S. government agency. Nothing in the contents should be construed as asserting or implying U.S. government authentication of information or agency endorsement of the authors' views. This material has been reviewed by the CIA to prevent the disclosure of classified information.

WHICH PATH TO PERSIA?

The Trouble With Tehran

U.S. Policy Options toward Iran

What should the United States do about Iran? The question is easily asked, but for nearly 30 years, Washington has had difficulty coming up with a good answer. The Islamic Republic presents a particularly confounding series of challenges for the United States. Many Iranian leaders regard the United States as their greatest enemy for ideological, nationalistic, and/or security reasons, while a great many average Iranians evince the most pro-American feelings of any in the Muslim world. Unlike other states that may also fear or loathe the United States, Iran's leaders have consistently acted on these beliefs, working assiduously to undermine American interests and influence throughout the Middle East, albeit with greater or lesser degrees of success at different times. Moreover, Iranian foreign policy is frequently driven by internal political considerations that are both difficult to discern by the outside world and even harder to influence. More than once, Iran has followed a course that to outsiders appeared self-defeating but galvanized the Iranian people to make far-reaching sacrifices in the name of seemingly quixotic goals.

Despite these frustrating realities, the United States is not in a position to simply ignore Iran, either. Iran is an important country in a critical part of the world. Although Tehran's role in creating problems in the Middle East is often exaggerated, it has unquestionably taken advantage of the growing instability there (itself partly a result of American missteps) to make important gains, often at Washington's expense. Meanwhile, the 2007 National Intelligence Estimate on Iran, properly understood, warned that Tehran was likely to acquire the capability to manufacture nuclear weapons at some point in the next decade.[1]

AN UNDISTINGUISHED RECORD

Perhaps not surprisingly, the track record of U.S. policies toward Iran is not particularly impressive. Since 1979 Washington has tried everything from undeclared warfare to unilateral concessions. These policies have done better at limiting Iranian mischief making than their critics will admit but have largely failed to convince Tehran to drop its support for terrorist groups, its pursuit of a nuclear weapons capability, or its wider efforts to overturn the regional status quo.

For its part, the Bush 43 administration had no explicit policy toward Tehran for its first two to three years. The administration simply did not know what to do about Iran and relegated it to the "too hard box," which led to crosswise tactical decisions—like accepting Iranian cooperation against the Taliban and al-Qa'ida early on but musing indiscreetly about bringing regime change to Tehran after Kabul and Baghdad. Only in 2003–2004, after the surprising progress of Iran's nuclear program was revealed, did Washington adopt a deliberate approach to Tehran. In part because of the inherent difficulties in dealing with Iran, and in part because of the deep divisions within the Bush 43 administration, the resulting policy attempted to straddle at least two very different approaches: attempting to mobilize international pressure on Iran to give up its nuclear program while retaining, at least rhetorically, the threat to pursue regime change (if not military action)—and being unwilling to take further actions in the diplomatic sphere that were seen as "soft" on Tehran or otherwise inconsistent with regime change.

The U.S. officials charged with implementing the Bush administration's policy of diplomatic pressure on Iran played a weak hand surprisingly well. Despite the constraints placed on them—particularly their inability to offer significant positive incentives to Iran or to other key international actors to secure their cooperation—they devised novel financial sanctions that caused real pain in Tehran and convinced reluctant foreign governments to apply ever greater pressure, including four UN Security Council resolutions enacted under Chapter VII of the UN Charter.

Despite these accomplishments, the Bush administration's approach was wearing thin before the president left office. Although battered, Tehran has so far withstood the international pressure and has made steady progress toward acquiring a nuclear capability. Throughout the region, Iran's star is seen as waxing while that of the United States wanes. Consequently, there is an emerging consensus within the American foreign policy establishment that the Obama administration will have to adopt a new policy toward Iran, and possibly a more ambitious one, that can succeed where its predecessors have failed.

The political, think-tank, and academic communities have not been reticent about proposing new Iran policies, but the overall result has been somewhat disappointing. No one has been able to devise an approach toward Iran that would have a high likelihood of achieving American objectives at a reasonable price. Moreover, the options that have been proposed often seek to accomplish very different goals depending on what the respective advocate believes the United States should be seeking to accomplish. The result has been a cacophony that has confused far more than it has clarified at a time when the American people and their new president desperately need a clear-eyed explication of the various options available so that they can make an informed choice regarding which course to follow.

President Barack Obama has already taken up this gauntlet. Since coming to office, he and Secretary of State Hillary Clinton have repeatedly stated that they would like to begin a process of direct dialogue with Tehran. Still, the president has emphasized that such engagement will be part of a wider strategy of carrots and sticks aimed at encouraging Tehran to modify its behavior. In particular, the president has made clear that he hopes to build an international consensus to impose much harsher sanctions on Tehran should the Iranian leadership refuse Washington's newly extended hand of friendship. Whether this approach can do better than its predecessors remains very much up in the air. At the very least, it should be thoroughly examined and tested to determine how best to implement it, and to try to ascertain the likelihood of its success. Moreover, because its prospects are uncertain and American policies toward Iran have a bad habit of falling short of their mark, it is also important to consider alternatives, contingencies, follow-ons, and fallbacks from the administration's chosen approach.

A Very Hard Target

The problem of formulating an effective new U.S. policy toward Iran starts in Tehran. Since the 1979 Islamic Revolution, much of the Iranian leadership has harbored considerable antipathy toward the United States. Ayatollah Sayyid Ruhollah Musavi Khomeini himself saw the world as a Manichean struggle between good and evil, with Iran standing as the champion of good (and of Islam, synonymous concepts in his mind) and the United States as the champion of everything evil. This set of beliefs lay at the core of his thinking and became a foundational element in the philosophy and claims to legitimacy of the regime.[2] While there is no question that some Iranian leaders and most of the Iranian people would like better relations with the United States, this core belief continues to inspire other, often more powerful, Iranian actors and institutions.[3] In particular, Iran's president, Mahmud Ahmadinejad, is by all accounts a devout adherent to Khomeini's conception, including his philosophical suspicion and loathing of the United States.[4] Even among those Iranian leaders who have long since moved beyond the imam's ideology, many still see the United States as a more traditional rival in southwest Asia, where a great many Iranians believe that their nation should, by nature or divine right, hold some form of dominion.[5] Khomeini's successor, Ayatollah 'Ali Khamene'i, may or may not share his predecessor's hatred of America, but his words and deeds indicate that he is deeply suspicious, even fearful, of the United States.[6]

As a result, the question of Iran's relationship with the United States has been the "third rail" of Iranian politics since before Khomeini's death in 1989. Pragmatic elements in the Iranian leadership have frequently argued for improved ties with the United States, largely based on the need for Iran to end its political and (especially) economic isolation and begin to revive its revolution-, war-, and corruption-ravaged economy. At various times, these figures have even attempted to open covert channels of communication to the United States to lay the groundwork for a rapprochement, most notably in 1986 (in what became the Iran-Contra scandal), 1995, and 1998–1999. However, in every case the effort was uncovered by more hard-line elements in the regime and was quickly throttled.

Meanwhile, Iran's hard-liners—who have consistently advocated a policy of across-the-board confrontation with the United States by subverting American allies, supporting militant groups that seek violent change to the

Middle Eastern status quo, and even mounting acts of terrorism—have not fully succeeded in steering Iran's America policy either. At times, Tehran's course has leaned hard in their direction, such as in 1987–1988 when Iranian forces attacked U.S. naval vessels in the Persian Gulf, 1992–1997 when the Iranians mounted a diplomatic and terrorist offensive against the United States and its allies in the Middle East, and 2006–2008 when Tehran provided Iraqi insurgents with weapons capable of killing large numbers of American soldiers in hope of driving the United States into a rapid withdrawal. However, even in these instances, Iran's collective leadership typically refrained from adopting the hard-liners' most extreme positions and even made important concessions to the pragmatists.[7]

Thus, seen from Washington, Iran's course has often seemed peripatetic and perplexing. For long periods, Iran has appeared to be America's Middle Eastern nemesis, supporting every nation, group, or person who wished the United States harm and trying to block virtually everything the United States sought to accomplish, often simply because it was the United States making the effort. Then, often with little warning, Washington would note a slight change in rhetoric or an obscure overture of unknown, but unquestionably Iranian, provenance. In 1986 and 1998, Washington reacted quickly and took considerable risks to reciprocate and make clear its desire for better relations. In 1995 the United States was much tardier, in large measure because the Iranian gesture was especially oblique. In 2003 the United States simply ignored the opening from Tehran. Nevertheless, in every case, because those Iranians desirous of rapprochement were unable to overcome the entrenched psychological and political enmity toward the United States of other Iranian leaders, the overtures quickly evaporated regardless of how rapidly, generously, or enthusiastically Washington responded.

Of course, America was not exactly an innocent bystander in these cycles of confrontation and collaboration. Oftentimes, bellicose American actions (meant as such or merely interpreted as such in Tehran) triggered belligerent Iranian responses. In 1987–1988, the Reagan administration, despite all its cowboy bravura, was dragged into escorting Kuwaiti tankers, but Tehran assumed that the United States eagerly sought the opportunity to attack Iranian naval and air forces in the Persian Gulf. On the other hand, some members of the U.S. Congress in the mid-1990s and some members of the Bush 43 administration in 2004–2006 appeared to be trying to deliberately provoke Tehran, and the Iranians took the bait. It is almost certainly the case, therefore, that even the most well-disposed observers in Tehran view American policy as equally confused and confusing.

The net effect has been that the U.S.-Iranian relationship has functioned like the proverbial pendulum. At times, the United States and Iran have developed tacit working relationships (such as over Afghanistan and toward al-Qa'ida in 2001–2003) or even kabuki-like courtships (such as in 1998–2000). At other times, the two sides seemed poised on the brink of war (as in 1987–1988, 1995–1997, and 2006–2007).

Because it seemed so hard for U.S. and Iranian overtures to coincide, and because the Iranian gestures appeared inevitably to be throttled by the regime's more hard-line elements, over time, American policymakers increasingly saw the Iran issue as a loser. Any effort to be proactive with Iran, either to try to engage it and entice it into a better relationship, or to confront it and try to force it to behave better, ended up in the same frustrating nowhere where it had begun. Because the Iranian leadership was consistently unwilling to jettison its ideological, political, and nationalistic antipathies toward the United States, it was never willing to accept American offers for better relations, most notably during 1989–1991 under the Bush 41 administration and in 1998–2000 under the Clinton administration. Because Tehran was also willing to allow further erosion of the Iranian economy and to accept varying degrees of international isolation and sanctions, whatever pressure the United States imposed kept Tehran weak but did not force a fundamental change in Iranian foreign policy. In Washington, Iran policy increasingly was viewed as a fruitless necessity, one that policymakers sought to ignore to the extent they possibly could.[8] Indeed, this sentiment seemed to be the prevailing view of Bush 43 senior officials in the early years of that administration. Even among the academic and think-tank communities, for most of the period between 1992 and 2003—except for the brief period between 1998 and 2000 when Clinton tried, ultimately unsuccessfully, to secure a rapprochement with Muhammad Khatami—work on Iran policy was largely relegated to a small community of experts, whose proposals were primarily tactical, not strategic, in nature—and even then these were frequently ignored by the policy community.[9]

The transformation of American and Iranian fortunes in 2002–2004 sparked both the interest in a proactive policy toward Iran and an agitated new debate over what such a policy should encompass. Prior to 2002, Iran was seen (by the United States and many countries throughout the Middle

East) as a difficult but largely marginalized troublemaker with the strength to play the spoiler in Arab-Israeli peace negotiations and Lebanese politics but unable to mount any more of a threat than that. Indeed, many Iran experts began to see the regime as increasingly anachronistic and likely to evolve slowly into something more benign over time—although it could certainly do some damage before that happened. From this perspective, there seemed to be little need for a dramatically new American strategic approach to deal with Iran.[10]

However, in 2002–2004, Iran's position seemed to reverse itself. The International Atomic Energy Agency confirmed the revelations of Iranian oppositionists that Tehran's nuclear program was far more advanced, and closer to being able to produce nuclear weapons, than had previously been known. At the same time, the United States overthrew the Taliban's regime in Afghanistan and Saddam Husayn's regime in Iraq—thereby eliminating Iran's two greatest regional security threats. Washington's catastrophic mishandling of the reconstruction of both of those countries bogged down the United States—militarily, politically, and economically—and greatly hampered the Bush administration's ability to deal with Iran or other regional actors looking to challenge the status quo. Worse still, because Tehran wielded considerable influence with armed groups in both countries, it could threaten vital American interests in Iraq and Afghanistan if it chose to do so and was able to contribute to the military and political problems of the United States in both. Compounding these vulnerabilities, the Bush administration botched political developments in both Lebanon and the Palestinian territories, causing new civil strife in each. Perhaps most damaging, it did not look to quell the 2006 Israel-Hizballah or the 2008–2009 Israel-Hamas conflicts, both of which produced results that were widely seen as victories for key Iranian allies. Moreover, destabilizing spillover effects from Iraq, Lebanon, the Palestinian territories, and Afghanistan incited internal unrest in a number of countries around the region, leaving many of America's staunchest allies (and Iran's worst foes) feeling shaken and vulnerable. By 2005–2006 the United States appeared weak and in retreat all across the region, whereas Iran seemed to be leading a new rejectionist coalition that threatened to transform the Middle East's strategic landscape.

This threat, or the impression of such a threat, shocked the American leadership and forced Washington—both the Bush administration and the wider policy community—to begin thinking about Iran in ways it had not in the past. In particular, the sense of a strategic threat from Iran, even among those who believed that it was being exaggerated by others, meant that simply trying to ignore Iran or merely reacting to its latest actions was no longer sufficient. Instead, the United States had to adopt a new strategy intended to eliminate, ameliorate, or contain this threat.

Building a Better Iran Policy

Since this realization, there has been no shortage of books and articles advocating particular policy positions toward Iran. Unfortunately, these pieces have often added more heat than light to the debate over how the United States should handle the many problems presented by Iran. As a result, policy positions are routinely dismissed by partisans of other approaches as being unworthy even of consideration. The right sneers at the idea of engaging with Iran as "appeasement," and the left clamors for the U.S. government to abjure all resort to force under any circumstance. Even in the muddled middle, there is confusion regarding the priority that should be given to negotiations versus containment, and what mix of incentives and disincentives is appropriate to coerce or persuade Tehran. That confusion has arisen in part from proponents' unwillingness to take their analyses deeper than sloganeering and in part from deliberate efforts to obfuscate the real costs and risks involved in virtually every policy toward Iran. Moreover, in recent years, the debate has increasingly focused on the narrow question of Iran's nuclear weapons program (admittedly a critical concern), frequently losing sight of the wider range of American differences with Iran.

The central purpose of this monograph is to try to present the most important policy options available to the United States to craft a new strategy toward Iran, and to do so in a dispassionate, objective fashion. We have attempted to portray each option in its naked glory, without the gloss of advocacy. Each of us believes that some of the options are better than others, but we all recognize that none are perfect and all have more risks and costs than guaranteed benefits. We have also sought to present them in a similar format to try to highlight the differences among them. One of the many failings of the current Iran debate is that proponents of different perspectives are often arguing about apples and oranges—comparing policies meant to achieve very different goals as if they were meant to achieve the same ends, or starting from assumptions as if everyone were in complete agreement about these assumptions. Part of the problem is that there is no national consensus, and one of President Obama's tasks in forging a new strategy toward Iran will be to build such a consensus or at least achieve a national tolerance for his preferred course.

We argue that at least nine discrete approaches to Iran have emerged in the public debate, and it is these nine options that we treat in this study. These nine differ in a variety of ways: not simply in that they would employ different policy instruments but also because they often seek to achieve different goals. These differences reflect divergent assumptions about Iran, about the international community, and about how best to prioritize and secure American interests regarding Iran. For instance, the debate between those who favor one of the diplomatic options and those who favor some form of regime change is not just about which would be the best way to head off the Iranian nuclear program; it is also about whether the United States should be willing to accept the Islamic Republic at all.

We have further grouped these nine options into four "bundles" reflecting the similarities among several of them. Part I of the monograph treats the two diplomatic options. It begins by examining the policy option that the Obama administration has already announced will be its approach to Iran, a policy we have dubbed one of "Persuasion," by which the United States would employ positive and negative incentives to convince Iran to give up its problematic behavior. Because this policy is not guaranteed to succeed, and because many Americans may disagree with the administration's approach, we go on to address a much wider range of alternative strategies, beginning with another diplomatic option, one of pure "Engagement," that would junk all of the sanctions and focus instead on accommodation and reassurance in an attempt to persuade Tehran to mend its ways. Part II looks at the various military options—a full-scale invasion, a more limited air campaign to destroy Iran's nuclear program, and allowing Israel to mount its own airstrike against the same. Regime change is the focus of Part III, in all of its different variants: attempting to trigger a popular revolution, supporting an insurgency (ethnic or political) against the regime, and aiding a military coup. Finally, Part IV examines the idea of moving directly to a policy of Containment of Iran, in which the United States would attempt to deter Iran from trying to wield a future nuclear arsenal while hindering its ability to cause trouble in the Middle East and Central Asia.

Nine Bad Options

Most readers are likely to conclude that all nine of the options presented in this monograph are riddled with costs, complications, risks, and low likelihoods of success. Unfortunately, the available options reflect the difficulties facing the United States when it comes to Iran, rather than a paucity of thinking on the subject. Perhaps some new Kennan or Kissinger will emerge to reveal the answer to America's Persian dilemma, but it seems unlikely. Washington is probably limited to variations of the nine approaches considered in this study, all of which involve heavy costs, significant risks, and potentially painful trade-offs.

Thus, in producing this study of the policy options toward Iran, we have tried to present the options in a neutral fashion in one place and in a uniform manner that allows easy comparisons and highlights differences, and in a way that does not attempt to soft-pedal potential risks and costs. We have endeavored to provide readers a full explanation of the options without the partisan distortions typical in many of the advocacy pieces now cluttering the public debate. Moreover, by presenting them in a uniform format, we believe the reader will be able to make comparisons across the different options and see their differences—not just in approach but in goals, costs and benefits, desired end states, and necessary trade-offs. Reasonable people may favor different options, because they seek different objectives, hold different priorities, or are more willing to pay a certain price to deal with the problem of Iran, rather than because a given option is more likely to succeed.

For these reasons, each option is presented in a fairly formulaic fashion. We start with its goal and the general time frame in which the policy might be expected to achieve that goal, then provide an overview of how the policy would work, followed by a section describing what would be required in terms of resources and tasks to give the policy the best chance of succeeding. We then conclude with a rundown of the various pros and cons associated with the policy. In this effort we received invaluable help from Henri Barkey, Geoffrey Kemp, Ellen Laipson, Abbas Milani, Mohsen Milani, Carlos Pascual, George Perkovich, Danielle Pletka, and Robin Wright. All of them provided comments and criticisms that not only improved this monograph's quality but also helped remove bias.

Although the nine different approaches we present represent discrete ways for the United States to handle Iran, it is *not* the case that all of these options are meant to stand alone. Quite to the contrary. The best American strategy toward Iran would doubtless combine several of these approaches into an integrated policy, in which the different approaches would be pursued sequentially or simultaneously, and thus in a complementary fashion. However, for analytic purposes, to most clearly illustrate the differences among them—and to best reveal which options can best be integrated with one another—we have chosen to present them as separately and discretely as possible. The concluding chapter addresses how the different options could be combined to produce such an integrated strategy.

Strategy, Then Tactics

For the most part, we present the nine options in a largely "bare bones" fashion, laying them out in their broad conception without delving into too many details. We did not sketch out invasion routes or list all of the targets for airstrikes, nor did we attempt to spell out how to turn Ahvazi Arab separatists into a full-blown insurgency or to detail the myriad steps that might be tried to engage or contain Iran. That is not the purpose of this volume. Filling in the details requires a great deal of information about the specific circumstances in which the policy is to be implemented—information that is not necessarily available as of this writing. Our goal was to help readers (and perhaps members of the new administration) see the principal differences among the options more clearly, their differing objectives and end states, their differing costs and risks, their differing responses to the threat from Iran, and their different acceptability to various constituencies— foreign and domestic.

Only by seeing the options in this stark form can American policymakers accurately devise a policy that fits with their goals, perception of the Iranian threat, willingness to bear sacrifices, and prioritization of the problem of Iran versus the problems of the economy, health care, Afghanistan, Iraq, Russia, and everything else the United States currently confronts. Once these questions are addressed, the United States can adopt a policy toward Iran that fits the bill and then adapt the basic premise of the policy to the specific circumstances of the moment. But without a clear-eyed assessment of how threatening Americans believe Iran to be, what they want to achieve, and what costs they are willing to pay to achieve that goal, the details will not add up to a strategy. Indeed, another of the problems Washington has had in the past is obsessing about disputes over niggling details and, in so doing, losing sight of any coherent, overarching strategy toward Iran.

A Note on Policy Names

For nearly a decade, some scholars and experts on Iraq have advocated a policy of "engagement" with Iran, by which they meant that the United States should lift all of its sanctions and end its other efforts to constrain or punish Tehran, and instead try to entice Iran into a purely cooperative relationship. Their assumption has been that Iran reacts very badly to threats, no matter how conditional, and only a patient, long-term effort to convince Iran that the United States is not a threat of any kind will have an impact on Tehran's behavior, and then only by gradually taming the Islamic Republic over many years, if not decades. This policy assumes that the United States cannot prevent Iran from acquiring a nuclear weapons capability, nor can Washington coerce Tehran into ceasing its support for violent extremist groups or trying to overturn the regional status quo in anything like real time. Therefore, the United States simply must accept these realities in the short term, in the hope that reduced pressure and friendship will eventually bring about either a change in the regime's behavior, or even a change in the regime itself. This is also the policy that we call "Engagement" in this monograph.

However, since the advent of the Obama administration, other people (including many in the media) have chosen to call the president's new approach to Iran a policy of "engagement" because the president has stated that he wants to begin direct negotiations with Tehran. Unfortunately, this has the potential to create confusion when considering the various options available to the United States, the nine options presented in this volume.

Because the Obama administration's starting policy toward Iran features more than just a process of direct negotiations, and in particular features the threat of further sanctions if Iran refuses to meet the United States halfway— a critical difference from the usual meaning of "engagement" with Iran—we have chosen to describe this as a policy of "Persuasion" instead. Indeed, the Obama administration's policy is an updated version of an older approach that is typically referred to as one of "carrots and sticks"; however, for reasons explained in Chapter 1, we argue that this moniker should no longer be used to describe this option.

SETTING THE SCENE

Formulating a new Iran strategy is not for the faint hearted, nor is it for novices. Iran is an enormously complex country, in terms of both its government and its people. Its interaction with the world is more complicated still. It is therefore useful for the reader to keep certain critical factors in mind when considering the options—factors that will likely play a role in shaping any of the options and Iran's responses to them.

The Iranian Threat to U.S. Interests

A crucial question that the Obama administration must ponder is the threat that Iran poses to U.S. interests. Not surprisingly, there is a very wide range of opinion about the extent of that threat. Some Americans argue that Iran does not constitute a meaningful threat at all, whereas others contend that it is one of the most dangerous opponents that the United States faces.

The threats from Iran to American interests generally fall under four main categories.

SUPPORT FOR VIOLENT EXTREMIST GROUPS. On at least one occasion, a court of law has proven that the Iranian government was responsible for an act of terrorism (an assassination in a Berlin restaurant in 1992). Beyond this, there is a great deal of intelligence information indicating that Iran has engaged in other acts of terrorism and supports a range of groups that engage in terrorist attacks—including Hizballah, Palestinian Islamic Jihad, and Hamas. Iran is widely believed to have been behind the attacks on the U.S. Marine and French army barracks in Beirut in 1983, Jewish and Israeli facilities in South America in the 1990s, and the American-occupied Khobar Towers housing complex in Saudi Arabia in 1996.

Iran generally pursues a foreign policy that seeks to upset the status quo in the Middle East, and because many Iranian leaders (probably including Khamene'i) see the United States as their principal foe, they also seek to weaken the United States however they can. Iran is not the only country that has taken such a course, but unlike most, Iran will back groups that use violence to advance those aims, including violence against Americans or against U.S. allies. Hizballah (in all its various incarnations) and Hamas fall into this category because they are not just terrorists, they are insurgents—

or legitimate resistance, depending on your point of view. There is abundant evidence that Iran has provided arms to a wide range of Iraqi militia and insurgent groups and that those weapons have been used to kill Americans; there is also evidence, albeit weaker, that Iranians are doing the same for the Taliban and other groups in Afghanistan who are fighting the United States and NATO forces there.

EFFORTS TO SUBVERT U.S. ALLIES. There is strong, but not incontrovertible, evidence that Iran has aided groups seeking to overthrow the governments of Saudi Arabia, Kuwait, and Bahrain (and arguably Lebanon and Israel as well) at various times. This, too, appears to be part of Iran's efforts to weaken the American position in the Middle East, but it is also probably a manifestation of the desire of many Iranian leaders to overturn the regional status quo for both ideological and strategic reasons. To the extent that the United States sees it in its interest to have allies in the Gulf, an Iranian threat to those governments constitutes a threat to American interests.

EFFORTS TO BLOCK AN ARAB-ISRAELI PEACE AGREEMENT. Many Americans—and certainly every U.S. administration since Nixon—believe that conflict between Israel and the Arabs threatens American interests because of its potential to draw in other countries (including great powers), escalate to nuclear weapons use, overturn friendly governments, cause chaos and civil strife, and affect Middle Eastern oil exports. Although some individual Iranian leaders have bravely stated that they would accept any peace with Israel that is acceptable to the Palestinians themselves (and presumably the Lebanese and Syrians), Tehran has mostly opposed peace between Arabs and Israelis, especially peace efforts brokered by the United States. There is some evidence that Iran may have even encouraged (perhaps even ordered) various groups to mount attacks that have derailed peacemaking efforts. Thus many Americans perceive Iran's efforts to prevent Arab-Israeli peacemaking as an indirect threat to the United States as well.

DEVELOPMENT OF WEAPONS OF MASS DESTRUCTION. When asked about the threat from Iran, most Americans would probably start with its drive to acquire a nuclear enrichment capability, which is widely believed to be intended to give Tehran the capability to build nuclear weapons. However, the threat itself actually consists of many parts, only one or two of which derive from the actual possession of the weapons themselves. The other parts of this threat instead derive from fears regarding how Iran's development of nuclear weapons (or just the capability to make nuclear weapons) might heighten the other threats that Iran potentially poses to the United States.

The direct threat from Iranian possession of one or more nuclear weapons stems from the possibility that Iran would acquire a nuclear weapon and use it against the United States (either right away or at a time of crisis). Because the American nuclear arsenal is vastly more powerful than Iran's and therefore American retaliation would be utterly devastating, Tehran would only do so either if its rulers were irrational or they believed that doing so was the only way to save their own lives or the regime.[11] The rationality of various Iranian leaders is hotly debated, but American policymakers simply do not have the information that would allow them to make a definitive judgment one way or another. Most of Iran's foreign policy decisionmaking since the fall of the Shah could probably be characterized as "aggressive but not reckless," but Washington cannot categorically rule out the possibility that there are truly insane or ideologically possessed Iranian leaders who would attempt far worse if they were ever in a position to do so.

Most other U.S. fears about Iranian weapons of mass destruction stem from concerns about how possession of such capabilities, and particularly a nuclear arsenal or the ability to build one, could exacerbate the other threats Iran poses to the United States. For instance, some Americans fear that Iran might give nuclear weapons to terrorists. While there are strong arguments as to why Tehran probably would not do so, this, too, cannot be ruled out, and the consequences if it did come to pass could be truly catastrophic. Another possibility is that Iran would develop nuclear weapons and then use them against Israel or another U.S. ally, like Saudi Arabia—which stands as the great champion of Sunni Islam, opposing Iran as the champion of Shi'ah Islam. Because the United States has implicitly extended its nuclear umbrella over the Saudis, and because Israel could retaliate almost as massively against Iran as the United States could, this, too, is only likely in circumstances where Iran's leaders are irrational or face their own demise.

For many Americans, a more likely (if somewhat less catastrophic) threat in Iran's acquisition of a nuclear weapons capability is that Iran will be emboldened in its support of terrorism, violent militant groups, efforts to subvert American allies, and efforts to overturn the Middle Eastern status quo. In other words, once Iran has a nuclear capability of some kind, Tehran will believe that it is safe from retaliation by the United States, Israel, or any other country, and so it will pursue a wide variety of aggressive actions with far fewer restraints than in the past—which would likely lead to various crises, including confrontation with the United States. The acquisition of nuclear weapons or a nuclear weapons capability has made some countries behave more responsibly (China and eventually Russia), but in other cases, it has either not changed their behavior appreciably (North Korea, South Africa, and arguably India) or has made them more aggressive (Russia under Khrushchev and Pakistan). Here the concern is not so much that Iranian leaders would act irrationally, but simply that they would become even more aggressive, and would overstep and miscalculate. Over the past 30 years, there is no question that, whatever their intentions, Iranian leaders have acted aggressively (at least for periods of time) and have found themselves in extremely dangerous positions that they did not envision when they first set out. A nuclear capability would vastly increase the potential ramifications of this kind of behavior for Iran, its neighbors, and potentially the United States. As Americans learned during the Cold War, crises between two nuclear armed states are extraordinarily dangerous events and should be avoided if at all possible.

THREATS AND OPTIONS. To a very great extent, fashioning a new strategy toward Iran should be driven by Americans' perception of the threat that Iran poses. American willingness to tolerate the threat posed by Iran must be weighed against the price of eliminating the threat. The less Americans feel threatened by Iran, the less they should be willing to pay to eliminate the threat; and the more threatened Americans feel, the more they should be willing to give to eliminate it.

Indeed, one reason for the wide divergences among Americans on Iran policy is that some find Iran far more threatening to U.S. interests than do others. If one believes that Iran's leaders are irrational or ideologically blinded to the point where they would use a nuclear weapon if they possessed one, then such a level of concern would likely cause one to support the most extreme options. This is not to say that one should be unwilling to try one or more of the diplomatic or regime change options first, or even try airstrikes before going all in. But if these efforts fail, such a per-

ception of threat may well lead to the conclusion that the costs of an invasion are more palatable than the risk that Iran will employ a future nuclear
arsenal.

To some extent, the converse is also true: that one's devotion to a particular option typically reveals (at least it *should* reveal) one's perception of
the threat from Iran. Those who fervently embrace the diplomatic options
but refuse to countenance any of the military or regime change options are
implicitly declaring that while they may not want to see Iran acquire a
nuclear capability, they are not so concerned about it that they would be willing to endure the costs and risks associated with covert action, airstrikes, or
an invasion. Even the most optimistic experts recognize that it will be difficult to convince Iran to give up its nuclear program through diplomacy
alone—whether by engagement, inducements, sanctions, or some
combination—and so stopping at diplomacy means leaving considerable
probability that Iran's nuclear program will not be stopped.

The View from Tehran

The Iranian political system is one of the most complex, Byzantine, fragmented, and opaque on earth. Consequently, summarizing even just those
elements relevant to a consideration of U.S. policy options toward Iran is a
daunting task, one that requires a tremendous amount of generalization
and superficiality. Nevertheless, it is important to remember that achieving
America's goals with Iran will not be a unilateral exercise: the Iranians get a
vote, too. Ultimately, success will depend on how Iran reacts to U.S. policy
initiatives, how Washington responds to Tehran's moves, and how each side
feels about the other's subsequent actions down the road. For this reason, it
is useful to have at least a thumbnail sketch of some key features of the Iranian political scene, and how Iranians see the United States.

It is always dangerous to try to generalize about Iranian opinion because,
more than in most countries, Iran's people and its establishment tend to
have widely divergent views on almost any issue imaginable. But from the
broadest aperture, Iran seems to see itself as simultaneously very strong and
successful, and very weak and troubled. To some extent, which one an Iranian tends to emphasize often reflects his or her primary concerns.

In the international arena, many Iranians see themselves as quite strong
and are proud of having made important gains. This is certainly the case for
Iran's radical hard-line leadership, such as President Ahmadinejad and the

commanders of the Revolutionary Guards, who see Iran's efforts to put together a rejectionist front against the United States and its allies as having made great progress in recent years. Iran's two most immediate threats, Saddam Husayn's regime in Iraq and the Taliban regime in Afghanistan, are gone, and the U.S. military is bogged down in both places, limiting its ability to threaten Iran. The hard-liners perceive the military clashes of Hizballah and Hamas against Israel as having redounded to Iran's benefit and play up the popularity of Ahmadinejad—and Iran's allies, Hassan Nasrallah of Hizballah and Khalid Meshal of Hamas—among the Arab populace as further signs of Iran's strength.

Those Iranians whose sight is set more inward tend to paint a different picture. The Iranian economy is a mess, with both inflation and unemployment approaching 30 percent. Iran remains completely dependent on oil exports for its economic livelihood, but the low price of oil and projections of dramatic declines in Iranian oil production (a product of mismanagement and the inability to secure Western technology because of the sanctions) are drastically curtailing Tehran's principal revenues. Iran's oil woes make the impact of both rampant corruption and the international sanctions—formal and informal, multilateral and unilateral—far worse than it already was. Nor do most Iranians see a remedy in their political system. The regime tightly circumscribes both who may rule and what actions they may take. In 1997 Iranians elected Mohammed Khatami president because he espoused the Left's vision of far-reaching change. However, Khatami failed to bring about the change that Iranians sought, so in 2005 they went to the polls and elected Ahmadinejad president, believing that he would deliver the Right's version of far-reaching change, at least in terms of extensive economic reforms and an end to corruption. He, too, has failed and has actually made the economic problems far worse.

Iran's economic woes, and the vulnerability to external pressure that they create, have gone so far as to push its political leadership to consider engaging the United States directly in ways it never had in the past. Statements by a variety of Iranian leaders, including even Ahmadinejad, suggest that Iran would be willing to engage with representatives of the Obama administration directly. It should be noted that Iranian officials met with members of the Bush 43 administration, both covertly during 2001–2003 to coordinate policy on Afghanistan and overtly in 2007–2008 to discuss Iraq. Thus the willingness to meet is not new, but what does seem to be new is a willingness to discuss the U.S.-Iranian relationship itself rather than the narrow mechanics of a particular mutual interest.

All that said, it appears that Iran's leadership has so far only made a tactical decision to discuss these issues with the United States, but it has not yet made the strategic decision to compromise on the issues that matter to the United States—such as the Iranian nuclear program and support for violent extremist groups. To some extent, this is probably because Tehran is not sure what America's goals and intentions are, and they do not know what Washington is offering (or threatening). Whatever else is going on, it is highly likely that the Iranians will not cross that bridge until they have entered into a process of negotiations and can see what is on offer. It is worth keeping in mind that "bazaar"— market—is a word of Iranian origin. And in Iran, the bazaar is always open.

Beyond this, however, Tehran's approach almost certainly reflects the nature of politics in Iran today. As we have noted, the Iranian polity is riven with factions, and alliances coalesce and splinter with stunning regularity and alacrity, all of which makes it extremely difficult to hold together a broad political coalition capable of effecting meaningful change over time. Moreover, many key political figures align on opposite ends of the political spectrum on crucial issues. The hard-liners tend to favor a patronage approach to the economy, view improved relations with the United States as anathema, and promote Iran's nuclear program as an economic/diplomatic/security panacea. Iran's reformists as well as its more pragmatic figures favor privatization of the economy and view better relations with the United States as critical to securing the trade, aid, and investment that the Iranian economy desperately needs; and while they would like to retain at least some aspects of the nuclear program, they have shown a much greater willingness to accept limits on it in return for better international economic and diplomatic relations. In the midst of all of this sits 'Ali Khamene'i, Iran's supreme leader, who is by far the most powerful figure in the Iranian system but has preferred to rule by balancing all of Iran's fractious factions. Khamene'i seems to be deeply suspicious of the United States, and he may share the ideological sympathies of the hard-liners, but he also seems to recognize the economic realities emphasized by the pragmatists. This has placed him on the horns of a dilemma, and his tendency has been to avoid dramatic decisions in favor of one camp or another so as to preserve the status quo in the hope that this will prevent a dangerous internal political schism without doing too much harm to either Iran's economy or security. It is the sum of all of these parts that creates a system that most Iranians describe as operating according to the laws of inertia: a body at rest will remain at rest unless acted on by an outside force, and a body in motion will remain in motion unless acted on by an outside force. In other words, the complexity and rivalries of the Iranian system predispose it to try to keep doing what it has been, and thus dramatic change requires enormous effort. Given that America's goal is to change at least Iran's behavior, if not its capabilities or even the very nature of its regime, there is a very high threshold for success.

The International Scene

Although it sometimes feels as if the United States and Iran exist in a vacuum, they do not. Because the rivalry has played out in the economically vital Persian Gulf region, and because both sides have attempted to enlist support from a wide array of foreign powers, nearly everything about American policy toward Iran involves the participation of other countries. Many of the policy options presented in this volume are impossible without the full-throated support of dozens of other countries. Even those options that attempt to rely solely on the unilateral abilities of the United States would greatly benefit from foreign support—and could be badly undercut if key countries chose to actively back Iran. Consequently, the perspectives of other nations regarding Iran and the U.S.-Iranian confrontation are also important factors for Washington to consider when devising a new strategy toward Iran.

Once again, because the problems between Iran and the United States touch on numerous different aspects of the foreign, economic, and security policies of many nations, simply describing all of the potentially relevant points about every other country and how it might react to various American strategies toward Iran would fill many volumes. Nevertheless, it is useful for the reader to bear the basic points in mind when weighing the various options addressed in this monograph.

IRAN'S NEIGHBORS. None of the countries of the Middle East or South Asia are enthusiastic about the prospect of Tehran acquiring the ability to build nuclear weapons, let alone an actual arsenal. Nevertheless, their reactions have tended to range from studied indifference (Pakistan, India) to deliberate silence (Iraq, Afghanistan, Armenia) to private panic (Turkey,

Saudi Arabia, and the other Gulf states). Yet their willingness to cooperate with the United States does not always correlate with either their public or private positions.

The states of the Gulf Cooperation Council (GCC) are both the most concerned and potentially the most influential American allies in the region. In public, they have tended to say little, although they have announced plans to match Iran's drive for a nuclear energy program as a lightly veiled warning to Tehran that its continued pursuit of nuclear enrichment could touch off a regional arms race. The Gulf states have done relatively little to promote diplomatic efforts to sanction Tehran, to counterbalance Iranian influence in Iraq and Afghanistan (although the Saudis have been very active in Lebanon), or to "buy" the support of other countries for tougher measures against Iran. For example, a few large GCC weapons or transportation purchases from Russian companies might go a long way toward changing Moscow's perspective on the Iranian nuclear program, but these have not yet been forthcoming. To some extent, the GCC's reticence so far may have been fallout from the ham-fisted regional actions of the Bush 43 administration, which so alienated the Arab masses that it made it difficult for Arab governments to publicly associate themselves with anything that the United States was leading. In private, GCC rulers have left no doubt that they do not want to see Iran develop a nuclear capability of any kind, fearing that it will encourage Tehran to redouble its efforts to stir up the downtrodden Shi'i populations of the GCC, encourage violent extremists in the region, and otherwise try to subvert or overthrow the conservative monarchies of the Arabian peninsula. Nevertheless, the GCC states have been equally clear that they would not support an American (let alone Israeli) military operation against Iran, which they fear would end up creating far more problems than it would solve.

The government of Iraq is still too fragile to be making waves internationally or picking friends and enemies among its neighbors. Moreover, because of Iran's lingering influence in Iraq and the ties of many Iraqi politicians (Shi'i and Kurdish) to Iran, Baghdad has been wary of involving itself in the international dispute over Iran's nuclear program. Yet it should be noted that as evinced by the overwhelming popular support for Prime Minister Maliki's offensives against Iranian-backed militias in al-Basrah, Sadr City, al-Amarah, and elsewhere, most Iraqis retain their traditional dislike for their Persian neighbors. Few Iraqis—and probably few of the current Iraqi leaders—would want to live next to a powerful, aggressive Iran if they could do anything about it. But they can't. While Iraq has made tremendous strides forward from the civil war of 2005–2006, its domestic situation remains precarious. Most Iraqi leaders fear that the U.S.-Iranian friction might escalate to actual conflict (overt or covert) and would be fought out in Iraq, where Iranian agents and proxies would likely try to mount a major campaign against the American soldiers who will remain there until at least 2012. Thus Iraq's greatest priority has been avoiding any dispute between Iran and America that could escalate to fighting and turn Iraq into their battleground. A very similar sentiment has guided Afghan silence on the issue.

Farther afield, Israel may be the only country in the region unhappier than the GCC about Iran's progress toward a nuclear weapon and what this could mean for Iranian support of terrorists and other violent extremist groups. Israel has been locked in almost daily combat with Iranian allies (Hamas, Hizballah, and the Palestinian Islamic Jihad) for over 25 years, and Jerusalem fears that an Iranian nuclear capability will motivate Tehran to encourage its allies to increase their attacks on Israel. Some Israelis even fear that Iran would use nuclear weapons against them as soon as it acquired a small arsenal—or would give the weapons to terrorists to do so—posing an existential threat to the tiny Jewish state in the literal sense, since a few well-placed nuclear weapons could obliterate nearly all life in Israel. In public, many Israeli leaders have threatened to attack Iran to prevent it from acquiring such a capability. In private, however, they unanimously state that a diplomatic resolution would be preferable, that a military strike would probably only buy them two to three years, and that they hope they will never have to decide whether to conduct such an operation, both because of the difficulties involved and the potential for Iranian retaliation.

EUROPE. At some level, European leaders seem to agree that Iran should not be allowed to develop a nuclear weapons capability (and there is remarkably widespread agreement among them that Iran's nuclear program is meant solely to acquire weapons), *but* they also agree that it would be preferable not to impose harsher sanctions on Iran *and* that the use of force would be disastrous. European unity dissolves beyond such bland platitudes. In particular, different European states take very different positions on whether it is more important to prevent Iran from completing its nuclear program or to avoid further sanctions on Iran.

One group of European countries, led by France and Britain, has pushed hard to impose more stringent sanctions on Iran to convince it to halt its nuclear activities. This group's motivation has been primarily the preservation of the global nonproliferation norm and only secondarily the preservation of stability in the Middle East. Its argument typically has been that Iranian acquisition of nuclear weapons (and again, these countries are convinced that this is the aim of the Iranian nuclear program) would be the straw that broke the camel's back of the Non-Proliferation Treaty and would spur numerous other countries to acquire nuclear weapons—either to deter Iran's presumed arsenal or merely because there was no longer any reason for them not to do so. These nations have pushed not only for stronger action by the UN Security Council but even for multilateral action by the European Union outside of the UN process.

Another group of European countries, represented principally by Germany and a number of Mediterranean states, has tended to emphasize their distaste for sanctioning Iran. On some occasions, this group has argued that continuing trade with Iran is the best way to ameliorate Iranian behavior over time (an idea embodied in the Engagement option; see Chapter 2). At other times, it has accepted the principle of sanctioning Iran but, when it came to putting words into deeds, opposed all but the mildest actual restrictions. And on still other occasions, officials from this group have simply acknowledged that their publics have a philosophical aversion to sanctions and their governments are not strong enough to go against the popular will. Whether their position is principled or simply politically expedient, these countries have steadfastly resisted placing further pressure on Iran and are likely to do so in the future.

If Iran's nuclear program is a topic of great importance for Europe, Tehran's involvement with terrorists and violent militant groups, let alone its efforts to overturn conservative Middle Eastern governments and block an Arab-Israeli peace process, stirs little European passion. Many Europeans believe that Iran's activities in these various areas are unhelpful, even dangerous, but those activities do not seem to have the same power to galvanize European opinion (let alone action) as much as Tehran's nuclear program does. This is an important area where Europe tends both to be internally united and of a different mind than the Middle Eastern states. Consequently, confrontational polices toward Tehran can often elicit at least some support when they are tied to Iran's pursuit of a nuclear weapons capability but find little backing when meant to respond to Iranian activities in other areas that the United States considers alarming.

While Europe is united in its opposition to Iran's nuclear program (if not in the method to stop it) and in its indifference toward Iran's support of militant groups, it is divided over the nature of the Iranian regime itself. The Islamic Republic is brutal, oppressive, repressive, intolerant, paranoid, and prone to widespread human rights abuses. Although it follows some democratic practices (such as relatively competitive elections), its adherence to others—such as transparency, accountability, the rule of law, the protection of minorities, freedom of the press, freedom of religion, freedom of speech—ranges from questionable to nonexistent. This morally odious behavior is irrelevant to some European regimes and of paramount importance to others. The Scandinavian states in particular are staunch advocates of human rights, and for them, the Iranian regime's treatment of its own citizenry is a matter of great concern.

RUSSIA AND CHINA. It is widely believed that Russia and China could play critical roles in a new American strategy toward Iran. Both are important sources of weapons for Iran, including nuclear sales from Russia. Russia and China are important trading partners with Iran, and Chinese businesses especially have moved into Iran to scavenge all of the business deals that Western firms were forced to abandon because of the sanctions. Thus, if Russia and China were to follow the West in sanctioning Iran, Tehran's already precarious economic situation might turn downright perilous.

In particular, the Persuasion approach would greatly benefit from Russian and Chinese willingness to impose harsher sanctions on Iran, and because the Obama administration has already announced that it will pursue this option, Moscow and Beijing hold potential trump cards over America's course. If Russia and China cooperate with the United States, Iran will come under much heavier pressure; this may or may not be enough to convince Iran to change course, but it certainly will give Washington reason to stick with this policy for some time. However, if Russia and China oppose the United States (which, in effect, would be siding with Iran), not only would it be far more difficult for the strategy to work, but also the United States will likely drop it much faster and turn instead to different options that require less international cooperation.

Both Moscow and Beijing have publicly stated that Iran should not be allowed to develop the capability to make highly enriched uranium, which is the key ingredient for a nuclear weapon. (The Iranians probably already have that capability, at least at the theoretical level.) In addition, despite the insistence of many experts and most Iranian officials that they would not do so, both Russia and China agreed to refer Iran's nuclear program out of the International Atomic Energy Agency (IAEA) and over to the UN Security Council. They then proceeded to vote in favor of four Security Council resolutions against Iran enacted under Chapter VII of the UN Charter (which makes the resolution binding on all member states and is the chapter under which uses of force are authorized). Moreover, two of these resolutions included sanctions against various Iranian individuals and entities, again something that most experts and most Iranians never expected Russia or China to support. Thus, over the past five years, Russia and China have taken some very important steps to counter Iran's ambitions to become a nuclear power.

Yet, Russia and China have continued to do business with Iran and have not prevented their own companies from—or even cautioned them against—doing so. In fact, Chinese firms have aggressively attempted to expand their business in Iran. Likewise, Russia completed work on Iran's Bushehr research reactor, which many believe to be a front that Tehran uses to conduct research into more nefarious nuclear activities. Russia has also discussed selling Iran advanced S-300 surface-to-air missile systems, which would make it more difficult for Israel and the United States to strike Iran's nuclear facilities. The Russians and Chinese have also steadfastly refused to approve the kind of sanctions against Tehran that could put real pressure on its teetering economy. In other words, the Russians and Chinese have done far less to hinder Iran than they might—or that their rhetoric would have suggested—and a great deal to help Iran, while also helping their own finances. Neither has shown any willingness to take Tehran to task for its support of terrorism, opposition to an Arab-Israeli peace, and other efforts to upset the Middle Eastern status quo, let alone for its human rights abuses.

Many Western experts on both countries have explained this behavior by suggesting that Russia and China have conflicting interests when it comes to Iran, and therefore, which side they come down on will be determined by who is willing to offer them the more enticing deal. Both countries see Iran's acquisition of nuclear weapons as potentially dangerous, but both see the opportunity for economic benefits from trade with Iran. For its part, Russia is largely unconcerned by instability in the Middle East—in fact, problems there actually can help Russia by driving up the price of its own oil exports. Moreover, for reasons of pique and pride, Moscow relishes tweaking its former superpower rival as a way of forcing Washington to pay it the respect that Russians feel they deserve. In private, Chinese officials will bluntly say that their strategic concern with Iran is energy resources. The Chinese simplistically believe that because oil is a finite resource, they must secure access to as much of it for themselves as they can (and so prevent others from consuming it) to ensure their continued future growth. Because Iran is a pariah to so many countries, Tehran is willing to cut the kind of deals with Beijing that make Chinese planners happy, in return for Chinese diplomatic support. The Chinese have repeatedly told Americans that a precondition of greater Chinese support for harsher sanctions against Iran is American cooperation on energy supplies.

THE TICKING CLOCK

The passage of time lends urgency to the need for an effective new Iran policy. The Obama administration may well have the last opportunity to try many of the policy options detailed in this study. The November 2007 National Intelligence Estimate on Iran's nuclear program warned that it was possible (albeit "very unlikely") that Iran might be able to produce enough highly enriched uranium for a nuclear weapon by 2009, although the period 2010–2015 was a more likely time frame.[12] In March 2009, Admiral Mike Mullen, the chairman of the Joint Chiefs of Staff, stated that based on the findings of the IAEA, he believed that Iran already had sufficient low-enriched uranium to make enough fissile material for a single nuclear warhead.[13] Others have disputed that assertion, but there is no question that Iran will soon have at least the theoretical know-how to make a weapon and most, possibly all, of the physical components to do so as well.

Once Iran has acquired that capability, it may be too dangerous for the United States to attempt the military options and too late to employ either the Persuasion or Engagement options to try to convince Tehran to give up its nuclear program. Although America's consistent support for some form of regime change behind the Iron Curtain throughout the Cold War suggests that Washington might still be able to pursue this strategy toward Tehran in some form, the same example also suggests that this would have to be far more restrained than many of its current partisans hope for today. Thus it may well be the case that the Obama administration represents the last chance for the United States to adopt an effective new strategy toward Iran that could eliminate the need to conduct the grand experiment of trying to see if Americans can indeed "live" with a nuclear Iran. With that in mind, we believe it absolutely critical that Washington and the American people have a clear sense of what each of the different options entails, what it would require, and what it might achieve before deciding which path to take.

I

DISSUADING TEHRAN

The Diplomatic Options

For the new Obama administration, dealing with the long-standing challenges to U.S. interests and security posed by the Islamic Republic of Iran will be complicated by a range of intractable and unfortunate factors: the increasing urgency of the timeline associated with Tehran's nuclear program, the adverse conditions for U.S. influence in the region, and finally the curious, contradictory legacy of its predecessors' policies. While experts differ on precisely when and how Tehran may cross the nuclear threshold, the scope and pace of the Iranian program ensures that this issue will rank near the top of the agenda for President Obama's first term. Moreover, the administration will confront the enduring impact of the Bush administration's decisions to invade Afghanistan and Iraq, evict Syria from Lebanon without building up a strong Lebanese government to replace it, and hold premature elections in the Palestinian territories, all of which have expanded Iran's influence largely at the expense of America and its regional allies.

After nearly eight years of war in Afghanistan and nearly six in Iraq, there are few Americans looking for another fight in the Middle East. For that reason alone, most of the debate over what Iran policy the Obama administration should adopt has focused on diplomatic options. In turn, this debate has principally revolved around three interrelated questions:

—Can the threat (or application) of economic and diplomatic sanctions against Iran move the regime to acquiesce to international requests to change its behavior? Which sanctions would have the greatest likelihood of doing so? How does the United States convince other great powers to cooperate with such a policy?

—Is it possible to offer positive inducements—either along with or instead of the negative incentives of the sanctions—to convince Tehran to change its behavior? What would be the nature of these inducements? How does the United States offer rewards to Iran that will not be taken as a sign of weakness and merely embolden the regime's hard-liners to further dig in their heels?

—How can Washington know if Tehran is serious about diplomacy or is merely trying to draw out a process of negotiations to buy time until the regime has established a nuclear fait accompli?

The differing answers to the above questions have crystallized into at least two contending approaches toward using diplomacy as a means to convince Iran to shed its nuclear program and eschew its other efforts to overturn the Middle Eastern status quo. The first is a revamped version of the diplomatic approach that the Bush administration mostly mishandled. It would attempt to employ both positive and negative inducements to persuade the Iranian leadership that changing its behavior would be both its most rewarding and least harmful course of action. This approach, which we have called a strategy of Persuasion, is the policy that the Obama administration has chosen for its initial foray into Iran strategy.

The second is a policy of Engagement that would abandon sticks altogether in the belief that any threats simply cause the Islamic Republic to dig in its heels, even if doing so means cutting off its nose to spite its face. Indeed, in its purest form, a policy of Engagement would take a long-term approach based on the belief that by reassuring the Iranians that their fears were baseless, integrating them into the global economy, and helping their people see the possibility of a better life for themselves through a cooperative relationship with the United States and the rest of the world, Tehran would slowly change its ways, much as China did. These two diplomatic options are presented in the next two chapters.

CHAPTER ONE

AN OFFER IRAN SHOULDN'T REFUSE

Persuasion

To convince Iran to give up its nuclear program, the George W. Bush administration in 2005 adopted a diplomatic approach that employed a combination of positive inducements and the threat of economic and diplomatic sanctions if Tehran refused to comply. By the time Bush left office, the policy had not yet succeeded, although it had accomplished more than many of its critics had predicted. Many Americans believe that this approach could be revived, revised, and made to succeed under a new administration.

Immediately after his election, President Obama himself indicated that this would be the starting point of his administration's approach to Iran.[1] Since then, the administration has finished its policy review and has adopted a multifaceted version of this option.

Like all Iran policy options, this approach faces considerable hurdles. For this option, the first hurdle is overcoming the legacy of the Bush administration's efforts and demonstrating that they failed not because of inherent flaws in the strategy, but because of poor implementation. Those who favor Persuasion (sometimes infelicitously referred to as a policy of "carrots and sticks") believe that the Bush administration hamstrung the process by combining it with elements of other policy options—particularly regime change—that ran at cross-purposes. It also eschewed key diplomatic bargains that might have secured greater international support and refused to put up meaningful positive incentives that could have had a greater impact on the actions of both Tehran and the rest of the international community.

Persuasion also requires building a broad international commitment to a set of powerful sanctions on Iran to punish it for noncompliance at a time when many countries do not see the threat from Iran as a priority, and some have reason to oppose such treatment. Moreover, in the final analysis, this option (and the Engagement option as well) rests on the willingness and ability of the leaders of Iran to sort out their politics in such a way that they agree to comply with the international community. Iran's habitual pugnacity toward external pressure and the Byzantine internal politics of the clerical regime mean that any such effort inevitably begins with a hard row to hoe.

Goal

This policy is intended to convince the government of Iran to change its behavior on issues of critical importance to the United States. It is not intended to try to change the government of Iran. Shortly after taking office, President Obama attempted to underline this point in his *Nowruz* (Iranian New Year) message to the people of Iran on March 19, 2009, in which he assured Iranians that "The United States wants the *Islamic Republic of Iran* to take its rightful place in the community of nations."[2] (Emphasis added.) In other words, the president was signaling that he was ready to accept the current Iranian regime, not merely the Iranian people, back into the international community if the regime were willing to work constructively with the United States and the rest of the international community.

A key question that the new U.S. administration will have to address regarding the goals of the Persuasion approach toward Iran is whether to focus only on convincing Iran to cease its nuclear program or also to insist that Iran cease its support for terrorism and other anti-status-quo activities (particularly its efforts to hinder Arab-Israeli peacemaking).

Although there are risks in Iran's mere possession of a nuclear weapons-making capability, the most likely threat is that once Iran is believed to have such a capability, it will pursue its regional anti-status-quo agenda more aggressively than in the past. Specifically, it may provide greater support to terrorist groups and Palestinian rejectionists, it may again attempt to subvert conservative Arab regimes, it may provide arms to countries and non-state actors fighting the United States and its allies, and it may pursue a range of other actions all intended to undermine the American position, topple or "Finlandize" unfriendly governments, and otherwise reorder the region more to its own liking. Even with a nuclear capability, Tehran may still not achieve these aims, but a greater willingness to try will nevertheless result in more violence, mayhem, radicalism, and crises in a region that does not need any more.

In other words, a critical threat behind Iran's pursuit of a nuclear weapons capability is that it will intensify Iran's anti-status-quo activities, which many Americans would argue should necessitate an effort not merely to convince Tehran to halt its nuclear program but also its support for violent extremist groups and other anti-status-quo activities. Indeed, American sanctions on Iran (at least prior to 2001) were always explicitly intended to convince the Iranians to give up all of these problematic behaviors, not merely their nuclear program. As such, this policy would mirror the goals of the successful American policy toward Qadhafi's Libya, which is often seen as a model for how a similar approach should be applied to Iran.

The American Dilemma

There is a critical complication in expanding the policy goals to encompass Iranian behavior beyond its nuclear program: it could undermine the international support that is the sine qua non of the option. There is broad agreement, at least in principle, among most of the international community, and certainly all of the great powers, on the need to prevent Iran from acquiring a nuclear weapons capability. This often breaks down in practice, but it still provides an important foundation that the United States can build upon to pursue this part of its policy. However, far fewer states are troubled by Iran's destabilizing activities in the region or even its support for terrorist groups. Certainly few believe these actions troublesome enough to merit the kind of harsh sanctions that may be needed to pressure Tehran to abandon them.

Consequently, focusing purely on the nuclear program would be the surest path toward building a wide and strong international consensus against Iran, but this might not be sufficient from the American perspective to secure U.S. needs regarding Iranian behavior. Moreover, many Americans may conclude that if the United States is going to provide Iran with the kind of major benefits that the Iranians will no doubt demand to halt their nuclear program, Washington ought to get more from Tehran in return. On the other hand, if Washington insists on including Iranian misbehavior beyond its nuclear program, it will be more difficult to secure the kind of broad international commitment to impose harsh penalties on Iran for failure to comply that probably will be necessary for the policy to succeed.

TIME FRAME

The Persuasion approach holds out the potential to achieve its goals relatively quickly—conceivably in a matter of months—although a time frame of several years seems more likely. At least in theory, the United States and its allies might agree very quickly on a package of benefits to offer Tehran, as well as a series of new penalties to impose on Iran if it refused the deal. Likewise, Iran might quickly decide that the deal is a good one and accept it, and then things would move forward relatively quickly. The reality, however, is that both processes are likely to involve very complicated internal political and external diplomatic negotiations, even if they are successful. Consequently, it seems unrealistic to expect this approach to produce actual success in less than a few years. However, if there are early indications of progress on both sides, the expectation of success may produce many positive ripples long before a deal is signed. For instance, should the Iranians conclude that they want to accept whatever the international community is offering, they may decide to unilaterally shift assets away from their nuclear program so as not to waste high-value resources on a program that is soon to be shut down.

One critical challenge to a Persuasion approach that relies on positive and negative incentives to redirect Iran on key issues is that it will be extremely difficult to know when the policy has failed. The Iranian regime, as a collective entity, is unlikely to declare that it will never agree to any offer from the international community or negotiate with the United States (although some individual Iranian leaders may claim as much). Tehran seems to understand that flat-out refusals, like those preferred by President Ahmadinejad, win Tehran nothing and so antagonize other nations that they build support for further sanctions. Consequently, even if the regime does decide to reject any new offer from the international community, it probably will feign interest and simply try to prolong the negotiations. Indeed, a number of Iranian leaders have already signaled a willingness to sit down with the United States and discuss the differences between us, but so far this appears to reflect a tactical decision to talk to Washington, not a strategic decision to compromise. Moreover, many Iranians will likely calculate that German, Russian, Chinese, and other foreign officials will use any hint of Iranian flexibility to argue against the imposition of further sanctions, and so even if Tehran has no intention of agreeing to compromise, it will keep tossing out hints that it will to buttress the arguments of those desperate to avoid additional sanctions.

Because it may be impossible for the international community to recognize when this policy has failed, it will be critical to place clear time restrictions on the negotiations and require Iran to take positive, discernible steps to demonstrate that it is not merely attempting to prolong these negotiations to ward off further sanctions. (We return to this matter later in this chapter to sketch out what such mechanisms might entail.)

OVERVIEW OF THE POLICY

The core concept of the Persuasion approach remains the idea of simultaneously offering Iran a series of compelling rewards for giving up its nuclear program (and possibly ceasing its other deleterious behavior as well) and threatening to impose harsh penalties on Iran for refusing to do so. In essence, it means offering Iran a "deal," but one that also contains an implicit ultimatum: change your ways and you will be rewarded; don't and you will be punished.

Because, after three decades of sanctions, the United States has virtually no ties to Iran it could threaten to cut, the pressure on Iran must come principally from other members of the international community—particularly Iran's leading trade partners in Europe, Russia, China, India, and elsewhere.[3] This makes the Persuasion option wholly dependent on international cooperation to make it work. It is simply not possible for the United States to pursue this policy unilaterally. For this reason, the UN Security Council is the ideal mechanism through which to pursue the policy, and the Bush administration did enjoy some important successes there. It is less feasible but still possible to pursue the strategy outside the United Nations, and the Bush administration was able to secure some modest cooperation from the European Union and America's Asian trade partners outside of the UN framework.

Because the Bush administration did eventually adopt a version of this policy, the key question that supporters of a Persuasion approach—

including the Obama administration now that it has opted for this strategy—must answer is what can be done differently so that a new version can succeed where the last one failed? The heart of the critique of the Bush administration's efforts is that it was never willing to offer Iran meaningful positive inducements, both because many administration hard-liners rejected on principle the idea of any "concessions," and because the administration concurrently pursued a limited policy of regime change, which militated against taking any steps that could alleviate Iranian problems.

This failure to address the inherent contradictions in the Bush administration's approach to Persuasion undermined its incentives-based approach in two ways. First, it meant that Iranians themselves did not believe that they were getting that much for giving up their nuclear program (let alone reversing their foreign policy more generally). Certainly, any potential benefits were not ammunition enough for those Iranians interested in their economic fortunes to win the policy fight with hard-liners determined to preserve the nuclear program.

Second, the meager benefits the Bush administration was willing to offer failed to impress European and East Asian publics. American allies in Europe and East Asia are critical to an approach that relies heavily on sanctions both because they have typically had extensive trade relationships with Iran and because they can furnish exactly the kinds of capital, technology, and markets that Tehran needs to address its economic problems. Moreover, if the United States is unable to secure the cooperation of its closest allies, it is hard to imagine that it could win over Russia, China, India, and other countries with different agendas. If the Europeans and Japanese are on board with the United States, these other countries must take notice; if the United States stands alone, they can ignore us.

The populations of many U.S. allies were suspicious of the Bush administration, believing (not incorrectly) that it remained committed to regime change and was simply attempting to give an offer to Tehran that it would never accept so that Washington could then use an Iranian rejection as justification for either implementing crippling sanctions or moving to war. In addition, it was generally the case that the publics of the European and East Asian democracies were only willing to sanction Iran for refusing to comply if they believed that Tehran had been offered a deal that was so good that only a regime determined to acquire nuclear weapons would refuse. Because the Bush administration's incentives were never big enough to satisfy the

European and East Asian concerns, few of these governments were willing to consider more than modest punishments against Tehran for refusing the offer.

At this point, Iran remains very much on the wrong track, pushing hard to acquire an enrichment capability, heedless of the international consensus against it. Within the scope of the Persuasion approach, there is no question that what is most needed are new, much harsher sanctions to convince Iran to stop, reconsider, and hopefully change course. Paradoxically, however, the only way that the United States is likely to secure international support for new sanctions is if it offers up much greater rewards to Iran for doing the right thing.

Upping the Ante

The incentives offered to Iran will need to be determined through a process of negotiation with both Iran and America's allies and partners in the wider international community. In many cases, these incentives are likely to be highly complex. Consequently, only the broad contours can be sketched out. In all probability, these benefits will fall into four broad categories: nuclear energy and technology, economic inducements, security guarantees, and political incentives.

NUCLEAR ENERGY AND TECHNOLOGY. On the nuclear front, the previous offers to Iran have included attractive terms to allow Iran to build light-water reactors to generate power and arrangements for Iran to participate in an international program to master the technology of enrichment. Light-water reactors can be more easily monitored, are harder to convert quickly to military purposes, and would be under arrangements whereby spent fuel would be returned to the providing country so that it could not be employed for bomb making. These terms would have to remain as part of a new offer: since Iran has repeatedly claimed that it wants only technology and energy from its nuclear program, Tehran would have to be provided with the opportunity to meet these needs regardless of whether these motives are genuine.

The much thornier question is whether the international community should be willing to allow Iranians a limited enrichment capability within their own country. If this is allowed, it will leave the Iranians a fairly rapid "breakout capability"—meaning that Tehran could switch over to a military program and begin manufacturing fissile material for nuclear weapons fairly quickly. For these reasons, a number of European countries have stated categorically that they will *never* agree to any deal with Tehran that allows it to retain such a capacity. On the other hand, the Iranian regime has steadfastly rejected any demand to halt its program short of acquiring a complete enrichment capability and has repeatedly told its people that acquiring this capability is absolutely vital to their future prosperity. Consequently, it may not be possible to reach a deal with Iran that does not allow it to claim that it retained an enrichment capability of some kind.

When the United States and its international partners meet to discuss this particular issue, a key consideration should be the extent, conditions, and intrusiveness of any inspections and monitoring regime that Iran would have to accept as part of the deal. Simply put, the more intrusive and comprehensive the inspections regime, the more willing the international community ought to be to compromise on this issue. Nevertheless, because the potential for a breakout capability is so worrisome, the international community should insist on an Iraq-style inspections regime with a dedicated organization (perhaps within the IAEA, but definitely with a separate, much larger staff and budget) to ensure that the monitoring of an Iranian enrichment program remains active and vigilant.

ECONOMIC INDUCEMENTS. Especially given the fragile state of Iran's economy, economic inducements are likely to be both the most straightforward and most important element of a new international overture to Iran. Under the Bush administration, Tehran was offered membership in the World Trade Organization, the lifting of international sanctions (most of which exert only modest pressure on the Iranian economy), and the resumption of its presanctions trade with Europe and Japan. These were not enough to convince Iran to take the deal.

Consequently, a new strategy based on the Persuasion approach will have to hold out the promise of much greater economic rewards. These should include:

—The prospect of support from other international financial institutions such as the World Bank.

—The lifting of not only international sanctions but unilateral sanctions against Iran as well, particularly the comprehensive unilateral sanctions imposed by the United States.

—A universal settlement of all claims between Iran and the United States (which include monies owed for some Iranian arms purchases, the freezing of assets, and other matters that the Iranians believe constitute a sizable amount of money).

—The provision of positive inducements for expanded international trade and investment in Iran, including trade credits and investment guarantees for foreign firms putting capital into Iran.

—Development assistance for Iranian agriculture, infrastructure, education, energy, and environmental modernization.

The lifting of American unilateral sanctions against Iran—which the Bush administration was never willing to offer explicitly because of its attachment to regime change—could have a major impact on Iranian thinking because the average Iranian and the regime's chief economic officials ardently desire it.

SECURITY GUARANTEES. Although Tehran denies it in public, the international community assumes that Iran's pursuit of a nuclear enrichment capability is meant, at least in part, to deter attacks against Iran. Consequently, another set of positive incentives that the international community will likely have to offer are guarantees for the security of the country and its regime.

Many Americans have suggested that the United States pledge not to attack Iran, as President John F. Kennedy did for Cuba as part of the resolution of the Cuban Missile Crisis. Such a pledge may be necessary, but Washington should not assume that it will be sufficient. It is likely that Tehran will want more concrete actions by the United States (and other countries) if it is to give up the safety of a potential nuclear arsenal—even a theoretical one. It is critical that the international community, and especially the United States, provide such concrete demonstrations of good faith both because it is unlikely that the Iranian people will be swayed otherwise, and because it can assuage the residual fears of European and Asian publics that the United States is simply using the diplomatic process to set up a military operation against Iran.

The more difficult process will be to diminish the conventional military threat posed to Iran by American forces in the Middle East and Indian Ocean. The United States has vital interests in the Persian Gulf region as that part of the world is both economically vital and politically unstable. Consequently, even after the United States draws down its presence in Iraq, it is highly likely that it will still maintain military forces in the Gulf, and those forces (which can be quickly reinforced from other regions) will always constitute a threat to Iran.

The United States could make unilateral concessions to Tehran, like agreeing to deploy no more than one aircraft carrier battle group in the Gulf or Arabian Sea at any time. However, Tehran is unlikely to view this as much of a concession because of how easy it would be for the United States to break that agreement if it ever chose to. The problem is further compounded by the fact that the United States will not be willing to go much beyond that (assuming it is willing to go even that far) for fear of jeopardizing its ability to respond to other problems in the fragile Gulf region. Finally, few Americans will want to restrict Washington's ability to employ force in the Gulf without reciprocal moves by Iran. For all of those reasons, a new security architecture in the Persian Gulf constructed from a process of security discussions, confidence-building measures, and (eventually) real arms control agreements is probably the only realistic way to meet Iran's legitimate security concerns in a manner that would be palatable to the United States and its allies in the region. Thus the United States ought to be willing to offer the inauguration of just such a process (using the Commission on Security and Cooperation in Europe as a starting point), which would hold out the potential for Iran to secure constraints on the deployment and operation of American military forces in the region in return for their agreement to take on different but commensurate limitations on their own forces.

POLITICAL INCENTIVES. Iranians of virtually every stripe aspire for their country to play a leadership role in the Middle East. Indeed, many seek to dominate their immediate neighbors as did the Pahlavi Shahs in their day. Iran's nuclear program appears to be part of that drive, although the explanation for how it would bolster Iranian prestige or power, and to what end, varies from person to person. Whatever the rationale, convincing Iran to agree to a deal that would end its nuclear program—and, ideally, its other anti-status-quo activities as well—will probably also entail conditions that allow Iran to fulfill at least some of these aspirations some other way.

A key question will be whether Iranians are ready to be accepted as a legitimate participant in the international politics of the Middle East, but not the dominant state in the region, as so many Iranians want. Again, views on this vary in Tehran, but it is just unclear what the Iranian leadership would be willing to accept, and direct negotiations with Iran should help to ascertain whether there is room for compromise. Under no circumstances, however, should the United States grant Iran a position of dominance, nor should we leave any ambiguity about what we see as Iran's role in the region. Our allies in the GCC are terrified that Washington hopes to resurrect the alliance with a domineering Iran that the Johnson and Nixon administrations tried to use to keep the peace of the Gulf. Consequently, there should be no doubt in anyone's mind that accepting Iran as a state with legitimate security concerns and a political role to play does not mean granting Tehran regional hegemony.

Here as well, the idea of creating a security architecture for the Persian Gulf like that of the Commission on Security and Cooperation in Europe would be a good place to start. It would provide exactly such a vehicle for the Iranians to have their legitimate security concerns heard, and even assuaged, by the other Gulf powers, but it would also make clear that Tehran was no more than equal to the other states of the region. It would not mean giving the Iranians whatever they want, but it would mean giving them the opportunity to have their voices heard and be included as members of "the club."

Engagement

Although the process of engaging Tehran is dealt with at much greater length in the next chapter, it is important to note that it also has a role in the Persuasion approach. First, it will be extremely difficult to conduct this strategy without a more expansive dialogue between the United States and Iran than the weak, long-distance line that has existed for the past five years (if not the past 30 years). Before proposing packages of incentives to Iran, the United States will need to get a better sense of what Iran wants and what it needs. Offers will likely have to be refined and adapted through a process of negotiation before they have any hope of becoming agreements. The United States may also need to convey to Iran more directly the seriousness of the penalties that it would pay for refusing to comply. All of this would be greatly facilitated by direct engagement between Washington and Tehran.

Moreover, a critical element of the Persuasion option is for the United States to demonstrate that it wants better relations with Iran and is willing to do everything to achieve this short of accepting Iran's nuclear ambitions, support for violent extremist groups, and efforts to overturn the regional status quo. The Bush administration's refusal to speak to Iran directly conveyed precisely the opposite conviction—and so tended to reinforce the perceptions of both Iranians and others (including Europeans, Japanese, Russians, Chinese, and Indians) that Washington was not sincere and was merely going through the motions of reaching out to Tehran in the hope that Tehran would reject the offer so that Washington could then pursue a more aggressive policy. The goal should rather be to convince the Iranians that the United States wants them to do the right thing, not to trick them into doing the wrong thing to make more aggressive policy options more viable. Consequently, this approach should express a clear desire for direct engagement, not only to facilitate negotiations but also to demonstrate good will toward Iran so as to make a cooperative resolution of the current situation more likely.

In this sense, engagement with Iran is a *tactic* of the Persuasion approach, at least initially. In this policy option, engaging Iran is meant to facilitate a deal that would resolve all of Washington's many disputes with Tehran and give Iran the chance to change its behavior in fundamental ways that would allow the United States and its international partners to bring Iran back into the community of nations. If Iran accepts that deal and fundamentally changes its behavior, then the tactic of engagement shifts easily into a *strategy* of engagement. Once Iran has demonstrated its goodwill and has chosen the path of compromise with the United States and the wider international community, that same process of engagement would be expanded into the kind of strategic engagement envisioned in the next chapter.

Preparing to Bring the Hammer Down

A critical element of the Persuasion option, and largely what sets it apart from the Engagement option, is the need to secure international agreement on a series of painful sanctions to be imposed on Iran if it turns down the package of benefits. The sanctions need to be made clear to Iran as the punishment for refusing to take the deal *at the same time it is proffered.* In addition, the negotiations within the international community on the sanctions need to be an integral part of working out the details of the benefits so that the United States and other countries more willing to sanction Iran (like France) can trade benefits for sanctions with those states less inclined to penalize Iran for its recalcitrance.

These sanctions need to be more painful than those imposed on Iran so far, but they probably should be graduated—meaning that they can start out less painful and grow more onerous over time if Iran continues to refuse the deal. A graduated approach of ratcheting up the pressure on Iran will make many countries more comfortable with the process since it would mean that Iran would have ample opportunity to reverse course before the most painful measures are imposed.

So far, most of the UN Security Council sanctions on Iran have had little impact because they have targeted the travel and foreign assets of individuals and Iranian entities connected to its nuclear program. The financial sanctions imposed on Iran both multilaterally and unilaterally by the United States and a number of European countries have been far more threatening to Tehran, and many Iranians seem to believe that they are contributing to Iran's current crop of serious economic problems.[4]

This demonstrates that future sanctions against Iran must be directed primarily against the Iranian economy. This is Iran's Achilles' heel, and little else has meaningful impact on the political debate of the Iranian leadership. In particular, new sanctions on Iran should focus on further curtailing Iranian financial activities and preventing the foreign investment that Iranians desperately need. Going after Iran's ability to secure insurance and reinsurance from international firms could further strain the country's finances. Some direct trade sanctions might also be appropriate, but they will need to be designed very carefully. Prohibiting trade can have an immediate impact on the civilian population, and if it causes deaths or illness (especially among children), can quickly undermine international support for the sanctions, as was the case with the UN sanctions on Iraq in the 1990s.

Nevertheless, there are some important exceptions to these rules. For instance, one noneconomic trade sanction that ought to be on the table is an international ban on arms sales to Iran. Similarly, if the international community wants to continue to punish specific Iranian institutions rather than the entire system, a better candidate than entities like the Revolutionary Guards would be the massive *bonyads*, so-called charitable organizations established after the revolution that control as much as half of the economic activity in Iran and are among the worst sources of the endemic corruption in Iran. These control dozens, if not hundreds, of subsidiaries that, along with quasi-state-controlled companies, dominate the Iranian economy and serve as critical sources of graft for various regime officials. Sanctioning these entities by preventing them from conducting international financial transactions would not only hit at institutions of far greater importance to the regime but would also take aim at organizations widely loathed by the Iranian people, a rare and fortuitous circumstance in the history of economic sanctions.

WEIGHING OIL AND GAS SANCTIONS. Potentially the most devastating sanctions the international community might levy against Iran would focus on its hydrocarbon economy. Iran is highly dependent on its oil exports for revenue and its gasoline imports for transportation. Prohibiting either one could cripple the Iranian economy and cause massive problems throughout Iranian society. For this reason, many have advocated such sanctions as being the only sure way to exert enough pressure to motivate the Iranian regime to give up its nuclear program.

This logic may well be correct, but there are real risks if it proves otherwise. The oil market remains volatile right now, and the loss of Iran's 2.5 million barrels per day of exports could push oil prices back up to economically damaging levels. For this reason, there is little international appetite for preventing Iran from exporting oil. By the same token, if the international community were to prohibit (or even limit) Iranian gasoline imports, there is a real risk that the regime would respond by suspending its oil exports, causing the same problem. After all, from Tehran's perspective, the restriction of gasoline imports could risk causing the collapse of the Iranian economy and thus the regime itself. In such circumstances, Iranian leaders may see little point in restraint because they may not feel that the loss of their oil revenue is as important if they cannot purchase one of their most essential imports. Or they may calculate that the only way that they can persuade the international community to give up a gasoline embargo is to do the one thing that would threaten the economy of the international community.

Prohibiting gasoline sales to Iran could also be so draconian that it would actually undermine the sanctions altogether. As noted above, it takes long periods of time for economic sanctions to have their impact and persuade a recalcitrant regime to take an action it hopes to avoid. This means that for sanctions to work, they must be sustainable for months or years. However, as history has shown—most dramatically in the case of Iraq under Saddam Husayn—sanctions that are considered excessively harsh and are believed to be causing widespread malnutrition, starvation, medical problems, and ultimately the death of innocent people (especially children) are unsustainable, regardless of the accuracy of those perceptions. If the international community were to cut off Iranian gasoline imports, it is virtually axiomatic that the Iranians would claim that innocents were dying, for example, because food could not be produced or distributed, homes could not be heated, and ambulances could not rush seriously ill people to the hospital. These claims might prove entirely false, but the sight of dead children whose deaths are said to be related to the sanctions would likely undermine international support for the sanctions, regardless of the Iranian regime's behavior.

For these reasons, sanctions against Iran's hydrocarbon economy, particularly its vulnerable gasoline imports, probably should be used only as part of a final set of sanctions at the end of a longer process of ratcheting up the pressure on Tehran—if they are employed at all.

NAIL DOWN THE SANCTIONS UP FRONT. An important lesson from the experiences of the Bush administration on Iran, as well as the Clinton administration's efforts to deal with Saddam Husayn, is the need to agree on specific sanctions and announce them as warnings long before they are to come into effect. Although the great powers all agreed during the Bush 43 years that Iran should not be allowed to acquire a uranium enrichment capability, and that it should be punished for refusing to comply with various UN Security Council demands embodied in resolutions enacted under Chapter VII of the UN Charter (which makes them binding upon all member states), whenever it came time to actually impose such sanctions on Iran, reluctant countries were able to weaken the actual resolutions to the point where they had little bite.

It is always easier to agree on harsher sanctions if the negotiations are conducted well before any sanctions are likely to be imposed. The key is then to codify those sanctions—and ideally write them into the very resolutions making the demands—so that they cannot be watered down when it comes time to impose them. Of course, the Iranians and their supporters would doubtless try even then, but the best chance that the United States has of securing harsh international sanctions is unquestionably to codify them and secure public, international consensus on them long before they actually need to be implemented. Codifying the sanctions to be incurred for failure to comply at each step of the process is also critically important so that the Iranians have a clear sense of the pain they will suffer if they fail to comply. Only in this way and only if the sanctions were very painful would those Iranians arguing for accommodation with the international community be able to demonstrate that the price Iran would pay for continued intransigence would be too high. The repeated ability of Iran's allies in the Security Council to water down sanctions resolutions has convinced most of the Iranian leadership that their allies will be able to do so in the future. Only if Tehran sees that the sanctions are daunting and were agreed to ahead of time would it be likely to reconsider its course of action.

UNAMBIGUOUS TRIGGERS. George Perkovich of the Carnegie Endowment has compellingly argued that another critical element of any new sanctions on Iran is to tie them, to the extent possible, to detectable Iranian actions. The more it is the case that new sanctions are triggered by Iranian actions (with both the actions and the sanctions to be imposed agreed to beforehand), the harder it will be for those who oppose further sanctions to avoid them. As Perkovich points out, because Iran has endlessly insisted that its nuclear program is intended only for civilian energy purposes, it ought to be possible for the UN Security Council to forbid certain actions that are only consistent with nuclear weapons production and demand other actions that are only consistent with nuclear energy production. Harsh sanctions should be used as penalties for Iran's unwillingness to do either. This scenario would make it very hard for the Russians, Chinese, and others to argue against the penalties.

Some examples of Iranian actions that could be tied to specific sanctions include:

—An Iranian withdrawal from the Non-Proliferation Treaty, which could only be interpreted as intent to build weapons with the uranium they have enriched.

—Iranian unwillingness to sign the additional protocol to the Non-Proliferation Treaty, which provides for much more aggressive and comprehensive inspections, and which Tehran has repeatedly said it has accepted, although no Iranian government has ever actually ratified it.

—Further enrichment of low-enriched uranium (LEU), which is adequate for energy generation, to highly enriched uranium (HEU), which is really only necessary for nuclear weapons.[5]

—A failure to convert the LEU that Iran now possesses into fuel rods for reactors. The Security Council, working through the IAEA, should demand that Iran convert all of its LEU into fuel rods—which ought to be acceptable to Tehran given its claims that it wants nuclear energy, not nuclear weapons.

—Continued storage of LEU near Iran's centrifuge cascades—where it could easily be enriched to HEU for weapons. Indeed, the IAEA should demand that Iran establish a storage facility for all of its LEU far from its centrifuge plants, with appropriate safeguards and regular inspections by the IAEA to account for all of the LEU Iran has produced.[6]

Under circumstances in which Tehran may be attempting to sow confusion and create ambiguity, this is an extremely useful approach to the problem of how to impose sanctions on Iran for its misbehavior. However, it cannot be the only method of imposing new sanctions on Iran. As noted above, negotiations over a deal cannot be allowed to become a means by which Iran simply avoids any penalties. Consequently, other sanctions will have to be tied to certain deadlines—Iran must accept either key pieces of or the entire deal being offered by the international community by a prescribed time, or it will face other penalties. Otherwise, Tehran may have no incentive to ever take the deal or reject it, and it will simply be able to keep playing for time.

The Ends, Not the Means

Because it will be difficult for a Persuasion approach to work under any circumstances, it would be preferable for the United States and its allies to concentrate purely on the outcome of the process and less (or not at all) on the process itself. What is important is securing international support and convincing the Iranians to accept the deal on offer; everything else ought to be incidental from an American perspective.

Some Americans have argued that the deal ought to be part of a "grand bargain" between Tehran and the West (or the whole international community) because Iran will only be able to make the necessary concessions in the context of securing its needs on a host of other issues. Others have argued that such a grand bargain would simply be too much for the Iranian system to handle, and so the United States and the international community should instead seek incremental agreements and/or deals on various pieces of the whole, both of which could be more easily digested by Tehran. Ultimately, it should be left to the Iranians to decide which approach is most palatable for them, and the United States and its allies should make very clear that they are amenable to either approach. It should not matter how the United States gets to the outcome, only that it gets there. Given how many hurdles the United States will face, it should not add more unnecessarily.

For the same reasons, the United States should be willing to allow the Iranians to define who and how they meet, as well as where. Some analysts argue that Americans must be present at the table when offers are put to the Iranians to demonstrate U.S. commitment to them. Others have insisted that an American presence at the table would make it impossible for Tehran to accede to any such offer. Again, all that matters is whether *the Iranians* want Americans at the table.

The one related element of process that does transcend the general rule that the United States should focus on function, not form, is whether the offer should be made to Tehran secretly or publicly. Again, there is debate among Americans and others, with one side arguing that a public offer would spark Iranian nationalism and virtually force the regime to reject it, and the other countering that a secret offer would allow opponents within the regime to kill it behind closed doors and then mislead the public about its contents.

On this issue, those who argue for a public declaration of the contents of the offer have a strong case. In previous iterations, regime hard-liners have been able to prevail in the political debates over various international offers to Tehran partly because the Iranian public never really understood what was being proposed. Since one of the critical elements of this offer is the idea that the deal will be so attractive to the vast number of Iranians that the regime will not feel able to turn it down (and that European publics will likewise see it as a deal that no Iranian regime with benign intentions could possibly reject), it is *vitally* important that the terms be made public. Keeping the contents of the deal secret would undermine the central principle of this option.

That said, it would still be consistent with this policy option to initiate contacts in secret, if that were preferable to Tehran, conduct negotiations secretly, and even make the initial offer to the leadership in private. However, Tehran should understand that in these circumstances, the international community would only keep the terms of the offer secret for a set period of time, and if the leadership did not come back with a positive response before that deadline, the terms would be made public. Indeed, this could be one way to impose time limits to prevent the Iranians from simply stringing along the negotiations.

The Cape and the Sword

The question of whether negotiations with Iran should be overt or covert is related to another aspect of the Persuasion approach: what to play up and what to play down. For a variety of reasons, many Iranians are extremely sensitive to their public treatment by the United States. Thus how Washington (and its international partners) describes its policy toward Iran, what it chooses to publicize, and what it tries to keep private are all important. Unfortunately, the Obama administration has already taken some important missteps in this respect.

When threatened, Iranian leaders tend to respond defensively, rejecting the threats unthinkingly regardless of their content or the potential impact on Iran. Especially since the 1978 revolution, Tehran has frequently cut off its own nose to spite its face when threatened. Moreover, because of the Iranian regime's deep insecurity—both literally and figuratively—the only way that a policy of Persuasion can succeed (in terms of securing Iranian agreement to a deal that would preclude its acquisition of a nuclear arsenal, terminate its support for violent extremist groups, and end its efforts to overturn the Middle Eastern status quo) is if the Iranian regime is able to claim that it won a great victory from the deal. As long as the United States gets what it needs, Washington should be fine with allowing the Iranians to crow all they want, because that will be a necessary precondition for achieving American aims.

This necessity should shape America's public statements about its Iran policy as long as a Persuasion approach is being pursued, as the Obama administration has been doing so far. Quite simply, the United States should emphasize its desire for engagement and rapprochement, promote all of the benefits to the Iranian people from agreeing to do so, and talk about its desire for a cooperative, long-term relationship between these two great nations. At the same time, the administration initially should say nothing in public about the sanctions and other punishments that will be inflicted on Iran should it fail to accept the deal. First, it is self-evident that if Iran does not accept the president's outstretched hand, the United States will adopt a different approach that will not be so friendly. Second, Iran is going to find out about the sanctions anyway—Tehran has various sources who will report on the negotiations between the United States and other key members of the international community over what sanctions to impose on Iran for failing to comply or engage, trying to draw out negotiations, or taking actions clearly intended to advance a nuclear weapons program. Eventually, those threats would need to be made public, but for the Obama administration, there is still time for that. Third, because the regime will not agree to be seen as bowing to pressure, issuing constant public threats, as Obama administration personnel have done in their first weeks in office, simply undermines the ability to get the Iranians to the table (let alone agree to the compromises that would make a deal possible) and does not materially advance any American interests.

On a related note, any American administration (including the current one) that intends to pursue the Persuasion approach should never utter the term "carrot and stick" in public. Although it is simply a metaphor, even a cliché, that Americans use to describe any diplomatic policy that employs *both* positive and negative incentives, because the metaphor is derived from the way one handles a donkey, it is often offensive to the object of the policy. That is certainly the case for Iran, which has repeatedly bridled at the term, including when President-elect Obama employed it in a televised interview.[7]

This too must be kept in perspective. Ultimately, rapprochement between longtime adversaries only becomes possible when both sides have made the unilateral calculation that is in their *own* best interests to end the squabble. When both have done so, the rapprochement typically takes place, and it typically takes place despite any number of missteps and offensive statements by people on both sides. The two countries inevitably overlook these slights because it is in their own best interests to do so. This is a critical point to keep in mind when considering the potential for a U.S.-Iranian deal. Countries do not make peace as a favor to one another; they do it out of a cold calculation that it serves their interests. Any rapprochement that can be derailed by obnoxious rhetoric is not the genuine item. During the American reconciliation with China in the 1970s and 1980s, and with India in the 1990s and 2000s, reactionaries on both sides fired off outrageous verbal broadsides at the other country to try to derail the process. Washington, Beijing, and New Delhi all chose to continue to improve relations because of the benefits to each of them of doing so. Until Iran decides that improved relations with the United States are in its interest, it does not matter what the United States says, there will be no rapprochement; and once the Iranians make that decision, affronts to its dignity will lose much (if not all) of their sting.

Nevertheless, words do have impact, and they can certainly complicate a delicate rapprochement—even once both countries have crossed the crucial Rubicon of seeing the rapprochement as in their interests. These complications rarely affect the ultimate outcome, but they certainly can affect the timing of the rapprochement. Given that America's problems with Iran are closely tied to matters of timing, Washington should try as hard as it can to not prolong this process by saying careless things that would make it harder for Tehran to cooperate. Indeed, the smartest thing that an American administration pursuing the Persuasion approach could do, would be to announce that it was pursuing a policy of pure Engagement instead, playing up all of the positives and the desire for a cooperative relationship, and pushing the sanctions and all of the threats well into the background until it becomes clear that the Iranians are interested in a deal.[8]

Requirements

As its name implies, the requirements of the Persuasion approach are principally diplomatic and secondarily political. Military risks and economic costs are both likely to be relatively low. In addition to those requirements already mentioned (significant economic incentives, the possibility of compromising on enrichment, the need for a highly intrusive inspection regime, and others), the most important and potentially most onerous requirement of this option is the need to strike diplomatic deals with Russia, China, and potentially other countries to secure their support for the new offer to Iran. In particular, the United States would need their agreement to impose crippling sanctions on Iran if Tehran continues to refuse the offer.

A critical failing of the Bush administration was its unwillingness to prioritize among foreign policy issues and make sacrifices on issues of lesser importance to secure gains on those of greater importance. As a result, it never really tested whether reluctant countries like Russia and China could be brought around to support tougher moves against Iran if Tehran failed to accede to UN Security Council demands. A key element of Persuasion would be prioritization—putting Iran ahead of other considerations and then making the necessary trade-offs to secure the support of Russia, China, India, and other relevant countries.

Although the Russians certainly make money off their relationship with Tehran, they have repeatedly stated that Iran should not be allowed to develop an enrichment capability and privately signaled their willingness to cooperate with the United States on Iran in return for American concessions elsewhere—probably on issues of greater importance to Moscow, like missile defense, Georgia, Chechnya, Belarus, Bosnia, Kosovo, and/or Ukraine. Steven Pifer has suggested that an easy compromise the United States could make would be to slow down the installation of ballistic missile defense systems in Eastern Europe in return for Russian cooperation on Iran.[9] This might be expanded to an explicit deal in which the speed of emplacement and ultimate extent of American missile defenses were directly related to the rapidity of Iran's nuclear development and whether Tehran ultimately agreed to suspend or end it. This would then put the onus on the Russians to find ways to convince the Iranians to stop their program (which likely would mean joining in on tough international sanctions) if the former wanted to head off the deployment of the American missile defense systems. Especially after the August 2008 Russian moves in Georgia, it would be repugnant for the United States simply to acquiesce to the reassertion of Russian dominance over the former countries of the Soviet Union, but it may be necessary to cut some deals in order to secure Moscow's support for a tougher Iran policy. If the current administration truly cares about preventing Iran from acquiring a nuclear weapons capability and is determined to pursue the Persuasion approach to the greatest extent possible, it may find it necessary to make such hard decisions.

Similarly, the Chinese have privately indicated that their greatest concern is secure energy supplies and that they, too, would be willing to go along with harsher sanctions on a recalcitrant Iran if the United States were willing to find ways to help China with its energy needs. Setting up a joint energy committee for Chinese and American officials to begin a dialogue, as Jeffrey Bader has suggested, would be a good place to start. Another option could entail determined efforts by the United States to reduce its own energy dependence (thereby freeing up oil supplies for Chinese purchasers) and encouraging oil-producing allies (such as Saudi Arabia, Kuwait, the United Arab Emirates, Mexico, and Canada) to work more closely with the Chinese to reassure them that their energy needs will be met.

Other countries also will want payoffs from the United States in return for their assistance on Iran. Such deals may be distasteful, but many will be unavoidable if the Persuasion approach is to have a reasonable chance of succeeding. Without support from a wide range of other countries, sanctions on

Iran will prove toothless. It is not that these nations do not recognize a danger in a nuclear-armed Iran; they just do not regard it as a high priority. As a result, the United States may have to offer them some benefit on one of their higher priorities to secure their cooperation on Iran, assuming that the current administration considers it one of America's highest priorities.

PROS AND CONS

The following are the advantages and disadvantages of the Persuasion approach.

Advantages

—There is evidence that a strategy of employing both positive and negative incentives has had an impact on Iranian politics, and in the manner—though not the extent—hoped for. Throughout the 2003–2007 time frame, Iranian elites debated about their nuclear program, with a number suggesting that Iran ought to be willing to make compromises to avoid international sanctions that they feared would cripple their already fragile economy. Given that the Bush administration was never willing to offer the kind of positive inducements that might have made Iranians take notice or might have convinced Europeans, Russians, Chinese, and others to go along with the kind of harsh sanctions that might have made Iranians wince, the level of debate during this period was surprising. It suggests that a more enthusiastic embrace of this option could produce a much more intense debate in Tehran that could result in a decision to accept a deal. The success of similar approaches with Libya and (to a lesser extent) North Korea also bolsters this supposition.

—This is precisely the course that most U.S. allies would like to see Washington pursue toward Iran. This makes it most likely that Washington would secure international cooperation for this option (which, as mentioned above, is a requirement) and could translate into leverage with those allies. In other words, foreign countries may be willing to accommodate the United States to convince Washington to follow this course—especially if they believe that the new administration is seriously considering regime change, the military option, or the Israeli military option (these are discussed in subsequent chapters) as alternatives.

—Although in an era of domestic economic distress every penny counts, the costs of the likely economic incentives to Tehran would be minor—and could well be offset if U.S.-Iranian trade blossoms anew in the wake of such a deal.

—For those looking to avoid a military confrontation with Tehran, a Persuasion approach would be unlikely to produce such a conflict. It would be self-defeating for Tehran to lash out militarily in response to sharper international sanctions, and it has never done so in the past.

—For those who favor regime change or a military attack on Iran (either by the United States or Israel), there is a strong argument to be made for trying this option first. Inciting regime change in Iran would be greatly assisted by convincing the Iranian people that their government is so ideologically blinkered that it refuses to do what is best for the people and instead clings to a policy that could only bring ruin on the country. The ideal scenario in this case would be that the United States and the international community present a package of positive inducements so enticing that the Iranian citizenry would support the deal, only to have the regime reject it. In a similar vein, any military operation against Iran will likely be very unpopular around the world and require the proper international context—both to ensure the logistical support the operation would require and to minimize the blowback from it. The best way to minimize international opprobrium and maximize support (however grudging or covert) is to strike only when there is a widespread conviction that the Iranians were given but then rejected a superb offer—one so good that only a regime determined to acquire nuclear weapons and acquire them for the wrong reasons would turn it down. Under those circumstances, the United States (or Israel) could portray its operations as taken in sorrow, not anger, and at least some in the international community would conclude that the Iranians "brought it on themselves" by refusing a very good deal.

—For similar reasons, the Persuasion approach nicely sets up Containment as a fallback strategy. If the United States and the international community offer the Iranian leadership a deal so good that they should not refuse it, but still do, they will convince much of the world that they are bound and determined to acquire nuclear weapons—and probably for nefarious purposes. More to the point, the kinds of harsh sanctions that would hopefully be on the table as part of this strategy would come into force if Tehran rejected the offer. The key is that these penalties would constitute a far more powerful set of constraints than Iran has faced in the past. In this way, Containment is one of two natural outcomes of the Persuasion approach: if

Tehran accepts the deal, the threat from Iran is eliminated; but if it refuses the deal, the sanctions are imposed, creating a strong Containment option.

Disadvantages

—To be successful, a Persuasion approach would invariably require unpleasant compromises with third-party countries to secure their cooperation against Iran. In many cases, the United States would likely have to choose among very unpalatable options and decide whether securing international support on Iran is worth betraying some other national principle or interest.

—The Iranians are unlikely to give a simple "yes" or "no" answer when the deal is finally presented. As in the past, their most likely answer will be "yes, but . . ." At least initially, they will attempt to see if they can wriggle out of the ultimatum, split the international coalition, or simply improve the terms and weaken the sanctions. If this is just part of a process to improve an offer that the regime has fundamentally decided to accept, it would be annoying but not harmful. On the other hand, the regime may very well decide to reject the offer but feign acceptance while insisting on negotiating the details, and use such a process to buy time. This is why the time limits and the automaticity of the sanctions are so important; if they are not part of the deal, then the Iranians could reasonably expect to escape the punishments (and the wider emplacement of a Containment regime against them) altogether.

—Although starting with a Persuasion approach can create some advantages for both the regime change and military options, the potential for Iran to prolong negotiations could also ultimately undermine these two options. In particular, the longer that the United States or Israel waits to strike Iran's nuclear facilities, the more likely it will be that Iran will have improved its defenses, potentially diminishing the impact of the strikes. Similarly, protracted haggling over the terms of a deal (at which the Iranians excel) will muddy the clarity of the international offer, making it easier for the regime to claim that the deal fell apart over technicalities—which will obscure why the regime turned down the deal and weaken domestic incentives for regime change, as well as international resolve to impose sanctions.

—Although there is no theoretical reason why the United States could not adopt the Persuasion option and still support democracy and human rights in Iran, the reality may be otherwise. In particular, Tehran may demand an end to such U.S. practices as part of the final deal, and if Iran truly were willing to give up its nuclear program, support for violent extremist groups, and other efforts to reorder the Middle Eastern status quo, it would be hard for the United States to reject this condition. Nevertheless, such an abdication could be odious to many Americans and Iranians alike. Indeed, the policy is predicated on the assumption that what the Iranian people want most is a healthy economy, and if they are promised that, they will give up almost anything else—and if they are threatened with the ruin of their economy, they will do anything to prevent it. However, if it turns out that political freedom, not economic prosperity, is the Iranian people's highest desire, then the United States not only might be selling them out but also might discover that a core assumption of this option is wrong.

—Some Iran analysts have argued that any policy that includes sanctions is self-defeating. They contend that when faced with threats of any kind, the clerical regime consistently reacts instinctively with belligerence, even when doing so is ultimately detrimental to its own interests. Consequently, in their view, whatever potential impact the positive inducements of the Persuasion approach might have would be undercut by the reflexive negative reaction to the threat of sanctions. It is this fiercely argued but unproven belief that lies at the heart of the Engagement approach, which argues for using only carrots, not sticks.

—There are reasons to believe that this policy will simply fail because of the intricacies and dysfunctions of Iranian domestic politics. Even if the positive and negative pressures work as intended (and as the debates from 2005-2007 suggest, they can), external influences are never more than one factor in Iranian decisionmaking. Since the revolution, the Iranian regime has acted in ways that have seemed bizarre and baffling to outsiders because they appeared to run contrary to Iran's national interests. In virtually every case, it has been because the Iranian leadership has understood its interests differently from the way in which outsiders have and/or because of domestic political considerations and endless political maneuvering among the elites. Since this policy option ultimately relies on the Iranian decisionmaking process to make a difficult choice based on external strategic logic, and since the Iranian system has just as often made decisions on alternative considerations that run contrary to such logic, one should not assume that this policy is bound to succeed.

CHAPTER TWO

TEMPTING TEHRAN

The Engagement Option[1]

A s the previous chapter noted, the Bush administration tried a version of the Persuasion approach toward Iran for roughly three years and failed to convince Tehran to end its quest for a nuclear weapons capability or cease its other problematic behavior. In response, a number of Iran analysts have suggested that the problem was not the Bush administration's half-hearted and contradictory embrace of the strategy but rather that the policy itself was flawed. These analysts argue that the threat and imposition of sanctions will inevitably prompt nationalistic Iranians and a fearful regime to reject any diplomatic overture from the West, no matter what the consequences. They have recommended instead that Washington drop the sticks and instead focus on the carrots as the only way of creating a set of incentives that the Iranian regime might accept.

At the heart of the Bush administration's oscillating initiatives toward Iran was a profound uncertainty about the utility of direct engagement with Tehran in addressing America's most pressing concerns about Iran's nuclear ambitions, its support for terrorism, its quest for regional dominance, and its treatment of its own citizens. This uncertainty over engagement transcended the narrow confines of a typical policy debate and emerged as a central issue of contention between the two presidential candidates in 2008.

During the election campaign, then-candidate Obama famously announced his willingness to engage with Iran, and he has renewed this pledge since taking office. But what remains unclear, and what many partisans and experts on both sides continue to debate, is whether the Engagement option should be merely one element of a larger approach or the central (perhaps only) aspect of the new U.S. policy. The purpose of this chapter is therefore to examine engagement—as a stand-alone initiative—as a prospective policy option for the current administration.

GOAL

At one level, the goals of a policy of pure Engagement are identical to those of the Persuasion option. Engagement seeks to convince the Iranian regime to give up a range of behaviors that the United States finds threatening. It proposes to do so by offering Tehran a range of diplomatic, strategic, and economic inducements so attractive that the Iranians will gladly give up their problematic policies to secure these benefits.

However, a critical difference between Engagement and Persuasion is that Engagement makes no effort to convince Iran to change its behavior soon. Instead, it is a process left open to the Iranian regime, and, as the next section explains, there is every likelihood that it would take years for the regime to change its ways as a result of this strategy, if it does so at all. Consequently, a critical element of the Engagement approach is the implicit assumption that there is nothing that the United States or the international community can do to prevent Iran from pursuing its nuclear program to whatever end Tehran has in mind. Similarly, Engagement has no mechanism by which to try to prevent Iran from supporting violent extremist groups, subverting Arab-Israeli peace efforts, or generally destabilizing the region. Although in theory the option endeavors to convince the regime to do so, in practical terms the policy consciously surrenders any potential leverage on Iran to make it do so. It is ultimately a strategy aimed only at long-term change, although its advocates would argue that such change is both the only realistic change and the most profound change imaginable.

Indeed, at first blush, it would seem that the Engagement approach has no ambitions to change the Iranian regime, and this is certainly true in the short term. The hope of Engagement is that once this regime no longer feels threatened by the United States or the international community in any way, it will come to believe that improved relations would enhance its own power and stability, and so will choose to change its ways. Indeed, with this approach, success would have to be defined in a way that falls short of achieving any maximalist conception of Washington's ideal aims. Even the best-case outcome of Engagement—a grand bargain achieved in a relatively short time frame—would likely leave unaddressed disturbing Iranian policies, such as Tehran's treatment of the most vulnerable of its citizenry, at least in the short term. Such an optimal end state of Engagement would entail an American-Iranian relationship marked by skeptical ties, cooperation within narrow constraints on areas of common interest, and over the long term, the slow expansion of interaction and mutual trust. However, American engagement with Iran, even if successful, will not preclude competition or even tensions. In analogous cases—Iran's uneasy détentes with the United Kingdom and Saudi Arabia, or America's relationships with China or Libya—rapprochement has not remedied all difficulties.

Nevertheless, while Engagement is routinely criticized as overly accommodating of the internal inadequacies of the Iranian regime, proponents suggest that its long-term payoff could exceed its more ambitious alternatives. Although Engagement is not directly predicated upon a change in the complexion of Iran's regime, its advocates argue that the process itself would provide the most direct and secure path toward altering the political and ideological character of the regime itself. They argue that increasing the level and frequency of interaction between Iranians and the broader world would erode the regime's legitimacy, create new sources and centers of power and influence, shatter the monopolistic controls of crony elites, and generally usher in more conducive conditions for a democratic transition in Iran. Moreover, many of Engagement's advocates contend that the only way profound political change can come to Iran is if the United States backs off, removing the bugbear that the regime uses to justify its repressive controls. In this space, they contend, indigenous democracy activists would flourish, and the result would be the gradual ascent of a coalition of democratic forces that they see as already emerging from the wreckage of the reformist movement.

The prospects of these assertions coming to fruition are difficult to assess. Normalization and the dramatic expansion of economic ties have certainly transformed China by creating a massive middle class, empowering new interest groups outside the parameters of the Communist Party, and corroding the influence of official ideology. Still, economic liberalization has yet to make a substantial dent in the authoritarian control of the Chinese state or its human rights policies. In other situations—particularly the more personalistic autocracy of Muammar Qadhafi's Libya—the prospect that rapprochement with Washington may stimulate meaningful internal progress is highly unlikely. Nonetheless, proponents of Engagement with Iran point to its well-developed civil society and its considerable experience with competitive politics—albeit currently only within the narrow constraints permitted by the regime—as indicators that Iran's contested domestic political scene would be well-positioned to benefit from the openings provided by Engagement.

TIME FRAME

Engagement can only work over the long term. First, simply alleviating Tehran's fears about the United States would take many years. This is especially so since American forces will remain in Iraq until at least the beginning of 2012, their presence in Afghanistan is open ended, and they will likely remain in the Persian Gulf for decades. Because of this, Iran will face powerful U.S. military units on its western, southern, and eastern border for a long time, and this will be threatening no matter how pacific American rhetoric is or how quickly Washington can dismantle the vast web of unilateral sanctions against Iran that have been built up in countless acts of legislation and executive orders. Indeed, the process of dismantling the sanctions— assuming Congress would agree to it—would be an equally long process. The debate over whether the United States is genuine in these changes would be only one element in what will doubtless be a protracted and intense political fight in Tehran over whether to engage Washington under even those circumstances. Enmity with the United States was a core element of Khomeini's philosophy. Many Iranian leaders believe in it fervently, and others see it as inherently part of the regime's legitimacy. Both groups will be loath to abandon it in favor of rapprochement.

Moreover, even security assurances and the dismantling of sanctions would not spell success for a policy of pure Engagement. First, under these circumstances, Iran's hard-liners would doubtless argue that because Iran faces no punishment for continuing with its current policy, there is no reason to change course. This is one area where the analogy with China breaks down: when Washington began its rapprochement with Beijing, China was not actively pursuing policies inimical to American interests, let alone designed to harm the United States. For the most part, China had itself shifted gears and (in tacit cooperation with the United States) was actively opposing the Soviet Union and conducting other initiatives beneficial to the United States. At least initially—and that initial period might last years or even decades—Iran would push forward on its nuclear program; would continue to back Hizballah, Hamas, the Palestinian Islamic Jihad, the Taliban, and other violent extremist groups; would continue to oppose an Arab-Israeli peace as being inimical to its own interests; and would likely continue to support policies designed to destabilize the Middle East. Indeed, it may well *increase* all of these activities.

Consequently, Engagement has a low likelihood of eliminating problematic Iranian behavior in the short term. Proponents of Engagement must ultimately accept that by pursuing this option, the United States may be acquiescing to several years or more of further Iranian nuclear development, possibly including the development of an actual arsenal, as well as other actions that run counter to U.S. interests.

The contention of those who favor Engagement is that sticking to this approach will, over time, moderate Iran's behavior and then lead to the gradual evolution of its political system in a more positive direction. There is no time limit on this and no way to speed things up (indeed, doing so would be counterproductive as it would mean putting pressure on Tehran), and for these reasons, it is impossible to know how long it would take to produce "success." Of course, those who advocate pure Engagement also contend that all of the other options would fail to secure results in a meaningful time frame, too, and that only Engagement would deliver results at all, even if it takes years or decades to do so.

OVERVIEW OF THE POLICY

Engagement as defined loosely—the simple act of talking to Tehran—represents an almost inevitable component of any broad strategic approach to dealing with the challenges posed by the Islamic Republic. Diplomacy is by definition the normal conduct of business between sovereign states, and even in the absence of formal relations between governments, the need to communicate directly persists. Throughout their 30-year estrangement, Washington and Tehran have communicated routinely on a range of urgent and mundane questions, largely but not entirely through the intermediation of the Swiss, who represent U.S. interests in Tehran.

Moreover, the manifest utility of dialogue has persuaded every U.S. president—with the exception of a three-year hiatus by the Bush 43 administration between 2003 and 2006—to deal directly with the Iranian government. President Jimmy Carter pursued negotiations through a variety of direct and indirect channels throughout the long siege of the hostage crisis, even maintaining formal relations—including allowing Iran to maintain its embassy in Washington—for a full five months during the ordeal. Throughout the 1980s, America's readiness to deal directly with Tehran persisted, even in the face of escalating regional tensions and U.S.-Iranian naval skirmishes in the Gulf. This receptivity helped inspire the Reagan administration's covert arms sales to the struggling Islamic Republic, in addition to the obvious short-term interest in enlisting Iranian assistance on behalf of Western hostages held in Lebanon. Even in the disastrous aftermath of the "Iran-Contra" affair, Secretary of State George Shultz explicitly kept the door open to dialogue, with U.S. officials continuing to meet with Iranian interlocutors, repeatedly requesting meetings with various Iranian leaders, and responding positively to back-channel queries from Tehran.

President George H. W. Bush continued this pattern of signaling American willingness to engage, most notably through his inaugural address assertion that "goodwill begets goodwill." Iran's initial response was disappointing, but sufficient positive signs emanated from Tehran, including an August 1989 overture by President Rafsanjani, for the Bush 41 administration to persist in pressing for Iranian assistance in freeing Western hostages held in Lebanon, albeit indirectly through the United Nations. Bush publicly appealed to Tehran for better relations, and in February 1991, Secretary of State James Baker floated the notion of some positive role for Iran in a post–Persian Gulf war security framework.

The Clinton administration entered office determined to avoid the disastrous Iranian entanglements of its predecessors, but prompted by Iran's unexpected 1997 election of a moderate president resumed and intensified its predecessors' efforts to reach out to Tehran. These efforts included authorizing the sale of airplane spare parts; relaxing sanctions on food, medicine, and Iran's most important non-oil exports; a proposal to open a consular station in Iran; back-channel invitations to Iranian reformers to develop a modus vivendi on terrorism; and several remarkable speeches by senior U.S. officials designed to assuage Iran's historical grievances and open a new era of interaction.

Finally and most recently, the George W. Bush administration—before embracing regime change and shunning Tehran rather than "legitimize" its undemocratic leadership—launched the only sustained, officially sanctioned dialogue since the negotiations that led to the 1981 hostage release. Before and during the American invasion of Afghanistan, American officials regularly met with Iranian representatives for help against their common foes, the Taliban and al-Qa'ida. Iranian assistance with intelligence, overflights, and logistics proved invaluable to the U.S. war effort. Later, after a three-year hiatus, the administration publicly recommitted itself to engagement through the May 2006 offer—extended jointly with America's European allies, Russia, and China—for direct talks with Tehran on the nuclear issue.[2] Although Iran refused to meet the primary condition of the offer by suspending uranium enrichment, the United States repeatedly reissued the invitation over the course of two years. Thus, even for a president who had denounced talks with radicals as appeasement, engagement with Tehran proved an unavoidable component of his strategy.

This history forms an important context for President Obama's determination to try to reopen a formal dialogue with Tehran. There seems to be little doubt that the new president wants to give Iran every chance to resolve its standoff with the international community cooperatively. Moreover— and paradoxically—it is hard to envision any more muscular approach to Iran that does not include a serious attempt at undertaking talks with Tehran. It seems unlikely that any U.S. administration would implement military action or a concerted program of regime change, for example, without first testing the waters of dialogue, if only to establish the bona fides of its actions and shore up the support of a skeptical public and hesitant international community.

Moreover, as noted in the previous chapter, engagement would likely be an important element of a Persuasion approach that sought to use both positive and negative incentives to convince Iran to give up its destabilizing activities in the near term. However, in the case of that option, engagement would begin simply as a tactic that the United States would use to gather information about Iran, determine its needs, signal subtle threats, and conduct negotiations to refine one or more offers to Iran. This tactical dialogue could then grow into strategic Engagement with Iran, but only if Tehran agreed to accept the package of incentives in return for ending its destabilizing behavior. If Iran refused, this option would likely evolve in a different direction—adopting aspects of regime change, possible military options, or shifting to a tighter containment of Iran than was possible in the past.

The Basic Framework

The Engagement option imagines two different paths to a better relationship with Iran. The first is the offer of a range of positive incentives for Iran largely identical to those encompassed in the Persuasion option, in return for which Tehran would desist from its nuclear program, support for violent extremist groups, and general efforts to overturn the regional status quo. This is the Engagement approach's method for trying to address Iran's problematic behavior in the near term. However, as noted above, the reality is that removing all threats against Tehran—let alone lifting the sanctions on Iran—could easily produce the opposite effect within the Iranian political debate over the short term, as regime hard-liners would take it as a sign that their policy of confrontation had been right all along, and Iranian pragmatists would likely have difficulty making the case that Iran would need to give up this policy to secure further benefits from the West. In practice, it would be hard to convince the regime that these moves were not a sign of American concession, at least for some time, during which Iran would likely continue its problematic behaviors.

Over the long term, the Engagement option envisions a process by which consistent American reassurance to Tehran, discontinuation of threatening American activities, and repeated offers of goodwill would change the Iranian perception of the United States. It assumes that Iranian behavior toward the United States is driven principally by a perception of threat from the United States and reactions to American moves perceived as hostile in Tehran. Consequently, over time, a series of confidence-building measures, including the deal envisioned in the preceding paragraph, would break down the barriers of this security dilemma and prompt Tehran to curb and eventually end its own hostile policies toward the United States.

Finally, as part of the long-term aspect of this policy option, the Engagement approach also argues that the only hope of fostering meaningful internal political change in Iran is for the United States and the international community to end their hostile behavior toward Iran, and to reduce the clerical regime's paranoia and undermine the basis for its repression of the Iranian people. Advocates of Engagement argue that only in these circumstances will a genuine democratic opposition to the current regime be able to grow and secure the support of an Iranian populace longing for change.

Putting Engagement First

Employing Engagement with Iran as the centerpiece of U.S. policy would entail a wholesale shift from all prior U.S. approaches, which have chiefly relied on military, economic, and diplomatic coercion—coupled at times with parallel efforts at enticement—to induce Tehran to abandon its troublemaking ways. A serious U.S. policy of pure Engagement, however, would focus primarily, if not exclusively, on incentives as a means of altering Iranian political dynamics, policy options, and strategic choices. Direct dialogue with Tehran would be the sine qua non of an American effort to engage Iran; however, the talks in and of themselves would represent a means rather than an end. The ultimate goal of Engagement would be the establishment of an enabling environment and diplomatic framework to support cooperation between Washington and Tehran on issues of common concern and to further integrate Iran into a rules-based global order.

The premise of such an approach is that Iran's most dangerous policies reflect an interests-based response to the threats its leadership perceives and the capabilities at its disposal, rather than an inexorable expression of the revolutionary and/or Islamic ideology that is such a distinctive element of the regime's rhetoric. As such, the policy assumes that Iran's support of terrorist groups and actions, its obstinate attachment to a massive and originally secret nuclear infrastructure, and its efforts to assert its sway across the Middle East are all policies that are subject to revision and adaptation in response to changing circumstances. The objective of Engagement is to change those circumstances in a positive fashion, restraining Tehran not by threat, use of force, or financial compulsion but by persuading Iranian leaders that their interests are better served by cooperation than by confrontation.

Advocates of Engagement argue that a whole-hearted U.S. embrace of this policy would alter Tehran's preferences in three primary ways. First, by expanding Iran's diplomatic horizons, Engagement would help mitigate the regime's perpetual insecurities and provide more acceptable mechanisms for Iran to assume its historic self-image as a great power. The diminution of the long-standing antagonism with Washington would empower Iranian moderates and create new avenues of influence that would provide even its hard-liners with a stake in maintaining constructive relations with the international community. Second, the economic incentives of expanded trade and investment with the international community, and specifically with America, would raise the cost for noncompliance and create internal constituencies for continued moderation. Faced with the prospect of losing material opportunities that would offer direct benefit to the Iranian people—and perhaps more important, to the influential political elites themselves—Tehran would constrain its own behavior. Finally, Engagement would entail increasing interaction with the world, which would have an inevitably liberalizing effect on society and, more specifically, the regime's leadership and its politically relevant base of support.

For advocates of Engagement, the foremost model is that of the American opening to China. For Washington, the decision to normalize relations with China represented a recognition of the limitations of American power in the aftermath of a disastrous war and an acknowledgment of the ascendance of new centers of gravity within the international system. For their part, the Chinese had come to a parallel epiphany about their strategic vulnerability in a world of enemies and the potential utility of a breakthrough with Washington. Neither side capitulated, but the strategic bargain that was concluded transformed the parameters of the relationship from open hostility to managed competition and episodic collaboration. Pursuing Engagement with Iran would require each side to accept just such a clear-headed appreciation of both the legitimate grievances and security interests of its adversary as well as a vision of the value and viability of an enduring strategic bargain between them.

Two Paths to Engagement

Engagement can be considered in two general formats: an incremental/compartmentalized route or the "grand bargain" approach. Either approach would seek as its ultimate objective a comprehensive framework to address all the issues outstanding between Washington and Tehran and generate a framework for eventual normalization of relations, because only a multifaceted process that tackles the broad host of issues at stake between the two governments could generate both the versatility and credibility to make real progress on the hardest issues.

The two options would differ primarily in their operational dimensions. An *incremental* or compartmentalized approach would undertake separate negotiating tracks organized around specific issue areas such as nuclear matters, Iran's role in the Levant, Persian Gulf security, and the financial and legal claims that Iran and the United States hold against each other. The tracks would be distinct and noncontingent, in the sense that logjams in one arena would not preclude progress in another. Most advocates of Engagement highlight the centrality of the bilateral conversation between Washington and Tehran. However, the protracted immersion of the permanent members of the UN Security Council as well as Germany into this conflict all but ensures that the multilateral component of the nuclear diplomacy will be retained under any new framework for Engagement. In such a compartmentalized approach to Engagement, it would be possible for Washington and Tehran to achieve bilateral consensus on a single area of concern while continuing to wrangle over more problematic items of the overall agenda.

Conversely, a *grand bargain* approach would endeavor to engage the wide range of issues involving Iran as a package, addressing each of the American concerns and Iranian grievances simultaneously with the objective of fashioning a comprehensive accord. Proponents of the grand bargain contend that a durable deal is best fashioned by tackling the totality of American differences with Tehran rather than in a piecemeal or gradualist manner. Many often cite as an added benefit the boost that any such comprehensive offer might provide to America's standing in the world and its efforts to generate sufficient diplomatic cooperation from key allies. The precise contours of the grand bargain would, of course, be determined by the parties through negotiations, but various descriptions of the potential trade-offs and commitments suggest that such a deal could comprise the provision of American security guarantees to Tehran along with a process to dismantle U.S. economic and diplomatic sanctions in exchange for Iranian steps to disavow Hizballah, Hamas, and other terrorist proxies and undertake measures to provide full transparency and confidence in the peaceful nature of its nuclear activities.

Advocates of each of the two options hold opposing views on the viability of the alternative. Those who prefer an incremental approach suggest that a grand bargain is simply unrealistic given the duration and acrimony of the estrangement and the sensitivity of the issues at stake for both sides. Incrementalists contend that early, specific progress in narrowly defined areas of common interest is an essential component to sustaining the process of engagement itself, and that only by achieving tangible benefits can engagement create the level of mutual confidence and political leverage from reluctant constituencies on both sides to facilitate concessions on more contentious issues or sustain any broader agreement.

Those who favor a holistic grand bargain approach deride incrementalism as prone to collapse and/or reversal under the weight of predictably episodic stumbling blocks. They point to the inability of either the United States or Iran to move beyond issue-specific cooperation in those instances where such interaction has been initiated, including the 2001–2003 talks on Afghanistan, arguing that only a fully inclusive approach will generate the momentum necessary to advance an undertaking of this magnitude to its fruition. For its supporters, only a grand bargain offers the requisite assurances for each side to make the epic concessions that its adversary demands.

The crux of the difference between these competing approaches to Engagement involves their understanding and interpretation of Iran's internal politics. Those who advocate an issue-specific, compartmentalized strategy of Engagement suggest that incrementalism is critical to building confidence and political support among Iranian hard-liners, whose ideological affinities and elite self-interest have long cemented their opposition to any normalization with America. Supporters of a grand bargain approach point to a 2003 trial balloon floated by influential Iranian reformists with reported support from the country's supreme leader as evidence that the Islamic Republic can in fact transcend its internal rivalries and ideological impediments when the state's interests so demand. Since the Bush administration failed to pursue the 2003 proposal, in part because of questions about its credibility, the issue of Iran's political will to resolve its antipathy with Washington remains largely untested and ultimately unknown.

The Inducements

The Engagement option's method of trying to convince the Iranian regime to cease its problematic behavior in the near or medium term relies on offering Iran only positive incentives, without the negative incentives of

Persuasion. In this sense, Engagement as a policy option is also predicated upon the efficacy of incentives to alter the preferences, priorities, and policies of the Iranian leadership. While the specific scope of any incentives would ultimately be determined by the American administration, most proposals suggest three broad areas that should be addressed: nuclear, strategic, and economic. Five years of frustrating and mostly fruitless negotiations between the international community and Iran have tended to prioritize the first, on the premise that the regime's staunchly nationalist defense of its "right" to nuclear technology limits its flexibility in acceding to the self-imposed limitations desired by the international community. Having invested its national prestige in the advancement and expansion of its nuclear expertise and infrastructure, the Iranian regime will only be willing to curtail its ambitions in exchange for carrots specifically tailored to satisfy its ostensible need for technical prowess and alternative power sources. To date, the offers of Western investment in light-water reactors and fuel guarantees have proven insufficient to tempt a political elite that is increasingly aligned around the utility of obstinacy on the nuclear issue, but it is reasonable to envision that the right package could produce a more amenable response.

The political and economic components of any potential incentives package are similarly essential to the prospect of the Iranian regime contemplating meaningful concessions of its own. Throughout most of the last three decades, the primary obstacle to generating any diplomatic traction between Washington and Tehran has been Tehran's insistence on specific U.S. policy changes as a prerequisite for engaging in any dialogue. The particular preconditions typically sought by Tehran have included a range of economic as well as political concessions on the part of Washington, such as the release of Iran's remaining assets frozen by the United States, the lifting of American sanctions, and the removal of U.S. forces from the Persian Gulf. Ultimately, however, the importance of these preconditions for Tehran appears to be as much symbolic as practical. Iranian officials have asserted explicitly and repeatedly that U.S. confidence-building measures are necessary to demonstrate American respect for Iran's revolution and its leadership. Tehran demands "practical steps" from Washington in order to "establish its sincerity and good faith."[3] American supplication has been needed to assuage Iran's persistently offended sensibilities. As an influential conservative journalist once questioned, "How can [supreme leader]

Ayatollah ['Ali] Khamenei accept relations with America if it shows no sign of repentance for its past actions?"[4]

In order to address Iran's underlying insecurity, many advocates of Engagement have called for specific U.S. commitments to refrain from efforts to remove the Iranian regime as well as provide security guarantees similar to those envisioned in the Persuasion approach. To some extent, such pledges would appear to replicate the language of nonintervention that can be found in various international accords, including the tripartite agreement that ended the hostage crisis. The 1981 Algiers Accords pledges "that it is and from now on will be the policy of the United States not to intervene, directly or indirectly, politically or militarily, in Iran's internal affairs." Interestingly, there is no evidence that a new U.S. pledge to respect Iran's sovereignty and refrain from threats or aggression would have particular resonance with Tehran. Demands for a security guarantee have never been part of the litany of conditions articulated by Iranian leaders—in fact, many have explicitly rejected this idea—and given their profound mistrust in U.S. leaders and motives, it is not clear why Tehran's persistent insecurities would be assuaged in any meaningful way by a new set of U.S. written commitments.

Instead, as with the Persuasion approach, security guarantees to Tehran would likely have to go well beyond toothless rhetoric. Again, such steps could include American efforts to initiate a dialogue on small-bore issues such as resumption of talks on naval protocols for incident-at-sea prevention or a U.S. proposal for a regional security framework that integrates the Islamic Republic more fully within the region. Here as well, it would be of equal or greater importance to Tehran that as part of any security guarantees, Washington pledge to curtail or end its high-profile efforts to promote democracy within Iran. These activities undermine U.S. efforts to draw Iran to the negotiating table by suggesting that the principal American objective is the eradication of the Islamic Republic and its leadership. These tangible measures, buttressed by unequivocal statements by senior American officials about the nature of U.S. aims and intentions toward Iran, could produce greater traction among Iranian decisionmakers.

A final and critical dimension of any Engagement approach involves economic inducements. These are envisioned as a more effective alternative to sanctions, which for over 28 years have failed to produce significant positive changes to Iran's most problematic policies. Of course, there is clear evidence that Iranian leaders are sensitive to economic pressure and, at various points, have adjusted their policies on the basis of costs, constraints, and opportunities. The best example of this can be seen in the efforts to promote regional détente during the late 1990s, which reflected, at least in part, reformist president Muhammad Khatami's concerns about sagging oil revenues and the urgent need for foreign investment. Nevertheless, proponents of the pure Engagement approach argue that economic rewards could prove more valuable in enticing Iran today, given the profound economic problems—particularly inflation in consumer goods and real estate costs—that have resulted from President Mahmud Ahmadinejad's disastrous approach to economic management. Offers that tap into the frustration of politically salient constituencies—bazaar merchants, for example, as well as the considerable class of privileged elites who have successfully parlayed political access into material wealth under the Islamic Republic—could create powerful internal advocates for policy changes within Iran.

Time and Timing

However effective economic incentives might prove, any U.S. administration seeking to implement the Engagement strategy vis-à-vis Iran will face a dilemma over the issues of time and timing. Currently, American individuals and entities are forbidden from engaging in nearly all forms of business interaction with Tehran, and even the exceptions carved out under the Clinton administration that permit food, medicine, and certain other non-oil exports have come under great pressure in recent years. Offering economic concessions in advance of any specific, tangible policy changes from Tehran would prove politically radioactive within the American domestic political debate. Moreover, even a simple effort to relax or suspend the most recently enacted sanctions, many of which have crimped Iran's interaction with the international financial system, would require the White House to make a positive assertion that the individuals or institutions have ceased involvement with terrorism and/or proliferation activities. No material economic gestures from Washington can be contemplated until a process of engagement is well under way, and Tehran has demonstrated its willingness and capacity to curtail its worst excesses.

In the absence of some hint of Iranian reciprocation, the best that any U.S. administration could likely produce is a more temperate attitude toward Iran's economic relationships with various international financial institutions and with U.S. allies, many of whom have curtailed export credits and other measures that facilitate trade with Iran because of legitimate concerns about the investment climate there as much as in response to U.S. pressure. One potentially powerful tool would be measures such as executory contracts that permit Americans to engage in business-related discussions with Iranian counterparts but defer any actual exchange of resources or services until further political progress has been achieved.

Moreover, Engagement suffers from some of the same problems with time as the Persuasion approach. In particular, it is virtually impossible to know if the policy is working until it has manifestly succeeded—and it could well take years or even decades to succeed. Following a policy of pure Engagement, the United States would make a number of offers to Tehran and, to the extent possible, couple them with the kinds of unilateral gestures described above to try to demonstrate Washington's good faith. Since no one could expect Tehran to respond immediately, the policy would have to anticipate a period of waiting during which time Tehran would have to make up its mind. Unscrupulous Iranian leaders might well attempt to draw out that period by hinting at a willingness to engage the United States even if they had no intention of doing so, merely to buy time to complete their nuclear program and advance other programs and policies inimical to American interests. Without even the threat of harsher economic sanctions embodied in the Persuasion approach, Engagement would have a far more difficult time even establishing when the policy had failed and that it was time to shift to another strategy.

An Uncertain Partner

Finally, any balanced assessment of a policy of pure Engagement must address the likelihood that Iran would respond as hoped. At present, that likelihood seems uncertain at best, and there is considerable evidence to justify real pessimism. Iran's current internal political dynamics present a thorny environment for any effort at Engagement. The conservative retrenchment and the ascendance of Ahmadinejad's brand of radicalism essentially eliminate any near-term prospect of a self-generated liberalization of Iran's internal politics and approach to the world. Iranian leaders see their state as besieged from all directions by Washington, a product of both its deeply engrained paranoia as well as actual facts on the ground. At the same time, the leadership—in particular President Ahmadinejad—is buoyed by a sense of confidence, even arrogance, about the country's domestic and regional status.

What this bifurcated view of the world translates to in practice is a tendency to equate assertiveness as equivalent to, or an effective substitute for, power—both in internal politics and in foreign policy. This Hobbesian worldview encourages adventurism and discourages compromise. Molded by their perception of an inherently hostile world and the conviction that the exigencies of regime survival justify their actions, Iranian leaders seek to exploit every opening, pursue multiple or contradictory agendas, play various capitals against one another, and engage in pressure tactics—including the limited use of force—to advance their interests. As Khamene'i has argued, "Rights cannot be achieved by entreating. If you supplicate, withdraw and show flexibility, arrogant powers will make their threat more serious."[5]

As Iran's ultimate authority, Khamene'i frames the parameters of any debate on an issue of this magnitude and can wield a veto over any overtures or responses. Gaining his imprimatur for both the process as well as any eventual outcome of Engagement will be essential but also immensely challenging. Khamene'i has never exhibited any evidence of positive sentiments toward America, and the United States has had no direct contact with either the supreme leader or anyone in his office for the past 30 years. Beyond Khamene'i, any overtures toward Iran will have to contend with the outsized personality and ambitions of President Ahmadinejad. Despite his manifest difficulties with both Iran's political elites as well as its population, it would be a mistake to presume that the era of Ahmadinejad is already on the wane. Even if he somehow passes from the scene, there is every reason to believe that the legacy of his ideological fervor and the constituency whose worldview he reflects will continue to shape the options available to any future Iranian leader. Any effort to promote engagement must find a way to co-opt or circumvent Ahmadinejad and those of his ideological ilk, most of whom have limited international exposure.

Still, it is worth noting that a positive shift in Iran's internal politics—one that swings the pendulum back toward the center or even toward a more liberalized domestic order—will not necessarily facilitate new cooperation on the international front. The power struggle that dominated Iran during the reformist zenith complicated its decisionmaking, and the exigencies of internal competition constrained even those leaders who might have been amenable to reaching out to Washington. Thus, after auspicious initial signals at the outset of Khatami's first term, the reformers refrained from overtures to the United States simply to avoid provoking hard-line reactions from their rivals. Moreover, shifts in Iran's internal politics may only undermine whatever international consensus remains around a common position on Iran, a factor that could stymie efforts to address the most problematic elements of Iran's foreign policy. Those states desperate to avoid any confrontational policy with Iran, regardless of all other considerations, often pounce on seeming shifts in Tehran's balance of power to justify further inaction.

Perhaps ironically, the consolidation of the conservatives has created a potentially and unexpected new opening for diplomacy with the United States. Today, for the first time in Iranian postrevolutionary history, there is cross-factional support for direct, authoritative dialogue with their American adversaries. Public endorsement of negotiations with Washington—a position that risked a prison term if voiced publicly as recently as 2002—is now the official position of the entire relevant political elite of the Islamic Republic. The shift can be credited at least in part to Ahmadinejad, whose conservative backing and firmly established revolutionary credentials facilitated his surprising and largely ham-fisted attempts to reach out to Washington as a means of courting public opinion. Ahmadinejad's overtures have been reinforced by public statements from Khamene'i over the past two years offering grudging but unprecedented support for negotiations with the United States.

To facilitate a serious dialogue, Iran will need something more than just the crucial blessing of Khamene'i and Ahmadinejad; given the complexities of the Iranian system and its endemic factionalism, Engagement will require an Iranian political figure who is both willing and capable of championing this agenda. For more than 20 years, Ali Akbar Hashemi Rafsanjani played that role, advocating consistently for an improved—if not wholly restored—relationship with Washington, both in public remarks as early as 1983 and, more relevantly, behind the scenes as one of the regime's central power brokers. However, the past decade has demonstrated that he is not well suited for Iran's contemporary political environment. Rafsanjani cannot command a vast popular mandate, as his embarrassing performances in the 2000 parliamentary and 2005 presidential ballots demonstrated. Nor have his wily backroom tactics proven particularly effective in neutralizing the bombast or the populism that has elevated Ahmadinejad. Rafsanjani will continue to have an important role in shaping Iran's policies and its political evolution, but his heyday is well behind him, and persistent reports of his imminent resurgence have proven vastly overstated. Who might assume this mantle as

Rafsanjani fades from the scene? There are a host of potential candidates but none who have yet demonstrated the necessary interest, tenacity, or political fortitude.

REQUIREMENTS

The fiscal and military requirements of pursuing Engagement are effectively negligible; if anything, a successful implementation could produce some cost savings for Washington with respect to military resources as well as expanded U.S. economic opportunities. Conversely, the domestic political resources required on both sides to make such an approach viable are imposing. Engagement reflects a tacit acceptance of two important arguments that are open to debate: first, that Iran's leadership is capable of changing policies and behavior that invoke central tenets of the regime's ideology; and second, that Iran and the United States are willing to accommodate each other's core interests in order to achieve a peaceful coexistence. Proponents can make a strong case for the viability of both propositions, but inevitably the propositions would require an American willingness to invest political capital and diplomatic energy in a process that has no guarantee of a positive outcome.

The most important "resource" that would be required on each side is political capital and the capacity of each government to support a protracted, complicated negotiating process over the course of what would inevitably be a period of great flux, if not turmoil, in the region. Destabilizing developments in a related arena—such as Iraq, Lebanon, Afghanistan, or the Arab-Israeli peace process—would impinge upon any incipient negotiating process, and both Washington and Tehran would require tremendous fortitude and cross-cutting domestic political support to ride out these predictable shocks.

Any U.S. administration preparing to undertake a serious strategy employing only positive incentives toward the Islamic Republic would have to be willing and prepared to absorb the vehement backlash from both domestic political constituencies as well as regional allies. A president who chose to engage Iran—whether as a stand-alone approach or as part of a more variegated effort—would need to have the solid backing of Congress, where grandstanding on issues related to Iran has long been a popular and politically advantageous diversion. The president also would need to make a compelling case to the American people about the viability and utility of Engagement while cultivating realistic expectations about the challenges of negotiating with an adversary as complicated and entrenched as Tehran. This could be especially challenging if Iran chooses not to respond positively for some period of time, and instead aggressively continues to pursue a nuclear weapons capability, provide weapons to Iraqi and Afghan groups killing American troops, oppose Middle East peace efforts, and engage in other destabilizing activities. Engagement would win plaudits from some international constituencies, but the parties to the past five years of negotiations over Iran's nuclear program—particularly Britain, France, and Germany—may perceive this approach as undercutting whatever minimal progress a united multilateral campaign of pressure has achieved to date. The United States would also have to manage the disparate interests and concerns of Israel and the Arab states of the Persian Gulf. Given a policy that regional states will doubtless see as "surrendering" to Iran, Washington would have to convince Israel not to attack and the GCC not to get nuclear weapons of their own.

Over the course of any Engagement, Washington would also have to deal with the ongoing challenges of Iranian mischief and defending the deal to skeptics. Specifically, the administration would have to consider the concessions the United States is prepared and capable of offering to Tehran and the level of Iranian misconduct Washington is prepared to countenance— and then persuade a largely skeptical political corps that such compromises are worthwhile. Other cases of Iranian détente with former adversaries— in particular, Britain and Saudi Arabia—have hinged on the ability and willingness of Iran's adversaries to accept a considerable degree of ambiguity from Tehran and to provide significant scope for face-saving rhetoric and actions.

In any U.S.-Iranian engagement process, Washington would have to be prepared to accept a strategic bargain that ultimately falls short of optimal American objectives. While the United States has struck similar bargains with other former adversaries, such as China, and has found a way to live with the manifold failings of imperfect allies such as Pakistan, Iran has special sensitivity within the American political context. Even the best imperfect bargain would be difficult to promote at home and may fall short of meeting American strategic needs in Southwest Asia. Since this option relies on the Iranians to want our positive incentives enough to make the compromises we need, without any threat should they refuse, the most that Iran might be willing to give up might fall well short of what the United States considers its minimal goals. For instance, it is impossible to imagine that Iran would give up nuclear enrichment in these circumstances, and unlikely that it would even agree to the more intrusive inspections of the NPT's additional protocol. The most that the United States might get from the Iranians on the nuclear front would be a reaffirmation of their statement that they are not seeking nuclear weapons, which would elicit much skepticism given the many lies they have already told the IAEA and the international community about their nuclear program.

Washington would also need to consider the logistical dimension of any engagement process. Thanks to the long American absence from Tehran and bureaucratic neglect, the U.S. diplomatic apparatus for dealing with Iran remains insufficient. To its credit, the Bush administration invested in upgrading capabilities by establishing a new set of administrative structures to coordinate all official policy and activities with respect to Iran. Over the long term, the new configuration will create a cadre of American officials skilled in interpreting Iranian issues and capable of staffing some future diplomatic engagement; in the short term, Washington will be pressed to assemble a team with sufficient background and exposure to Iran who can staff prolonged negotiations.

PROS AND CONS

The following are the advantages and disadvantages of the Engagement approach.

Advantages

—There is evidence that Engagement can work. The direct bilateral talks on issues surrounding Afghanistan that were pursued by the Bush administration between 2001 and 2003 have been described by an official U.S. participant as "perhaps the most constructive period of U.S.-Iranian diplomacy since the fall of the shah."[6] Over the course of 18 months, the direct communication between Washington and Tehran on Afghanistan generated tangible cooperation between the two adversaries on a critical issue of American security, including valuable tactical Iranian assistance in Operation Enduring Freedom, the establishment and stabilization of the post-Taliban government in Kabul, and Iranian offers to participate in a U.S.-led training program for the Afghan army and to launch a counterterrorism dialogue with Washington.[7] The bilateral dialogue was not an easy or perfect pathway for diplomacy, but even where the results did not fulfill U.S. expectations, the existence of a direct dialogue provided an indispensable channel on this vital issue for both sides. With the appropriate investment of diplomatic resources and energy, this precedent could be extended to the wider array of American concerns.

—The costs of the likely economic incentives to Tehran would be minor—and would probably be more than offset if U.S.-Iranian trade flowers as part of a rapprochement.

—A serious, well-crafted effort by Washington to engage Tehran would generate considerable support among European allies and potentially create leverage for alternative policy directions if Engagement were to fail. At various points over the past five years, the self-imposed limitations of the Bush administration on dealing directly with Tehran were the subject of considerable frustration by its European partners, who often expressed futility at trying to influence Tehran without any capacity to address the underlying dilemma—the enduring antagonism between the United States and Iran.

—A serious process of engagement could temper tensions in the Gulf and might mitigate unintended clashes between U.S. forces in the Gulf and Iranian agents and proxies in Iraq and elsewhere by providing a mechanism for addressing grievances and concerns, and by generating greater transparency, enabling each side to observe its adversary's preferences and decisionmaking processes. At present, Iranian decisionmakers—like many in Washington—are trying to interpret American policy and politics through the glass darkly, which tends to inflame conspiracy theories and reinforce inaccurate interpretations of intent. For all those Iranian political actors, such as Ahmadinejad, who have dismissed the possibility of a U.S. military strike on the country, there are others from each end of the political spectrum who have expressed fears that a desperate Washington might attack Iran to vindicate and/or extricate itself from its failed intervention in Iraq. As an associated benefit, a sustained process of dialogue between Washington and Tehran would dampen the security premium that the market has factored into the high price of oil, which itself would erode some of Iran's current imperviousness to the impact of economic sanctions.

Disadvantages

—Iran's internal politics are so complex and convoluted that Engagement—which is premised on the notion that Iran will reciprocate kindness for kindness—has no guarantee of success. Indeed, there is also evidence that incentives proffered unilaterally from Washington to Tehran will prove inadequate. The Clinton administration undertook dramatic steps to create an opening with the reformists during the Khatami period— including the relaxation of an array of sanctions and a fairly wide-ranging apology for past policies—and received no reciprocal positive signals or overtures from Tehran, in part, no doubt, because of the enduring power struggle within the Iranian regime. While the reconsolidation of power in the hands of Iran's conservative faction could mitigate this problem, the current political context within Iran and the region creates a different complication. Tehran's hard-liners will interpret any unilateral initiative from Washington—or perception of concessions—as a sign of weakness, which will only bolster the current consensus among the Iranian elite that a more aggressive position will better serve their country's interests.

—Tehran may conclude that the end of confrontational American policies toward Iran as envisioned in this option is a sign of weakness on the part of the United States, and a vindication for their own aggressive behavior. Not only might this make Iran less willing to accept any deal proffered by the United States, in the expectation that further Iranian aggressiveness might force additional American concessions, but it could lead to unintended clashes between the United States and Iran (or Israel and Iran). Thus the option also runs the risk of provoking the very military conflict it seeks to avoid.

—The timetable for any negotiating process exacerbates the inherent discrepancies between U.S. and Iranian interests. Even in an optimal situation—a sincere and unified Iranian commitment to the negotiations— the process itself would be protracted. Prior cases of rapprochement with old adversaries involving either the United States or Iran have entailed years of discussion, much of it occurring behind the scenes. The anticipated duration for this negotiation would necessarily be longer, a product of the complexity of the issues at stake, the entrenched nature of the antagonism, and the peculiarities of Iran's perpetually fractured internal political dynamics and consensus decisionmaking process. Tehran could easily use the process of negotiations and dialogue as an opportunity to maximize its own leverage and dupe the international community, pushing forward until its nuclear capabilities have reached the fabled "point of no return." The end result would be close to the worst-case scenario from the perspective of U.S. interests in ensuring that Iran does not possess nuclear weapons capability.

—It is very possible that there simply is no constituency within Iran that is both willing and capable of making a bargain with Washington. In fact, there are undoubtedly important constituencies within the Iranian political elite who would welcome a crisis as a means of rekindling Iran's waning revolutionary fires and deflecting attention from the domestic deficiencies of Islamic rule. The reality is that despite an array of missed opportunities on both sides, Tehran has never clearly communicated that its leadership would be prepared, fully and authoritatively, to make epic concessions on the key areas of U.S. concern. Even more uncertain is whether Iran has had or will ever attain the level of policy coordination and institutional coherence that would enable any overarching agreement to be implemented successfully.

—Unless the United States carefully prepares its allies regarding its adoption of an Engagement approach, Washington may find that some of its most important partners in dealing with the challenges posed by Iran could prove surprisingly unenthusiastic about such a dramatic shift in U.S. tactics. The Europeans may interpret such a turnaround as subverting their own considerable investment in a multilateral diplomatic framework for addressing Iran's nuclear ambitions, and prove reluctant to provide crucial international reinforcement for American overtures. Within the region, America's Arab allies would likely react as apprehensively to U.S.-Iranian engagement as they would to the prospect of a military attack. Given their reliance on the American security umbrella and their longstanding trepidations about Iranian influence and intentions, the Persian Gulf states would likely seek to bolster their domestic defenses—and turn to alternative suppliers to do so. They may follow through on their many private threats to acquire nuclear weapons of their own if the Iranians are allowed to do so. At the very least, their confidence in the credibility of U.S. diplomatic and military commitments would suffer.

—Finally, the Israel factor presents a disturbing wild card for the prospects of Engagement. For most of the past three decades, Israel and the United States have maintained broadly similar assessments of the threat posed by Iran and correspondingly close cooperation on policy. Although the bilateral relationship today remains as strong as ever, a reversal of the traditional American approach to Iran would raise profound misgivings among most of the Israeli body politic and their supporters in the U.S. Congress. If Israeli leaders believe that their interests are being ill served by U.S.-Iranian negotiations, they may feel compelled to take independent military action, irrespective of the prospects of success or the cascading impact on American interests in the region. Such a scenario would torpedo any engagement process and likely create an avalanche of intensified security dilemmas for Washington.

PART II

DISARMING TEHRAN

The Military Options

The diplomatic options available to the United States for addressing the problem of Iran share a common, possibly fatal, flaw: they require Iranian cooperation. Even the Persuasion option, which contains important elements of coercion in addition to those elements meant to persuade, ultimately relies on the willingness of the Iranian regime to cooperate. Both diplomatic options assume that Tehran is capable of making cost-benefit analyses, placing strategic considerations ahead of domestic politics and ideology, and making a major shift in what has been one of the foundational policies of the Islamic Republic—enmity toward the United States. As the previous chapters noted, all of these assumptions are, at best, unproven. At worst, there is considerable evidence calling many of them into question.

This means that neither of the diplomatic options is a sure thing. They are not doomed to failure, but neither are they guaranteed to succeed. Neither may have a better than even chance of success, and we cannot know with any degree of certainty just what their true probability of success is.

Beyond this concern, many Americans simply distrust the Iranian regime. They do not believe that Tehran will ever live up to any agreements struck with the United States, no matter what the circumstances or the manifest advantages to Tehran. For them, this also calls into question the advisability of a policy employing both positive and negative incentives (Persuasion) or one relying only on positive incentives (Engagement) toward Tehran.

Others extend that mistrust not only to Iran but to Russia, China, and even our European and Japanese allies. They contend that whatever America's allies may agree to in theory, they will never be willing in practice to impose the kinds of penalties on Tehran that might make a diplomatic approach feasible.

For that reason, they reject any option that requires Iranian cooperation, or even the cooperation of America's allies. Instead, they place their faith only in options that the United States could implement unilaterally. Unfortunately, after 30 years of devising ever more creative new sanctions against Iran, Washington has few unilateral economic and diplomatic methods left to pressure Tehran. There are essentially no more economic arrows left in America's quiver. If the United States is going to act unilaterally against Iran, it will likely have to resort to force.

Consequently, for these Americans, force is the only sensible option to apply toward Tehran. In their view, force has the great advantage that it is wholly under American control and can succeed without Iranian cooperation and only minimal allied support. Unlike the regime change options (covered in Part III), the military options rely on the most capable instrument of the U.S. government—its peerless armed forces—and, again, do not require any Iranians (or U.S. allies) to cooperate in any way. Advocates of this policy option see force as superior to Containment because they fear that once Iran crosses the nuclear threshold, the Islamic Republic will prove difficult or even impossible to deter from greater aggression, and possibly even nuclear weapons use.

The election of President Ahmadinejad in 2005 and the continued progress of Iran's nuclear program since then have made the military options more plausible and prominent. At the same time, however, growing military difficulties in Iraq made the idea of another major American military effort in the Middle East less credible, and the unilateralist and militaristic image of the United States that developed after the 2003 invasion of Iraq further constrained Washington. Yet the possibility of using force has remained part of the conversation, with American officials convinced that it must remain at least a last-ditch recourse, if only to focus the minds of Iranian leaders. President Obama has so far refused to rule out the use of force, even while making clear that it is not the approach to Iran he plans to take. Meanwhile, Ahmadinejad's bellicose posturing toward Israel has made many worry that even if the United States does not strike Iran's nuclear facilities, Israel might do so instead (possibly with American acquiescence).

With this context in mind, Part II of this monograph examines the military options against Iran. Even those Americans who consider it a very bad idea—or at least very premature—must wrestle with the pros and cons of keeping an explicit military threat as a part of an American policy toolkit in this difficult situation.

Part II begins by looking at the most extreme military option, that of invading the country to depose the regime, as the United States did in Iraq and Afghanistan. We chose to consider this extreme and highly unpopular option partly for the sake of analytical rigor and partly because if Iran responded to a confrontational American policy—such as an airstrike, harsh new sanctions, or efforts to foment regime change—with a major escalation of terrorist attacks (or more dire moves against Israel and other American allies), invasion could become a very "live" option. In 1998 there was almost no one who favored an invasion of Iraq or believed it likely, but five years later it was a fait accompli. Certainly stranger things have happened, and so we cannot simply ignore this option.

Airstrikes against Iran's nuclear facilities are the most frequently discussed military option for the United States and Israel, and indeed they are the most likely scenario for the use of force. Consequently, the second chapter of this section examines this option.

Some Americans believe that the costs to the United States of taking military action against Iran would be too high, or they simply doubt that Washington would ever summon the will to do so, and so they hope that Israel will take action instead. Regardless of what the U.S. government wants, Israel might do so anyway if it believes it has no other alternative. In that scenario, the United States would have to ask itself whether to encourage or discourage Jerusalem from taking that fateful step. According to newspaper accounts, the Bush 43 administration blocked just such an Israeli attack, and the Obama administration might face a similar decision at a more delicate time in the future.[1] Consequently, the last chapter in this section considers this decision.

CHAPTER THREE

GOING ALL THE WAY

Invasion

There is little appetite in the United States for mounting an invasion of Iran. After the frustrations and costs of the wars in Afghanistan and Iraq, few Americans are looking for another fight in the Middle East. American ground forces are badly overstretched as it is. Under these circumstances, an invasion of Iran would require calling up huge numbers of National Guard and military reserve personnel and keeping them in service for several years. After the strains of frequent deployments to Iraq and Afghanistan over the past eight years, this might undermine the foundations of the all-volunteer force.

Nor is it clear that a full-scale invasion is necessary. The most compelling rationale for this course of action is the fear that Iran's leadership would prove difficult or impossible to deter once it had acquired a nuclear weapons capability. Doubts remain, but American, European, and even Israeli experts have all argued that while Iran may not be easy to deter, the available evidence indicates that it probably could be deterred from the most extreme behavior. This in turn calls into question whether the costs of an invasion could be justified.[1]

Despite this, only an invasion offers the United States finality when it comes to its 30-year conflict with the Islamic Republic. If the goal is to eliminate all the problems the United States has with the current Iranian regime, from its pursuit of nuclear weapons to its efforts to overturn the status quo in the Middle East by stirring instability across the region, there is no other strategy that can ensure this objective. Of course, as U.S. experience in Iraq and Afghanistan has demonstrated, that certainty comes with the distinct possibility of creating new risks, threats, and costs that may be as troublesome or more so than the current range of problems.

In particular, as American failures in Iraq and Afghanistan have underscored, the critical question that the United States would need to address in the event of an invasion of Iran is how to build a stable, secure, and at least relatively pro-American state after toppling the government. While American missteps in Mesopotamia and Central Asia have certainly furnished Washington with a wealth of lessons about how to do better the next time around, the idea of applying these lessons to Iran—a country with three times the population and four times the land mass of Iraq—is daunting. Moreover, since one of the lessons is clearly that large numbers of troops are needed to secure the country for months after an invasion and that those troops could only be provided by a massive, long-term call-up of National Guard and military reserve units that might wreck the all-volunteer force, it is just unclear how the United States could reasonably expect to handle postwar Iran if the American people ever did change their perspective enough that an invasion became politically feasible.

GOAL

The goal of the Invasion option of Iran would be to forcibly remove the Iranian government, crush its military power to prevent any remnants of the regime from reasserting their control over Iranian society, and extirpate its nuclear programs. Unfortunately, as Washington learned in Iraq (and to a lesser extent in Afghanistan), that cannot be the limit of American goals. As the wars in Iraq and Afghanistan have demonstrated, the United States would inevitably have to ensure that a reasonably stable and reasonably pro-American (or at least less anti-American) government would be able to assume power and rule the country after U.S. forces departed.

Like Iraq, Iran is too intrinsically and strategically important a country for the United States to be able to march in, overthrow its government, and then march out, leaving chaos in its wake. Iran exports about 2.5 million barrels of oil per day, and, with the right technology, it could produce even more. It also has one of the largest reserves of natural gas in the world. These resources make Iran an important supplier of the energy needs of the global economy. Iran does not border Saudi Arabia—the lynchpin of the oil market—or Kuwait, but it does border Iraq, another major oil producer and a country where the United States now has a great deal at stake. Moreover, Iran borders Turkey, a NATO ally, as well as Afghanistan (where the United States has a growing investment) and Pakistan—one of the most unstable and dangerous countries in the world. Thus the impact of spillover from chaos in Iran would likely threaten vital American interests in several locations.

Consequently, if the United States ever were to contemplate an invasion of Iran, it would likely find itself in the same bind as it is in Iraq: the country is too important to be allowed to slide into chaos, but given Iran's internal divisions and dysfunctional governmental system, it would be a major undertaking to rebuild it. As with Iraq and Afghanistan, the reconstruction of Iran would likely be the longest and hardest part of any invasion, and would generate risks and costs so great that a decision to invade could only be responsibly made if there were a concomitant commitment to a full-scale effort to ensure the country's stability afterwards.

Time Frame

In theory, the United States could mount an invasion at any time. The president could order an invasion tomorrow, which would seem to make this option very time efficient. But the reality, of course, is that it is highly unlikely that he would do so, and there are many hurdles to be cleared before the first troops would hit the beaches. Although an invasion might accomplish its objectives more quickly than Engagement or the various regime change options, it still would require months of military and logistical preparations, and it might take even longer to lay the political and international foundations.

It seems highly unlikely that the United States would mount an invasion without any provocation or other buildup. Even in the case of the Bush administration's march to war with Iraq in 2003—which was about as fast as it is possible to imagine—there was almost a year of preparations, starting with ominous statements from the administration, new UN Security Council resolutions, a congressional vote, the buildup of forces, and an ultimatum to Saddam Husayn. Moreover, in the case of Iraq, there was a legal basis that the Bush administration could rely upon (the same basis that Bush 41 and Clinton had used to justify various air- and missile strikes against Iraq during the 1990s). In the case of an invasion of Iran, there does not yet seem to be a legal predicate to justify the use of force—which is important more because it is required under domestic U.S. law than because of the need for international legal sanction. If a provocation or a UN Security Council resolution is needed to provide that legal basis, that also will take time.

In fact, if the United States were to decide that to garner greater international support, galvanize U.S. domestic support, and/or provide a legal justification for an invasion, it would be best to wait for an Iranian provocation, then the time frame for an invasion might stretch out indefinitely. With only one real exception, since the 1978 revolution, the Islamic Republic has never willingly provoked an American military response, although it certainly has taken actions that could have done so if Washington had been looking for a fight.[2] Thus it is not impossible that Tehran might take some action that would justify an American invasion. And it is certainly the case that if Washington sought such a provocation, it could take actions that might make it more likely that Tehran would do so (although being too obvious about this could nullify the provocation). However, since it would be up to Iran to make the provocative move, which Iran has been wary of doing most times in the past, the United States would never know for sure when it would get the requisite Iranian provocation. In fact, it might never come at all.

As far as the time requirements for the military side of the option, it might take a few months to move the forces into the region, and then anywhere from one to six months to conduct the invasion, depending on a variety of circumstances—particularly how much U.S. forces had been built up in the region before the attack was launched. Nevertheless, it is important to keep in mind that the rapid launch of the war against Iraq was a function of the inadequate number of troops and planning for postwar reconstruction. Since Washington would not want to repeat that tragic mistake in Iran, the buildup for an invasion of Iran would have to be bigger and thus take longer to complete than the buildup for the Iraq invasion. Finally, the preparations for Iraq were greatly aided by a superb network of American bases in the Persian Gulf. Absent some dramatic Iranian provocation, it seems very unlikely that those same countries (Kuwait, Bahrain, Qatar, and Britain, in particular) would allow the United States to use those same facilities for an invasion of Iran, potentially further lengthening the time required for the invasion itself.

As in both Iraq and Afghanistan, postinvasion reconstruction would be the longest (and possibly the bloodiest) part of the whole endeavor. If it were handled very well, applying all of the lessons learned in Iraq and Afghanistan, it might require only a few years of major military and financial commitments, followed by a significant diminution of U.S. presence and aid thereafter. If the reconstruction were to go badly, either because of American mistakes or forces beyond U.S. control, it could take many more years to produce an acceptable end state.

OVERVIEW OF THE POLICY

A ground invasion of Iran designed to overthrow the government would be onerous but rather straightforward. Indeed, it would likely have considerable parallels with the overthrow of Saddam's regime in Iraq and the Taliban regime in Afghanistan. Because the United States probably could not mount the invasion using bases in any of Iran's neighboring countries (discussed in greater detail below), a U.S. Marine Corps force would first have to seize control of a regional port, after which the United States could establish a logistical base and build up its ground and air forces before embarking on a "march" of several hundred miles north to Tehran.

The key to this policy option is not the mechanics of its implementation but mustering both the political support and the resources needed to make it work, and dealing with the potentially painful consequences of either its success or failure.

REQUIREMENTS

The requirements for the Invasion option are complex. In some ways, they are well within American capabilities; in other ways, they are potentially well beyond our current reach.

The Question of a Provocation

As noted above, in the section on the time frame for an invasion, whether the United States decides to invade Iran with or without a provocation is a critical consideration. With provocation, the international diplomatic and domestic political requirements of an invasion would be mitigated, and the more outrageous the Iranian provocation (and the less that the United States is seen to be goading Iran), the more these challenges would be diminished. In the absence of a sufficiently horrific provocation, meeting these requirements would be daunting.

For purposes of this analytic exercise, we assume that a U.S. invasion of Iran is not triggered by an overt, incontrovertible, and unforgivable act of aggression—something on the order of an Iranian-backed 9/11, in which the planes bore Iranian markings and Tehran boasted about its sponsorship. First, this seems exceptionally unlikely given Iran's history of avoiding such acts, at least since the end of the Iran-Iraq War. Second, were that ever to happen, the circumstances of an invasion would become almost easy—the United States would suddenly have enormous domestic and (perhaps grudging) international support for undertaking an invasion. Indeed, the entire question of "options" would become irrelevant at that point: what American president could refrain from an invasion after the Iranians had just killed several thousand American civilians in an attack in the United States itself?

Beyond such a blatant act of inexcusable aggression, the question of provocation gets murky. Most European, Asian, and Middle Eastern publics are dead set against any American military action against Iran derived from the current differences between Iran and the international community—let alone Iran and the United States. Other than a Tehran-sponsored 9/11, it is hard to imagine what would change their minds. For many democracies and some fragile autocracies to which Washington would be looking for support, this public antipathy is likely to prove decisive.

For instance, Saudi Arabia is positively apoplectic about the Iranians' nuclear program, as well as about their mischief making in Lebanon, Iraq, and the Palestinian territories. Yet, so far, Riyadh has made clear that it will not support military operations of any kind against Iran. Certainly that could change, but it is hard to imagine what it would take. For instance, one might speculate that further Iranian progress on enrichment might suffice, but the Iranians already have the theoretical know-how and plenty of feedstock to make the fissile material for a bomb.[3] Given that this situation has not been enough to push the GCC to support military operations against Iran, what would? Certainly Iran testing a nuclear device might, but at that point, it almost certainly would be too late: if the United States is going to invade Iran, it will want to do so *before* Iran has developed actual nuclear weapons, not after. It is hard to know what else Iran could do that would change GCC attitudes about the use of force unless new leaders took power in the Gulf who were far more determined to stop Iran than the current leadership is. And the GCC states tend to be more worried about the threat from Iran than European or East Asian countries are.

Given all this, there does not seem to be much utility in examining an American invasion of Iran in the context of an overt Iranian attack that produced mass American civilian casualties. It does not seem to be a scenario that the United States is likely to face, nor is it an "option" for American foreign policy because the outcry from the American people for an overwhelming military response would drown out all other possible approaches. The more challenging scenario for the United States, and one that is still a potential policy option, is to mount an invasion of Iran without an outrageous provocation, simply to eliminate Iran as a source of problems in the Middle East. In this situation, Washington would be effectively deciding to "go it alone" because it will be too difficult to create the circumstances that would result in any meaningful aid from other countries. It is this scenario that is most relevant to this study, and therefore the scenario that will be treated below.

Diplomatic Requirements

Given the context laid out above, the diplomatic requirements for an invasion of Iran would appear to be impossible and therefore irrelevant. If the United States decides to invade Iran without some dramatic Iranian provocation, the likelihood of international support will be slim to none. To be blunt, Israel is probably the only country that would *publicly* support an American invasion of Iran, and because of its difficult circumstances, it would not be in a position to furnish much assistance of any kind to the United States. Many Arab states would welcome the demise of the Islamic Republic in private, but probably none would publicly support what would be widely considered an illegitimate action and one more act of American aggression against another Muslim state. All of them would be terrified that the result would be as harmful to them as the invasion and botched occupation of Iraq. The Europeans, Russians, Chinese, and entire third world could be counted on to vehemently oppose another rogue act of American unilateralism.

As a result, the United States would have to opt for an invasion in the expectation that it would have effectively *no* support from any of Iran's neighbors. The Gulf states would warn the United States not to do it and probably would prevent the use of American bases in their countries for the operation. No Iraqi or Afghan government, no matter how beholden to the United States, would want to risk supporting a war that so few of their people, their neighbors, or their Islamic brethren would support. The Russians would likely come down hard on the Caucasus and Central Asian states not to support another act of American aggression so close to their borders—although this might just be enough to provoke countries like Georgia and Azerbaijan to allow the United States some modest basing rights in expectation of American protection against Moscow.

Military Requirements

As with Iraq and Afghanistan, the military requirements for an invasion of Iran could prove deceptive. The invasion itself would be a major military operation, but one well within the capability of American forces. Once in, however, a long-term commitment would be necessary, which would greatly increase the military requirements.

Although Iran's armed forces are roughly twice as large as Saddam's were in 2003 (750,000 to 1 million in the Iranian armed forces today compared to about 400,000 to 500,000 in Iraq's various military services back then) and probably would perform somewhat better, they are clearly outclassed by the American military. Consequently, an initial invasion force might be comparable to that employed against Iraq in 2003. Four U.S. divisions and a British division spearheaded the 2003 invasion and disposed of the Iraqi dictator and provoked the dissolution of his military and police forces in a matter of weeks. A fifth American division aided in the latter stages of the invasion; all told, about 200,000 Western military personnel were involved.

Against Iran, a U.S. invasion force would face two primary military obstacles: insurgents and terrain. Iran is a country principally of mountains and deserts—two of the most difficult military terrain types. In addition, Iran has considerable experience with guerrilla warfare through its long association with Hizballah and the support it provided for the latter's (successful) guerrilla war against Israel in southern Lebanon. After watching the American blitzkrieg to Baghdad, the Iranians have concluded that the best way to fight the U.S. military would be through a protracted insurgency, bleeding American forces (especially as they wend their way through the long, difficult mountain chains that fence in the Iranian heartland) and wearing them down.

To deal with the terrain and Iran's likely defensive strategy, an American invasion of Iran would require a variety of different kinds of forces. First, it would probably involve a significant contingent of Marines (two to four regimental combat teams, or about 15,000 to 30,000 Marines) to seize a beachhead and then a major port at one of four or five general locations where such a landing could be staged along the Iranian coastline. To get past the mountains, the United States would then want large numbers of air mobile forces—the brigades of the 101st Air Assault Division and the 82nd Airborne Division, and possibly the 173rd Airborne Brigade as well. Beyond that, the United States would want at least one, and possibly as many as three, heavy armored divisions for the drive on Tehran itself (depending on the extent to which the Marines and air mobile units are tied down holding the landing area and mountain passes open, as well as providing route security for the massive logistical effort that would be needed to supply the American expedition). Again, this suggests a force roughly comparable to that employed for Operation Iraqi Freedom: four to six divisions amounting to 200,000 to 250,000 troops.

Assuming that Washington receives little or no support from neighboring states to mount an invasion, a large naval commitment would also be required (one thing that would be different from the invasion of Iraq). It is unlikely that the United States could move forward with an enormous military operation without the Iranian government getting a sense of what was headed their way. This being the case, the United States would have to expect that the Iranians would fight back with everything they had, and under these circumstances, the Iranian naval and air forces would do everything they could to close the Strait of Hormuz and otherwise attack American naval forces to prevent them from landing U.S. ground forces on Iranian soil. Iran certainly has some potentially dangerous capabilities, but if the U.S. Navy and Air Force bring their full might to bear, they could methodically crush Iran's air and sea defenses in a matter of weeks, with relatively few losses. However, this will require a major commitment of American minesweeping, surface warfare, and (especially) air assets.

Beyond this, the navy would likely have to contribute much greater air support to the ground campaign than was the case for the invasions of either Iraq or Afghanistan. Certainly, some U.S. aircraft (like B-2 Stealth bombers) could fly from the continental United States (and Washington might get British permission to use the island of Diego Garcia for B-1s, B-52s, and tankers), but unless the GCC states, Iraq, and/or Central Asian countries could be persuaded to allow the U.S. Air Force to operate from nearby airfields, the vast majority of American aircraft would have to operate from carriers in the Persian Gulf and North Arabian Sea. Given the extent to which modern U.S. ground operations rely on air support (including during occupation and counterinsurgency campaigns), this suggests that three or more carriers would need to be committed to this campaign, at least until Iranian air bases could be secured and developed to handle U.S. Air Force planes.

Similarly, if the United States were denied access to its many bases in the Persian Gulf region, as seems likely, the navy would have to bring in everything needed to support the invasion, and U.S. engineers would have to build facilities at Iranian ports to make them capable of supporting a massive force.

Indeed, because it is likely that the United States would have little regional support, because the distances involved would be much greater than in Iraq (distances from major Iranian ports to Tehran are anywhere from one and a half to three times as great as the distance from the Kuwaiti border to Baghdad), and because of the much more difficult terrain, the logistical requirements for an invasion of Iran could be considerably more demanding than those for an invasion of Iraq.

Finally, it is worth noting that this undertaking would likely create a desperate need for a range of specialized forces that are already in short supply. Special forces units would be in high demand for an invasion of Iran, but that would mean diverting them from Iraq and Afghanistan, where they are also desperately needed. And if the supply of Arabic speakers was inadequate for the demands of the war in Iraq, it will seem luxurious in comparison to the numbers of Farsi speakers available in the U.S. military and the government at large (despite a heroic effort by the Defense Language Institute to turn out more Farsi speakers since 2001).

Requirements of the Occupation

Given the significant (but decreasing) U.S. commitment in Iraq and the considerable (and increasing) U.S. commitment in Afghanistan, assembling an invasion force for Iran would be a daunting task. However, it would pale compared to the needs of the postconflict security and reconstruction mission.

This will likely prove true even if Washington has learned the lessons of Iraq and mounts the invasion and occupation of Iran exactly as it should have done in Iraq. All low-intensity conflict operations, whether a counterinsurgency campaign or a stability operation like securing postinvasion Iran, require relatively large numbers of security forces because the sine qua non of success is securing the civilian populace against widespread violence. Scholars and counterinsurgency experts have suggested that it takes about 20 security personnel per 1,000 people to secure civilians against insurgencies and other forms of violence common in postconflict reconstruction.[4] This ratio suggests that an occupation force of 1.4 million troops would be needed for Iran.

There is reason to believe that high-quality troops with lavish support assets (like the U.S. military) can get away with less than the canonical figure. However, even if the United States, by relying on far superior training, technology, and tactics, could cut that number in half, the remainder still represents essentially the *entire* active duty component of the U.S. Army and Marine Corps. Even if it were only necessary to maintain such a large force in Iran for the first six months, after which the United States could begin drawing down its forces quickly (as experience in the Balkans and even Iraq suggests is possible), such a commitment would certainly require a massive mobilization of the National Guard and both the Army and Marine Reserves. It might necessitate their total mobilization for at least six to twelve months and might also require major redeployments away from Iraq and Afghanistan.

Again, assuming a best-case scenario in which the proper application of the lessons learned from Iraq and Afghanistan enables the invasion and occupation of Iran to go more easily and be more peaceful and successful, it would take several years to establish a stable, legitimate government with competent, loyal security forces that can take over the security of their country from the United States. During that time, the United States would doubtless have to maintain 100,000 to 200,000 troops in Iran, even under ideal circumstances of full Iranian cooperation and minimal resistance (or even criminality). If one assumes that during the same period, total U.S. military commitments in Iraq and Afghanistan will also remain in the 100,000 to 150,000 troop range (with the assumption of a declining commit-

ment to Iraq and a growing commitment to Afghanistan, albeit smaller than
the one in Iraq at its peak), it is hard to imagine how the current level of
American ground forces could sustain such deployments over the period of
years that would be required. Only a major, rapid increase in the size of the
armed forces would make that possible without destroying the National
Guard and military reserve systems—an increase that perhaps would necessitate some form of partial conscription.

Moreover, it obviously would be unwise to assume the best case. The
Bush administration's insistence that only the best case was possible in Iraq
lies at the root of the concatenation of mistakes that produced the worst case
in Iraq from 2003 to 2006. Iranians are fiercely nationalistic, and while many
would welcome the end of their current regime and the establishment of a
better relationship with the United States, the evidence suggests that most
would fiercely oppose a U.S. invasion. Accounting for more realistic scenarios increases the challenges and requirements for the occupation of Iran
even more, to levels that realistically only could be met by a major, rapid
expansion of the U.S. armed forces, for which the American people appear
to have little interest.

Political Requirements

Because the military requirements of the occupation and reconstruction
of Iran are so daunting, and the likelihood of international support in this
scenario appears so low, the first and most important requirement would be
the overwhelming political support of the American people for an invasion.
Simply put, compared to U.S. involvement in Iraq, the invasion and reconstruction of Iran is likely to be a more taxing task—even assuming that the
United States avoids repeating the mistakes of Iraq—and there will be even
less foreign assistance to accomplish it.

This means that the president would have to have such strong and
enduring support from the American people that he would be able to conduct the invasion and occupation of Iran employing essentially only
American resources and in the face of widespread international animos-
ity. He might need to mobilize fully the National Guard as well as the
Army, Marine, and possibly Navy Reserves and keep them in uniform for
months or even years if there is considerable Iranian resistance, as there
may well be. In worst-case scenarios, the president might even need to ask
the American people to accept some form of limited conscription. If the

occupation of Iran were to go badly, there might be considerable American casualties for long periods of time—possibly even more than in Iraq at its worst because of the more difficult terrain, the likely greater hostility of the populace, and the greater proficiency in guerrilla warfare of the Iranian military.

If the president can secure this kind of support, an invasion of Iran is a viable option. Without such support, the invasion and occupation of Iran would likely be as mismanaged and tragic as it was in Iraq from 2003 to 2006.

PROS AND CONS

The following are the advantages and disadvantages of the Invasion approach.

Advantages

—The most important and obvious advantage of mounting an invasion of Iran is that it would "solve" all of Washington's current problems with Tehran. Iran's nuclear program would be obliterated. The regime that supported so many terrorist, insurgent, and revolutionary groups that sought to harm the United States and/or its regional allies would be gone. Hizballah, Hamas, the Palestinian Islamic Jihad, and the like would have lost one of their most important backers. And Washington would no longer have to worry about how to deal with a regime it considers both threatening and maddeningly opaque.

—Moreover, a policy focused entirely on mounting an invasion of Iran would be implemented entirely under American control. Washington might find itself in a position where it would not need to worry about convincing reluctant allies, since there would be no expectation that they could be convinced nor any expectation that they would help. Furthermore, Washington would not need to persuade the Iranian leadership (or even Iranian dissidents) to cooperate with the United States—it could force them to do so, or simply get rid of them and bring in a whole new group.

—Finally, it would mean employing the most powerful, most skillful, and most decisive tool in the U.S. strategic toolkit—the American armed forces—to "fix" the Iran problem. Neither American covert operatives nor diplomats nor aid mavens have had a track record as good as U.S. soldiers, sailors, airmen, and Marines over the years.

Disadvantages

—An invasion of Iran would be extremely costly in a whole variety of ways. Iran is arguably a more complex, convoluted, and conflict-ridden society than either Iraq or Afghanistan. But like Iraq, it would be too important to be cast aside after deposing the regime and razing all its nuclear and terrorist-support facilities. The invasion itself would be large and costly, but the effort needed to occupy, secure, and then build a new Iranian state—one capable of governing the country effectively without falling into chaos or inciting new anti-Americanism—would be far more so. Even if Washington has learned all of the lessons of Iraq and Afghanistan and handles an invasion of Iran in a much better fashion, this option would cost tens—if not hundreds—of billions of dollars a year for five to ten years. It would require the commitment of the better part of U.S. ground forces for several years, and could necessitate a much greater commitment and expansion of American ground forces than at any time since the Second World War. It might even require the institution of partial conscription for some period of time and would divert badly needed assets away from both Iraq and Afghanistan.

—Another inevitable cost would be in American lives lost (not to mention Iranian civilian deaths). Hundreds or possibly thousands of American military personnel would die in the invasion itself. Thereafter, casualty levels would depend dramatically on both the extent of Iranian resistance and the competence of the American security effort. The remarkable success of American forces in Iraq since 2007 demonstrates that the right numbers of troops employing the right tactics in pursuit of the right strategy can secure a country at much lower cost in blood than inadequate numbers of troops improperly employed. Prior to the Surge—and during its heated early months when U.S. troops were fighting to regain control of Iraq's streets—American military deaths were running at 70 to 80 a month. Once that fight had been won, they fell to roughly 5 to 15 a month. This suggests that U.S. casualties during the occupation and reconstruction of Iran could vary enormously; however, only in the best-case scenario—where the securing of Iran is as smooth as the NATO securing of Bosnia—should policymakers expect minimal casualties. In more plausible but still favorable scenarios where Iranian resistance approximates Iraqi levels of violence after the Surge, the United States should still expect a dozen soldiers and Marines to be killed each month, on average, for several years. In worst-case scenarios, in which the United States mishandles operations in Iran as badly as it did initially in Iraq, those numbers could run into the hundreds each month, or worse.

—Washington would have to expect Tehran to retaliate against American targets outside of Iran. Iran has a more formidable ballistic missile arsenal than Saddam had in 1991 and a far more extensive and capable network to mount terrorist attacks beyond its borders. Whether the Iranians could pull off a catastrophic attack—along the lines of 9/11—would depend on how much time they had to prepare for such an operation and how well developed their contingency plans were at the time. Washington has long believed that Tehran maintains extensive contingency plans for all manner of terrorist attacks against American targets for just such an eventuality, and may even have practiced them at various times. Even if such attacks ended with the fall of the regime, since an invasion might take as much as six months from the time the first U.S. Navy warships began to clear the Strait of Hormuz to the removal of the clerical regime, the United States would have to prepare to prevent such attacks—and live with the failure to do so—for at least this time period.

—In addition to the potentially heavy costs, an invasion also entails running a very significant set of risks. As noted, Iranian society is hardly pacific. A botched reconstruction, like the one in Iraq, could unleash a Pandora's box of problems both inside the country and out. Various Iranian ethnic groups might attempt to declare independence, inevitably setting off a civil war with the country's Persian majority and creating the risk of drawing in Iran's various neighbors to protect their own interests. As in Iraq, Iran's oil wealth would be a tremendous driver of both internal conflict and external intervention. Chaos and conflict could jeopardize Iran's oil and gas exports, and would certainly complicate the security problems of Iraq, Afghanistan, and Pakistan.

—Under the circumstances postulated in this chapter, a U.S. invasion of Iran could antagonize much of the world. In the short term, this could jeopardize the international cooperation Washington so desperately needs to deal with the international financial crisis and a dozen or more pressing geostrategic crises. It may be difficult for other countries to heed America's wishes on Darfur, the Arab-Israeli conflict, North Korea, alternative energy and global warming, NATO enlargement, or other similarly thorny issues in the aftermath of an invasion of Iran that many may see as even less justified than the invasion of Saddam Husayn's Iraq.

—Moreover, an invasion of Iran has the potential to damage the longer-term strategic interests of the United States. Such an invasion could well redefine America's position in the international order in a particularly deleterious manner. Especially given that such a war would probably have less support than the invasion of Iraq, and would be undertaken by an administration other than that of George W. Bush, it would likely loom far larger than the Iraq War in the thinking of other people and governments. It could well settle the debate over whether the United States is an aggressive, unilateralist imperial power or a mostly benign and uniquely unselfish *hegemon.* Americans have always seen themselves as the latter, and there are many people around the world who still view the United States that way despite the events of 2001–2008—in large part because some agree that there were justifications for the war in Iraq, and others simply blame American actions on an aberrant administration. An invasion of Iran could eliminate the lingering basis for that support and profoundly alter global perspectives on the United States, which over time would inevitably translate into commensurate shifts in policy against this country.

CHAPTER FOUR

THE OSIRAQ OPTION

Airstrikes

Because there is little expectation that the Obama administration would be interested in paying the costs and running the risks associated with an invasion—let alone convincing the American people to do so at a time of national economic crisis—those who believe that force is the best, or even the only, way to address the problems of Iran are more likely to advocate a more limited campaign of airstrikes against key Iranian targets. In particular, such a policy would most likely target Iran's various nuclear facilities (possibly including key weapons delivery systems such as ballistic missiles) in a greatly expanded version of the Israeli preventive strikes against the Iraqi nuclear program at Tuwaitha in 1981 (usually referred to by the name of the French reactor under construction, the Osiraq reactor) and against the nascent Syrian program at Dayr az-Zawr in 2007. The United States might be able to provide a reasonable justification for such a campaign by building on the fact that the UN Security Council has repeatedly proscribed Iran's nuclear enrichment activities in resolutions enacted under Chapter VII of the UN Charter, which are binding on all member states.[1] Moreover, there is some expectation that a determined air campaign against Iran's nuclear facilities might set back its program by a meaningful period of time—at least some years.

The United States might mount further strikes against Iranian command and control, terrorist support, or even conventional military targets. However, these would more likely be staged in response to Iranian attacks against the United States or its allies that were mounted in retaliation for the initial round of American strikes on Iranian nuclear facilities. Simply destroying these other Iranian assets would have little material impact on American interests or Iran's ability to harm those interests. Terrorist camps, ministries, and headquarters buildings can all be rebuilt quickly, and it is unlikely that any damage done to them or the personnel within would somehow cripple Iran's ability to subvert regional governments or wage asymmetric warfare against the United States or its allies. The United States could certainly obliterate large chunks of the Iranian conventional military, which would take a long time for Iran to replace, but Iran's conventional forces are so weak that they have little geopolitical value, and therefore destroying them would have little impact on either the American or Iranian positions in the Middle East and Southwest Asia.

Thus airstrikes against Iranian nuclear sites are typically seen as part of a strategy meant principally to deprive it of its nuclear capabilities in a way that diplomacy could not. Airstrikes against these other target sets (terrorist training facilities, command and control, and conventional military forces) do not fit well into the concept of a disarming strike because they would not materially weaken Iran for very long.

Alternatively, the United States could choose to attack these non-nuclear target sets in pursuit of a different strategy, a coercive one. This strategy would not disarm Iran, but would put at risk those things that the regime values most, in an attempt to force Tehran to change its policy of supporting various terrorist groups, stoking instability in the region, and pursuing nuclear weapons. However, there is little support in the United States for employing a coercive strategy of repeated airstrikes against Iran to try to force Tehran to alter its course.

In many ways, this absence is remarkable given the long-standing support for coercive air campaigns among both air power enthusiasts and policymakers. At various points in the past, numerous American analysts, military officers, and political leaders have suggested an approach to Iran that relies on coercive air campaigns; thus its absence in the current debate is striking. The nationalistic chauvinism, ideological fervor, and political dysfunctions of the Islamic Republic, coupled with the long history of coercive air campaigns failing to live up to the claims of their proponents, seem to have produced a consensus that a coercive air campaign against Iran would likely fail. Simply put, it does not seem like the Iranian regime would be susceptible to the kind of pressure applied by coercive air power, and coercive air campaigns are notoriously bad at successfully compelling the target country to do what the attacking country wants.[2]

Consequently, the Airstrikes option against Iran has focused principally on a campaign intended to disarm Iran—to strip it of its nuclear capability—in the expectation that this would greatly reduce for some period of time the threat Iran poses to the United States and its allies. Of course, a key question debated even by its advocates is "how long a period of time," which in turn raises the question of whether this option is sufficient by itself to address effectively U.S. concerns about Iran, or whether it is merely the first piece of a more complex approach. Some proponents suggest that airstrikes constitute a stand-alone policy in that the United States could simply resume its attacks whenever the Iranians began to rebuild their nuclear facilities, as most observers suspect they would. The expectation is that at some point, the Iranians would tire of being bombed and give up, or the people would tire of a regime that keeps provoking American airstrikes and oust it. Other proponents of this policy argue that repeated bombings of Iran would be difficult to sustain (and might not lead to the regime's removal), and therefore, the Airstrikes option would be designed simply to buy time, hopefully several years, during which the United States could orchestrate other actions against Iran—such as a Persuasion approach that would carry the demonstrated threat of further uses of force as a very potent "stick," or a more determined effort at regime change that would also benefit from the demonstrated willingness of the United States to employ force against the Iranian regime.

GOAL

The goal of an air campaign would be to obliterate much or all of Iran's nuclear program, which is spread over a number of major nuclear energy related sites, on the assumption that any of them could be used to develop weapons. The list of targets would likely include at least the well-known nuclear research reactor at Bushehr, a range of locations related to Iran's uranium processing and enrichment program, and the Arak plutonium

separation plant, as well as sites believed to be involved in producing war-
heads or other components for nuclear weapons. It might also include other
targets involved in developing Iran's long-range missile force, which is the
most obvious method Iran would have of using nuclear weapons should it
acquire them.

If all of these targets were successfully destroyed, such a military operation might delay Iran's attainment of a nuclear weapon by a decade or more.
After Israel's 1981 Osiraq raid, Saddam Husayn was unable to build a "base-
ment bomb" over the following decade (although by the time of Operation
Desert Storm in 1991, he had come close). Such a lengthy delay might provide enough time for Iran's imperfect political process to produce a new
leadership before the existing one could create a bomb surreptitiously.

A more modest (or less successful) American or Israeli aerial campaign
would create havoc in the Iranian nuclear program but would not necessarily accomplish the physical annihilation of all facilities. Unless Iran has large
secret facilities of which Western intelligence and the IAEA are unaware,
such a campaign could also set back Iran's nuclear program, but probably
much less so than a larger and more successful strike. It would be difficult
to quantify, but a limited or less successful attack might delay Iran's attainment of a nuclear capability by anywhere from one to four years. If Iran *has*
managed to build large, secret facilities, like a second main uranium enrichment site, the delay to Iran's attainment of its first bomb could be much less.
This would be particularly true if Iran had moved enough uranium hexafluoride from known sites to have fuel for the centrifuges at the second site.

In short, if Iran is presently on track to have a nuclear bomb between 2010
and 2015, a highly successful major air campaign in which all of Iran's
nuclear facilities were destroyed might conceivably push back that time
frame to the 2015–2025 range. However, a less successful strike, a purposely
more limited strike, or one that misses major Iranian nuclear facilities
because they were unknown at the time might only push that window back
to 2010–2017. It is worth underscoring that all such time projections are
rough estimates at best, given the huge gaps in knowledge about Iran's
nuclear program.

It is also important to note that the Airstrike option is designed solely to
limit Tehran's capability to destabilize the Middle East and aggressively
oppose U.S. interests there by wielding nuclear weapons. It is not intended
to produce regime change in Tehran, nor is it meant to address Iran's other

problematic behavior—except in the indirect sense that if the Iranian leadership believes that the United States is prone to employ force against it for actions that Washington dislikes, Tehran might rein in its efforts across the board. However, this is hardly a guaranteed outcome; it is just as likely that Iran would respond by ratcheting up its problematic behavior, both to retaliate for the American raids and potentially to make it difficult for the United States to maintain its military presence in the Persian Gulf. Consequently, the goal of this option is simply to try to delay or even prevent Iran from acquiring a nuclear capability in the expectation that doing so will make Iran less of a threat.

TIME FRAME

To a great extent, the time frame for the Airstrikes option against Iran depends on a set of factors similar to that governing a possible invasion. In theory, airstrikes against Iran could be mounted in such a way that they are entirely under the control of the United States and require virtually no foreign contributions. In this set of circumstances, all that matters is how fast the required American military forces can be deployed to the region— although even in this case, the desire to preserve at least tactical secrecy (if not strategic surprise) would likely make such deployments more time consuming than they otherwise might be.

However, as with an invasion, airstrikes against Iran would certainly benefit from foreign support, particularly the willingness of regional U.S. allies to permit the use of bases near Iran. Moreover, because it is more likely (still a relative statement) that the United States could secure such support for airstrikes as opposed to an invasion, Washington may want to take the time to try to win over its regional allies in support of the airstrikes.

This raises many of the same issues discussed in the previous chapter regarding a provocation. Airstrikes launched without some act of Iranian aggression would likely find little public support anywhere outside of Israel. Again, most Arab governments might privately cheer, but they will find it hard to do more than that. However, if the airstrikes were launched in response to an Iranian provocation, the United States might find Arab, European, and Asian acquiescence, even enthusiasm, for them. Thus the more that the United States wants international political support for the air campaign (especially in the form of bases), the more important it would be for these strikes to come as a response to an act of Iranian aggression—and this means that Washington would have to be willing to wait (perhaps indefinitely) for the Iranians to take such an action.

As with an invasion, it would ultimately be Washington's choice as to when to begin airstrikes against Iran, but after that, the U.S. government would have far less control over when this conflict might end. In the case of an invasion, Washington would get to set the date for the invasion and could have some confidence that the regime would be gone six months later; however, the United States would then find itself committed to a potentially open-ended reconstruction process. Similarly, Washington could decide when and for how long to mount airstrikes against Iran. However, implementation of this policy would not be concluded when the smoke from the last bomb cleared. Iran might retaliate, and the United States might feel the need to respond to Iran's retaliation. In conjunction, or alternatively, Iran might decide to rebuild its nuclear program, and the United States would have to decide whether to launch another round of airstrikes, a potentially recurring cycle. Even if the Iranians chose not to retaliate or rebuild, they might not end their support for violent extremist groups or efforts to subvert the regional status quo, which would then require the United States to find some other way of convincing them to desist.

In short, airstrikes could be conducted relatively promptly, in a matter of weeks or months, and might buy time for other options (although they also might preclude many other options). However, as a policy, they could take years or even decades to "succeed" and even then might only satisfy part of the U.S. agenda.

Overview of the Policy

The core of this policy would be for the United States to mount an air campaign lasting anywhere from a few days to several weeks to strike at known Iranian nuclear facilities, with many aim points at the typical site.

Such a campaign would be well within U.S. military capabilities, but it would present a number of important challenges. For any aerial attack to be successful, it would naturally require good intelligence on the locations of all major Iranian nuclear facilities. It would demand weapons capable of reaching and destroying those facilities, including those in hardened structures well below the surface, as well as sufficient aircraft to carry them. It would involve an even greater number of support aircraft—to suppress Iran's air defenses, shoot down its fighters, control the air battle, carry supplies, refuel American jets flying long distances, monitor Iranian reactions, and assess the impact of strikes. And it would require extensive command and control, communications, and intelligence capabilities to direct, coordinate, and evaluate the strikes.

Having observed the Israeli Air Force's virtuoso performance against the Osiraq reactor, as well as numerous American air campaigns in the Middle East and the Balkans, Iran's revolutionary regime broadly understands how the United States would seek to mount such an effort and has devoted considerable effort to hide, diversify, and protect its nuclear assets. Many Iranian facilities are in hardened concrete structures and/or are deeply underground. Some may even be in tunnels deep within mountains, although a number of nuclear weapons experts doubt that major operational centrifuge complexes would be located in such places. The National Intelligence Estimate of 2007 assessed that if Iran were to pursue a bomb, it would likely use secret facilities to make highly enriched uranium (although the estimate famously concluded that Iran probably halted any such efforts in 2003, when Iran apparently stopped working on bomb design efforts). Iran has natural uranium deposits and has now mastered the basic technology of uranium enrichment—at least at the theoretical level—up to and including centrifuge enrichment, so even if an attack were highly successful, the United States would still have to consider the possibility that Iran could rebuild its entire program.

Given the multiplicity of targets and the lengths to which the regime has gone to protect them, Israel's 1981 Osiraq strike or even its 2007 Dayr az-Zawr raid in Syria are not particularly good models for an air campaign against Iran. The attack against Iraq's nuclear reactor, for instance, was conducted in a single mission by just eight bomb-dropping Israeli F-16s and a half-dozen F-15s providing cover. The Israelis relied on surprise, a stealthy flight profile, and the relatively underdeveloped Iraqi air defense network to ensure their mission's success. In addition, they were attacking a single large, highly vulnerable, above-ground facility. It might be feasible to attack Iran's nuclear research reactor at Bushehr in this way, but that reactor is not the heart of the Iranian nuclear program: it is not complemented by a reprocessing facility (since Iran's nuclear cooperation contract with Russia requires that spent fuel be sent back to Russia for treatment), and its loss would have little impact on Iran's uranium enrichment program. A robust campaign against Iran's nuclear complex would have to contend with a large number of potential Iranian facilities—possibly several hundred—and an even greater number of potential aim points. A relatively *modest* campaign might still target several dozen key nuclear energy related sites. Some of these targets might have to be struck repeatedly to allow a first detonation to begin "burrowing" underground, exposing targets that could only be seriously damaged on a second or third pass.

Because of the number of aim points (which would mean relying on large numbers of nonstealthy aircraft) and the possible need for repeated strikes, an American campaign would likely involve a deliberate effort to suppress Iranian air defenses—something the much smaller Israeli strikes simply avoided in 1981 and 2007. In particular, the United States would seek to destroy large warning radars, advanced surface-to-air missile batteries, key command and control facilities for Iran's air defenses, and possibly the most dangerous Iranian fighter squadrons (such as those employing F-14s and MiG-29s). Consequently, an all-out air campaign could involve thousands of sorties by manned aircraft, unmanned drones, and cruise missiles over several days, while even a more limited operation would probably require hundreds of sorties. By way of comparison, Operation Desert Fox—a three-day air campaign against Iraq in 1998 that targeted 100 Iraqi facilities (many of them air defense sites, but about a dozen were weapons of mass destruction facilities)—required 650 manned aircraft sorties and 415 cruise missile strikes.

It is beyond the scope of this chapter to lay out all possible targets for an American air campaign against the Iranian nuclear program, but it is useful to enumerate the most important ones to give a sense of what the U.S. strikes would aim to destroy. These would likely include the following sites:

—*Bushehr Research Reactor.* Although this is nothing but a research reactor, it has received fuel from Russia and could soon be operational, giving it the theoretical capacity to make enough plutonium for dozens of bombs.

—*Arak Heavy-Water Reactor/Plutonium Separation Facility.* This is Iran's principal plutonium separation facility, although it is much further from completion than the Bushehr Research Reactor. This facility will produce purer plutonium than Bushehr does, making it easier to employ in a weapon. The location also hosts a nearby heavy-water production plant.

—*Natanz Uranium Enrichment Plant.* The uranium enrichment operation here is the centerpiece of Iran's nuclear program and the facility of greatest concern to the international community. Natanz was designed to house as many as 50,000 gas centrifuges, although only several thousand of the more primitive P-1 models were operating by early 2009 (still enough to make a bomb's worth of enriched uranium per year if reconfigured from producing low-enriched uranium to highly enriched uranium). Iran is already moving to install more advanced P-2 centrifuges, which have two and a half times the productive capacity of a P-1. The main centrifuge hall at Natanz is located ten to twenty meters underground, but since 2007, the Iranians have been digging even deeper tunnels into mountainsides near Natanz and may move centrifuge cascades and/or uranium storage facilities there, where they would be even better protected against American penetrator munitions.

—*Esfahan Nuclear Technology Center.* This is Iran's main uranium fuel fabrication plant that produces the uranium hexafluoride gas feedstock for the centrifuges at Natanz. Although this facility would doubtless be a key target, Iran already possesses enough uranium hexafluoride for dozens of nuclear weapons without needing to produce any more.

—*Parchin Nuclear Weapons Development Center.* Parchin is a massive military research and testing facility. Parts of it are believed to be associated with the nuclear program, including explosives testing. In addition to Parchin, U.S. airstrikes would likely target other Iranian facilities believed to be related to warhead design and production.

—*Karaj and Tehran Nuclear Research Centers.* These are important research and development facilities for the Iranian nuclear program. Both consist of about a dozen buildings, mostly office buildings, labs, and storage facilities. Because they are located in the suburbs of the Iranian capital, they create a considerable risk of collateral damage and require a major effort to suppress the fairly extensive (by Iranian standards) air defenses of Tehran.

—Advanced missile design, production, and testing facilities such as those at Karaj, Semnan, Sirjan, Esfahan, Shahroud, and the Shaid Hemat facility near Tehran.

—Any centrifuge production facilities, if U.S. intelligence is able to discover them.

Scaling Down

Even a campaign designed to go after this relatively limited target set would be a very large operation, probably on the scale of Desert Fox. Nevertheless, it would be smaller in scope than the kind of campaign military planners would prefer. From their perspective, a much larger operation designed to hit every facility possibly associated with the nuclear or missile programs would be preferable because this would provide the greatest confidence that the goal of the operation—setting back the Iranian nuclear program by a number of years—could be achieved. However, the United States may feel it is not sustainable to conduct an operation for the length of time needed to complete such a large campaign. A number of factors may contribute to this assessment: if other military contingencies made it impossible to bring sufficient aircraft to bear, if inadequate intelligence meant that the president did not feel comfortable bombing targets beyond those listed above, or if the United States wanted to maximize the element of surprise (to prevent Iran from concealing key elements of its nuclear program and/or to minimize American casualties) by mounting the operation without a buildup of forces in the region. As such, Washington might opt for such a "limited" variant of the policy.

As noted, even in this case, a small raid on the scale of Iraq in 1981 or Syria in 2007 would not be enough, given the sheer number of locations (including underground facilities) to be struck. Instead, the United States would likely conduct its "limited" operation in multiple stages. Dozens of cruise missile attacks—precisely timed to precede the arrival of manned aircraft—would begin the assault by targeting the most crucial and capable radar sites, as well as other relatively soft parts of the target set, such as above-ground communications centers. These would be followed by scores of shorter-range fighter bombers (Navy F-18s, possibly coupled with Air Force F-15s and F-16s if bases in the Persian Gulf were available) and several dozen B-1 and B-2 bombers flying from Diego Garcia, if it is available, or from the United States, if it is not. Many of these aircraft would carry deep-penetrating munitions and would be tasked to launch multiple weapons against a single aim point to ensure that deeply buried targets were destroyed.

No matter how confident Washington was of achieving surprise, the United States would want to employ a number of air superiority fighters to counter any Iranian fighters that got into the air, and airborne warning and control aircraft to orchestrate the air battle, along with aerial surveillance platforms to monitor Iranian ground activity. Military planners would also need satellites and unmanned intelligence and surveillance platforms, possibly supplemented by manned reconnaissance missions, to assess the damage done in the initial strike—and their findings might necessitate follow-on strikes. This entire effort would inevitably require considerable in-flight refueling from tankers based at Diego Garcia or wherever else possible. As a last resort, smaller navy tankers flying from carriers could at least refuel their own jets.

Such an operation would hardly seem "limited" to the Iranians, but it would be relatively small from the perspective of American air campaigns. It would have a reasonable likelihood of significantly degrading Iran's highest value nuclear targets, but it would be far from guaranteed to meet the goals of this policy. Moreover, by going lean and emphasizing surprise over mass, such an approach would run a number of risks. Fighter cover would have to be minimized in order to achieve surprise and to maximize the basing available for attack aircraft. Consequently, Iranian fighters might get lucky and knock down one or more American planes. The United States would not have enough Stealth bombers to conduct even this smaller raid exclusively; it would also need to use more detectable bombers and/or navy attack jets in the mission. This would raise the potential for American aircraft to fall prey to Iranian air defenses, although Iran's surface-to-air missile arsenal is very limited in both its coverage and capability. Perhaps regional states would allow the United States to fly fighter cover for the operation from land bases or—best of all for American planners—to fly stealthy F-22s that could conduct much of the strike themselves. But it could be hard to secure such support, as discussed below. Overall, this operation would be feasible for the United States, but its overall effectiveness would be hard to predict, and aircraft losses could not be ruled out.

Scaling Up

Alternatively, Washington might decide that if it is going to mount an air campaign against Iran—with all the costs and risks this course of action will inevitably entail—it should at least make sure that the campaign itself is powerful enough to maximize the likelihood that the United States achieves its objectives.

A more comprehensive air campaign would likely be structured and sequenced somewhat differently than the scaled-down approach. In the first wave of sorties, some strikes might be directed against key Iranian nuclear facilities, especially those containing assets that are believed to be easy for Iran to move. But this type of campaign would likely focus its initial attacks on destroying Iranian air defenses, including radars, surface-to-air missiles, and fighter aircraft, in order to establish air supremacy and thereby facilitate additional waves of bombing directed at the nuclear targets themselves. The follow-on waves would likely strike and then restrike the targets listed above to ensure their destruction, but they would also go after dozens of other Iranian targets that either play a more peripheral role in the nuclear program or for which the evidence of a tie to the nuclear program is less certain. Moreover, some sorties might be directed—or merely held in reserve—against Iranian air and naval forces deployed along the Strait of Hormuz to prevent them from attempting to close the strait in response to the American strikes.

Even in this approach, there would be incentives to achieve surprise, so the United States might want to begin the operation with only a single aircraft carrier, or else time its start to an instance when one carrier was relieving another, so that two would be temporarily present. The real problems would come if the United States felt it needed three or four carriers for this operation. (It is worth noting that six U.S. carriers supported Operation Desert Storm, two supported Desert Fox, and three supported Iraqi Freedom—and all of those campaigns were able to count on the use of Persian Gulf ground bases that might not be available for the campaign against Iran considered in this chapter.) Because it takes weeks to deploy a carrier to the Persian Gulf, and because it is very difficult to conceal a carrier's destination, the conflicting demands of surprise and mass would create a dilemma for a large air campaign against Iran. The best solution would be the availability of land bases in the Persian Gulf, Central Asia, and the Caucasus, to which air force jets could be rapidly deployed. However, because the United States may find little overt support for any military campaign against Iran, this option might not be available. In that case, Washington will have to decide whether surprise or mass is more important and deploy its aircraft carriers accordingly.

Facing Iranian Retaliation

It would not be inevitable that Iran would lash out violently in response to an American air campaign, but no American president should blithely assume that it would not. Iran has not always retaliated for American attacks against it. Initially after the destruction of Pan Am Flight 103 in December 1988, many believed that this was Iranian retaliation for the shooting down of Iran Air Flight 455 by the American cruiser USS *Vincennes* in July of that year. However, today all of the evidence points to Libya as the culprit for that terrorist attack, which if true would suggest that Iran never did retaliate for its loss. Nor did Iran retaliate for America's Operation Praying Mantis, which in 1988 resulted in the sinking of most of Iran's major warships. Consequently, it is possible that Iran would simply choose to play the victim if attacked by the United States, assuming (probably correctly) that this would win the clerical regime considerable sympathy both domestically and internationally.

However, it is at least equally likely that Iran would shoot back as best it could. As noted above, Iran may attempt to shut down the Strait of Hormuz in response, but this seems unlikely. Doing so would threaten the international oil market and so lose Iran whatever international sympathy it might have gained for being the victim of an American attack. Of greater importance, American air and naval capabilities are so overwhelming that it would simply be a matter of time before the U.S. military could wipe out its Iranian counterparts and reopen the strait. The result would simply add insult to injury for Tehran. Especially given that under these circumstances, American naval and air forces available in the Persian Gulf will be vastly more powerful than is normally the case, such a move by the Iranians would appear to be playing right into Washington's hands.

It seems far more likely that Tehran might choose to respond in kind (roughly) by lobbing ballistic missiles at U.S. bases, oil facilities, and other high-value targets located in the Gulf states, Israel, or other U.S. ally states. This contingency would merit deploying considerable antiballistic missile defense assets in the region and providing as much warning to U.S. allies as possible. However, because many Iranian leaders would likely be looking to emerge from the fighting in as advantageous a strategic position as possible, and because they would likely calculate that playing the victim would be their best route to that goal, they might well refrain from such retaliatory missile attacks.

The most likely method of Iranian retaliation would be some form of terrorist attack. It could be immediate and coincident with the U.S. air campaign. As noted in the previous chapter, Iran is believed to have exten-

sive contingency plans for attacks on American targets, and it might be possible for Tehran to execute some of these operations in a matter of days.
Such retaliation also could come well after the fact. In particular, if Tehran
wanted to retaliate in spectacular fashion, especially by conducting attacks
on American soil to reciprocate for the American attacks on Iranian soil, it
would likely take months to arrange. Major terrorist operations require
extensive planning and preparatory work, and they are especially difficult to
execute in the United States ever since the security improvements that followed 9/11. Consequently, an indivisible part of the Airstrike option would
be to take a wide range of steps to harden U.S. targets against the possibility
of Iranian retaliation by terrorist attack—steps that would have to be maintained for many months thereafter.

Follow-Up or Follow-On?

The last piece of this policy option is the question of what follows the
airstrikes. It is hard to imagine that even a couple of weeks of American
airstrikes, encompassing thousands of sorties, would simply end the problem
of the Iranian nuclear program forever. It is highly likely that, at least initially,
the Iranian population would rally around the hardest of the hard-liners in
their government—those people most antagonistic to the United States—in
response to what Iranians would inevitably see as an unprovoked and unjus-
tified act of aggression, no matter what preceded the American strikes. Those
leaders, riding a crest of support for them and fury at the United States,
would almost certainly insist that Iran begin to rebuild its nuclear program,
if only out of sheer defiance of the United States. Of course, they would have
a very powerful new argument to employ: the United States would not dare
to attack us in such a fashion if we actually had a nuclear weapon. They might
use the attacks to justify pulling Iran out of the Non-Proliferation Treaty,
thereby eliminating the ability of international arms control experts to monitor Iran's nuclear facilities and provide much-needed information about the
status, location, and progress of Iran's program.

If the United States were to adopt the Airstrike option, it would have to
anticipate that the initial round of airstrikes would not eliminate the problem altogether, and so the policy would have to include a series of next steps
to cover the long term. As already noted, some proponents of the Airstrikes
option argue that the right long-term approach is simply repeated airstrikes:
every time the Iranians begin to rebuild their nuclear program, strike again

to knock it down. They argue that, if nothing else, this would simply keep pushing the operational date of an Iranian nuclear weapon farther and farther into the future. At best, repeated airstrikes might eventually convince the Iranian people that their leaders' policies were bringing ruin on their country, and so they would overthrow the regime.

Other proponents suggest that the initial round of airstrikes (and possibly a follow-on round) would be intended simply to buy time for other options, particularly regime change. Still others, who tend to be leery of the military option against Iran, have suggested that the Airstrikes option would only make sense if the United States could ensure that a tight new Containment regime could be imposed immediately afterward to hinder Iran's ability to reconstitute its nuclear program or to retaliate, and thereby avoid the need for additional American military strikes. In short, these approaches do not consider Airstrikes as a stand-alone option but rather as one element in a more complex strategy, a topic explored at greater length in the conclusion to this volume.

Requirements

Military

In many ways, the military requirements of the Airstrike option are the least taxing and probably the easiest for the United States to satisfy (which is partly why this option is appealing to many people). America's massive air and naval forces are more than adequate to handle the military aspects of this option and are so able to accomplish the missions that there would be multiple ways in which they could do so. This creates considerable flexibility in the military leg of this policy stool. It means that the military component can, and probably would have to be, tailored to suit the diplomatic and political requirements, which would likely prove to be far more limiting. But, as described in some detail above, whatever the diplomatic and political circumstances, the U.S. military would undoubtedly be able to generate the forces necessary.

Instead, in the military realm, a key concern would be whether any of Iran's neighbors would be willing to allow U.S. aircraft to use their air bases. If not, then the United States would have to rely far more heavily on aircraft carriers, which in turn raises the potential trade-off between surprise and mass. That trade-off is intimately intertwined with the list of targets that the

United States would seek to hit: the longer that list, the more planes and cruise missiles would be needed. Similarly, if the president did not believe that he could sustain this campaign politically and diplomatically for very long, the military would have to adjust the ambitions of the operations.

Diplomatic

The United States would have two overriding diplomatic objectives should it decide to conduct airstrikes against Iran. In an immediate sense, it would need to generate as much support for the attacks as possible, especially among Iran's neighbors, in hopes of securing the use of their airfields to base American jets. As noted above, the availability of these bases is a very important consideration for many key military aspects of the airstrikes, such as their size, duration, and ability to achieve surprise.

In a broader and ultimately more important sense, U.S. diplomacy would have to ensure that the air campaign against Iran does not derail every other American policy initiative in the region. When considering this option, it is critical to keep in mind that the policy's ultimate objective is to obliterate the Iranian nuclear program in the expectation that doing so would greatly limit Iran's ability to hamper other American policy initiatives in the region, such as a new Israeli-Palestinian peace process, a drawdown from Iraq that does not jeopardize its political progress, improving the situation in Afghanistan, and so on.

A critical challenge for this policy option is that, absent a clear Iranian act of aggression, American airstrikes against Iran would be unpopular in the region and throughout the world. This negative reaction could undermine any or all of America's policy initiatives in the region regardless of how the Iranians respond. The vast majority of countries whose partnership is necessary to advance these other policies, including those that dislike or even fear Iran, do not want to see American military operations against Iran out of dislike for unilateral American military operations and/or fear of the repercussions in the region. Thus Washington cannot allow airstrikes against Iran to become a self-defeating course of action that undermines the other U.S. policies that this option is ultimately meant to enable.

Especially in the absence of a clear Iranian provocation, averting this paradoxical danger would be a major task for U.S. diplomats in the run-up to such an air campaign. They would have to make the case that Iran's continued refusal to accede to the will of the international community to halt its nuclear enrichment activities (as stipulated in multiple Security Council resolutions enacted under Chapter VII of the UN Charter) threatened the security of the Middle East and jeopardized the global nonproliferation regime. They would have to persuade these governments that the United States had reasonably tried all of the alternative approaches and none had succeeded. They would have to argue that the American actions were ultimately designed to enhance the stability of the region and that it would be a mistake for everyone if countries allowed their pique at Washington to impede other initiatives that are ultimately in the best interests of the entire region and the entire world.

The truth is that these all would be challenging cases to make. For that reason, it would be far more preferable if the United States could cite an Iranian provocation as justification for the airstrikes before launching them. Clearly, the more outrageous, the more deadly, and the more unprovoked the Iranian action, the better off the United States would be. Of course, it would be very difficult for the United States to goad Iran into such a provocation without the rest of the world recognizing this game, which would then undermine it. (One method that would have some possibility of success would be to ratchet up covert regime change efforts in the hope that Tehran would retaliate overtly, or even semi-overtly, which could then be portrayed as an unprovoked act of Iranian aggression.) This suggests that this option might benefit from being held in abeyance until such time as the Iranians made an appropriately provocative move, as they do from time to time. In that case, it would be less a determined policy to employ airstrikes and instead more of an opportunistic hope that Iran would provide the United States with the kind of provocation that would justify airstrikes. However, that would mean that the use of airstrikes could not be the primary U.S. policy toward Iran (even if it were Washington's fervent preference), but merely an ancillary contingency to another option that would be the primary policy unless and until Iran provided the necessary pretext.

A final complication for the diplomatic requirements of the Airstrikes option lies in the tension between mounting an effective diplomatic campaign that secured permission for the U.S. military to use local bases, and the desire to achieve surprise. Any effort to garner international support for an air attack would eliminate the possibility of gaining strategic surprise for the operation because the Iranians would inevitably get wind of the American diplomatic exertions. In these circumstances, the best that the United States might hope for would be tactical surprise in that the Iranians might still be kept from knowing the timing and specific conduct of the operation. This too would be another trade-off that the president would have to decide in moving forward this option, hopefully gauging the likelihood of getting access to regional bases (and their importance to the operation) against the utility of achieving surprise.

Legal

It is worth repeating that this policy does not yet have any meaningful legal justification. In particular, UN Security Council resolutions specify that they do not authorize member states to use force to bring Iran into compliance with the resolutions' demands. This absence is important because, by law, American military actions must have such a legal basis. While it is certainly the case that various presidents have provided only the flimsiest legal justifications for military action, other administrations have taken this requirement very seriously. Since most Americans undoubtedly hope that their leaders will take this requirement seriously, and since the new Obama administration has suggested that it will treat such requirements as obligations, not formalities, the absence of such a legal basis could prove to be an impediment to adoption of this option. Moreover, having a strong legal justification would help greatly with the diplomatic task of securing support for an air campaign while not letting it derail every other American policy initiative in the Middle East.

Pros and Cons

The following are the advantages and disadvantages of the Airstrike approach.

Advantages

—From a military perspective, the option is well within American capabilities. Airstrikes would likely do considerable damage to important parts of the Iranian nuclear program. In particular, the Bushehr (and Arak) plutonium complexes, the Esfahan uranium production facility, and many of the research centers could be totally annihilated because they are "soft" targets without reinforcement, camouflage, or other protection. In the case of Arak and Bushehr, there would be scant prospect of Iran being able to rebuild such facilities at the same sites or elsewhere to replace them. Given the huge size and enormous cooling requirements of modern nuclear power plants, it is virtually impossible to build them underground or otherwise hide them from modern reconnaissance methods. Even the hardened targets, like those at Natanz and Parchin, would likely be destroyed if the United States made enough of an effort. At a minimum, they would be severely compromised, with operations set back several years. Moreover, during the course of the operation, Iranian actions might tip off U.S. intelligence to the existence of other, hitherto unknown facilities that could be found, struck, and destroyed as well.

—American casualties during the operation itself would probably be minimal. Iran's air defense network, while improved, is no match for the U.S. military's ability to neutralize it. Some aircraft and pilot losses would have to be expected, including dozens of fatalities, based on the experience of casualties during Desert Storm and other recent air campaigns. But the total toll from even an extended operation would probably be less than the monthly toll of Americans dying from Iranian-made weaponry at the peak of the Iraq War in 2005–2007.

—There would certainly be collateral damage in the form of Iranian civilian deaths, but it is unlikely that huge numbers would be killed. In particular, strikes against Iran's facilities at this time would not produce large amounts of radioactive fallout, and many of the targets to be struck are located outside heavily populated areas.

—The operation itself is not dependent on external support. Even without the use of regional allies' airfields, one to three American aircraft carriers, bombers from Diego Garcia, and cruise missiles from ships and submarines in the region could be enough to execute a successful attack.

—There is some chance (albeit not high) that the Airstrikes option could delay Iran's nuclear program by as much as five to seven years, which might be long enough that Tehran's most virulent hard-liners would never come into possession of a nuclear weapon. There is even the possibility that several Iranian political cycles might pass before even a determined leadership could create a more dispersed, hidden, durable nuclear capability and thereby finally attain a nuclear weapon.

—Even if Iranian politics did not moderate significantly during that same period of time, the setback could buy the rest of the region the time and opportunity to make progress in other ways—such as further steps toward

Arab-Israeli peace and a strengthening of currently weak democratic govern-ments in Lebanon, Afghanistan, and Iraq. If Iran were to acquire nuclear weapons only after such positive developments, it probably would have greater difficulty stoking trouble in the region.

—By attacking Iran's nuclear facilities but sparing its conventional mili-tary and its economy, the United States would retain a measure of "intrawar deterrence" to limit Iranian retaliation. In other words, leaving aside the Invasion option, it would have the ability to attack additional Iranian targets in retaliation for any excessive Iranian response in the region or the world at large, or to blockade Iranian oil shipments.

Disadvantages

—Iran's determination to acquire a nuclear weapons capability would probably not be reduced by such an attack and, especially in the short term, could well be increased.

—The hard-line Iranian leadership that presently struggles to maintain political support at home might be strengthened by a nationalistic reaction among the Iranian people against what they would doubtless perceive as an unprovoked American attack.

—Even massive airstrikes might only set back the Iranian nuclear pro-gram by as little as a year or two, and this seems more likely than the more optimistic possibility that this policy option would delay Iran's program by three years or more. Given the track record of U.S. and international intel-ligence in accurately assessing the nuclear programs of foreign states, any attack, even a sustained American operation, might fail to destroy a substan-tial fraction of Iran's nuclear program. The United States cannot strike what it does not know about, and there is good reason to think that Iran has or will soon have major nuclear facilities—including alternative uranium hexa-fluoride storage/production and uranium enrichment plants—that have not been identified.

—Hizballah, widely considered the most proficient international terror-ist organization, could take off the gloves in responding to any such attack. Even the possibility of a 9/11-type response cannot be dismissed given Iran's demonstrated capabilities in this arena.

—Any U.S. pilots shot down and captured in the course of their bomb-ing runs could suffer a significantly worse fate than the American hostages taken in Tehran at the time of the revolution three decades ago.

—Tehran could resort to economic warfare. An Iranian attempt to close the Strait of Hormuz to oil traffic—or at least to complicate passage of oil tankers through it, driving up the global price of oil in the process—would not be out of the question (even if it probably would not last long and would leave Iran worse off than before). For revolutionaries in its leadership who had just suffered the indignity of seeing their nuclear complex destroyed, the corresponding risk to their own country's economy might seem worth the benefits. In other words, cutting off their collective noses to spite their face is not out of the question.

—Tehran might escalate its involvement in Iraq and Afghanistan, perhaps shipping advanced surface-to-air missiles and advanced antiarmor weapons, such as those it has provided Hizballah but has so far refrained from providing Iraqi and Afghan insurgents.

—In response to the Airstrikes option, Iran's politics could become even more radical rather than less so. If such an extremist government were to come into possession of a nuclear weapon, it might be even more inclined than the current regime to prove its revolutionary mettle by attacking its neighbors overtly or covertly, stepping up involvement in Lebanon's politics, escalating support for anti-Israeli terrorists, or even trying to draw Israel into a shooting war.

—Over the long term, it would be difficult to sustain a strategy of repeated air campaigns to prevent Iran from reconstituting its nuclear program. Doing so could dramatically undercut Washington's ability to pursue its other objectives in the Middle East—which ultimately constitute one of the rationales behind preventing Iran from acquiring a nuclear weapons capability. Washington may be hard pressed in its ability to push for the range of other foreign policy initiatives it hopes to pursue in the Middle East (a new Arab-Israeli peace process, democratization of Lebanon, stabilization of Iraq and Afghanistan, and even an end to the genocide in Darfur)—which a new Iran policy was specifically meant to enable, not preclude. If this is the case, then the policy option would have proven self-defeating.

—An air campaign against Iran could badly undermine U.S. efforts to employ any other strategy in dealing with Tehran. Airstrikes against Iran could prove so unpopular around the globe—especially if the United States cannot point to some egregious Iranian action as a provocation—that it may be far harder for the United States to galvanize international support for additional sanctions against Iran, let alone a full-scale containment regime. And having launched what Iranians would inevitably consider an unprovoked act of aggression, the prospect of engagement of any kind with Iran in the aftermath would appear unlikely.

CHAPTER FIVE

LEAVE IT TO BIBI

Allowing or Encouraging an Israeli Military Strike

For the United States, the Islamic Republic of Iran has been an enemy for 30 years, one that has sought to thwart U.S. policies in the Middle East, such as advancing the Arab-Israeli peace process and creating stable regional security arrangements. Crisis after crisis has arisen between Iran and the United States, but Iran has never been and almost certainly never will be an existential threat to the United States. It harbors no territorial designs on the United States, has never conducted a terrorist operation aimed at the American homeland, and, even should it acquire nuclear weapons, lacks the delivery systems to threaten the United States directly. Further, its economy is anemic, and even if substantially reformed, will probably never provide the base for Iran to make itself a challenger to the United States on par with Nazi Germany, Imperial Japan, the Soviet Union, or Communist China.

But for Israel, Iran is a much more dangerous opponent—it is close and threatening. There is a virtual consensus in Israel that Iran cannot be allowed to acquire nuclear weapons. From left to right across the political spectrum, a great many Israelis see a threat to their very survival from a nuclear Iran. Former prime minister Ehud Olmert said, "Israel will not tolerate a nuclear weapon in the hands of people who say openly, explicitly and publicly that they want to wipe Israel off the map."[1] In his first speech to the Knesset after being sworn in as prime minister, Binyamin ("Bibi") Netanyahu said, "We cannot afford to take lightly megalomaniac tyrants who threaten to annihilate us."[2] Other Israeli leaders are more reasoned but also are determined to prevent Iranian acquisition of a nuclear weapons capability. Ephraim Sneh, former deputy defense minister and a much-decorated retired general of the Israel Defense Forces (IDF), notes that "the most salient strategic threat to Israel's existence is Iran."[3] These leaders fear that Israel's strategic room for maneuver in the region would be constrained by an Iranian nuclear deterrent. The success of Iranian-backed terrorist groups, Hizballah in Lebanon and Hamas in Gaza and the West Bank, in the last few years has only added to Israel's concern.

Even relatively dovish analysts like the historian Benny Morris write about an Iranian bomb in apocalyptic terms: "The Iranians are driven by a higher logic. And they will launch their rockets. And, as with the first Holocaust, the international community will do nothing. It will all be over, for Israel, in a few minutes—not like in the 1940s, when the world had five long years in which to wring its hands and do nothing."[4]

Only a few Israeli commentators have suggested the threat may be exaggerated or that it actually serves Israeli interests to have a threat from Iran. Former Mossad chief Ephraim Halevy argues that "Ahmadinejad is our greatest gift. We couldn't carry out a better operation in the Mossad than to put a guy like Ahmadinejad in power in Iran."[5] But even Halevy believes Iran is a serious threat to Israel's interests.

It is clear from discussions with Israeli military and intelligence officials and from numerous press leaks and reports that Israel is well under way in planning for a military operation to prevent Iran from acquiring nuclear weapons. Israel's defense minister, Ehud Barak, said in 2007 that "the things that we do behind the scenes, far from the public eye, are far more important than the slogan charade," implying that Israeli covert capabilities are already hard at work trying to cope with the Iranian threat and preparing to attack it if they must.[6] It is impossible to know what those plans entail in detail without access to the IDF's secret planning, but Israelis say the mission is "not impossible." The IDF's September 6, 2007, attack on the Syrian nuclear facility at Dayr az-Zawr is widely believed in Israel to have been in part a message to Tehran that Iran may be next.

Israeli leaders have been warning about the Iranian threat since the early 1990s. Prime Minister Yitzhak Rabin highlighted the danger Iran posed to Israel in his first visit to the United States in 1992 after his election. Israeli intelligence operations against Iran were stepped up even earlier and have included use of third parties to publicize the Iranian threat without revealing the Israeli hand. Iran's secret enrichment and heavy-water reactor programs were publicly exposed in August 2002 by an Iranian dissident group (the Mujahedin-e Khalq), which reportedly was unwittingly fed the information by Israeli intelligence.[7]

In short, there is considerable reason to believe that under the right (or wrong) set of circumstances, Israel would launch an attack—principally airstrikes, but possibly backed by special forces operations—to destroy Iran's nuclear program. This could create either an opportunity for or a threat to American interests with regard to Iran and the broader Middle East. It could constitute an opportunity, and thus a possible policy option, if the United States would like to see Iran's nuclear program destroyed but prefers not to do it itself. It could be a threat if the United States believes that an Israeli attack would destabilize the region and would not advance (or would harm) American interests in relation to Iran.

Not surprisingly, some Americans have expressed the hope that Israel would strike Iran—that Jerusalem would have the "guts" to do what Washington does not. Other Americans regard the prospect with horror, believing that an Israeli attack would have all the disadvantages of American airstrikes (as well as some unique ones) and none of their advantages. American decisionmakers need to have a clear sense of what such an Israeli operation would look like, as well as the pros and cons for the United States, to decide whether to try to encourage or discourage it.[8]

GOAL

As in the case of American airstrikes against Iran, the goal of this policy option would be to destroy key Iranian nuclear facilities in the hope that doing so would significantly delay Iran's acquisition of an indigenous nuclear weapons capability. However, in this case, an added element could be that the United States would encourage—and perhaps even assist—the Israelis in conducting the strikes themselves, in the expectation that both international criticism and Iranian retaliation would be deflected away from the United States and onto Israel. The logic behind this approach is that allowing Israel to mount the airstrikes, rather than the United States, provides a way out of the dilemma described in the previous chapter, whereby American airstrikes against Iran could become self-defeating because they would undermine every other American initiative in the Middle East, an outcome exactly the opposite of what a new Iran policy is meant to accomplish.

As with American airstrikes against the Iranian nuclear program, this option would not entail any direct effort to deal with Iran's support for terrorists and radical groups, nor would it directly seek to mitigate other Iranian efforts to subvert the status quo in the Middle East. At most, this policy assumes that Iran's ability to pursue such activities would be greatly enhanced by possession of a (presumed) nuclear weapons capability, and therefore that removing this threat would help limit Iran's ability to cause problems for the United States in the region. Likewise, this approach makes no effort to change the Iranian regime or otherwise reshape its character.

TIME FRAME

If the United States decided to encourage Israel to mount airstrikes against Iran, the entire operation could happen very quickly, probably much faster than a similar American campaign. Israel appears to have done extensive planning and practice for such a strike already, and its aircraft are probably already based as close to Iran as possible. As such, Israel might be able to launch the strike in a matter of weeks or even days, depending on what weather and intelligence conditions it felt it needed. Moreover, since Israel would have much less of a need (or even interest) in securing regional support for the operation, Jerusalem probably would feel less motivated to wait for an Iranian provocation before attacking. In short, Israel could move very fast to implement this option if both Israeli and American leaders wanted it to happen.

However, as noted in the previous chapter, the airstrikes themselves are really just the start of this policy. Again, the Iranians would doubtless rebuild their nuclear sites. They would probably retaliate against Israel, and they might retaliate against the United States, too (which might create a pretext for American airstrikes or even an invasion). And it seems unlikely that they would cease their support for violent extremist groups or efforts to overturn the regional status quo in the aftermath of Israeli airstrikes. Their opposition to an Arab-Israeli peace treaty would likely be redoubled. Hence the United States would still need a strategy to handle Iran after completion of the Israeli airstrikes, and this could mean a much longer time frame to achieve all of America's goals.

OVERVIEW OF THE POLICY

An Israeli air campaign against Iran would have a number of very important differences from an American campaign. First, the Israeli Air Force (IAF) has the problem of overflight transit from Israel to Iran. Israel has no aircraft carriers, so its planes must take off from Israeli air bases. It also does not possess long-range bombers like the B-1 or B-2, or huge fleets of refueling tankers, all of which means that unlike the United States, Israel cannot avoid flying through someone's air space. The most direct route from Israel to Iran's Natanz facility is roughly 1,750 kilometers across Jordan and Iraq. As the occupying power in Iraq, the United States is responsible for defending Iraqi airspace. The alternatives via Turkish airspace (over 2,200 kilometers) or Saudi airspace (over 2,400 kilometers) would also put the attack force into the skies of U.S. allies equipped with American-supplied air defenses and fighter aircraft. In the case of Turkey, an Israeli overflight would be further complicated by the fact that Turkey is a NATO ally that the United States has a commitment to defend, and it hosts a large, joint Turkish-American airbase along the most likely route of attack.

For political and military reasons, Israel's need to overfly Turkish, Iraqi-Jordanian, or Saudi airspace creates two problems. First, an Israeli strike must achieve surprise so that Israeli planes are not intercepted by the air defenses and fighters of those countries. Second, in part based on reason number one, the Israelis would get basically one shot at Iran. On the first pass, they likely would surprise any of those countries and be able to reach Iran and return before the Turks, Saudis, or Jordanians could activate their air defenses; but a second wave would meet alerted air defenses, creating military and political problems that Israel would likely find insurmountable. An initial Israeli attack across Iraqi territory would severely complicate the U.S. military presence there; a repeat performance would likely compromise it altogether. Thus, after the first round of strikes, Israel would have nothing but its small fleet of ballistic missiles and submarine-launched cruise missiles for follow-on attacks, and because the ballistic missiles are such valu-able assets, Jerusalem would not likely squander them on anything but the highest value Iranian targets.

Another problem Israel faces is distance. The IAF possesses 25 F-15I long-range strike aircraft, which have a combat radius of over 2,500 kilometers, giving them the range to hit Iranian targets even if they have to fly via Turkey or Saudi Arabia. However, 25 aircraft is a tiny number given the size, disper-sal, and hardening of the Iranian nuclear program, especially since the planes could not carry much ordnance, nor would they have the ability to hit mul-tiple facilities on a single sortie at that distance. So Israel's F-15I fleet alone could not hope to do as much damage to the Iranian nuclear program as even the small-scale American airstrike discussed in the previous chapter.[9] Thus just employing the 25 F-15Is probably would not make the operation worthwhile from Jerusalem's or Washington's perspective.

In addition to the F-15Is, Israel has acquired 100 F-16I fighter bombers. There is a great deal of speculation regarding the combat range of the F-16I, which most sources suggest is roughly 1,600–1,800 kilometers. However, at least one well-regarded Israeli source has stated that it has a range of 2,100 kilometers.[10] Even if the longer distance is possible, this means that the F-16Is only have the range to strike Iran unrefueled if they fly the shortest route across Jordan and Iraq—which is also the most politically problematic because it clearly incriminates the United States as Israel's witting accomplice in the strike. From the American perspective, this negates the whole point of the option—distancing the United States from culpability—and it could jeopardize American efforts in Iraq, thus making it a nonstarter for Wash-ington. Finally, Israeli violation of Jordanian airspace would likely create political problems for King Abdullah of Jordan, one of America's (and Israel's) closest Arab friends in the region. Thus it is exceedingly unlikely that the United States would allow Israel to overfly Iraq, and because of the prob-lems it would create for Washington and Amman, it is unlikely that Israel would try to fly over Jordan.

Consequently, in most scenarios, for Israel to mount an airstrike of any size against Iran—assuming that Israel cannot secretly refuel its aircraft at an air base near Iran—it would have to provide in-flight refueling to enable the F-16Is to participate. This is a further complication because while it is pos-sible for fighter aircraft to refuel one another, doing so immediately halves the number of planes actually dropping bombs (the other half are doing the refueling and so carry fuel, not weapons). In addition, since "buddy refuel-ing" by other fighter bombers is inefficient, it may take multiple refuelings—meaning that out of 100 F-16Is committed, perhaps only 25 might be able to make it to the targets in Iran. The alternative is the more tra-ditional method of using large tanker aircraft to provide the fuel, but these are extremely vulnerable. Because of this and given the remarkable capabil-ities demonstrated by the IAF over the years, the possibility that Israel would find ways to "hide" tankers in international air space or fly them with the strike packages for much of the way until their services are no longer needed should not be ruled out. However, such risky operations would only be fea-sible for the first round of strikes. Once the surprise is over and the Iranians, Turks, Jordanians, and/or Saudis have their air defenses on alert, the tankers would be highly vulnerable.

What all of this means is that, realistically, an Israeli strike against Iran could consist of no more than 125 Israeli F-15I and F-16I sorties (with lim-ited weapons loads because of the distance), backed by a small number of cruise missile shots. This is not a meaningless force, and it likely could do a considerable amount of damage to the best known of Iran's facilities. But again, it probably could not do as much damage as even the limited Amer-ican Airstrikes option discussed in the previous chapter—it probably would not even be able to cover all the targets listed. Moreover, the IAF would have virtually no capability to conduct opportunity strikes on targets revealed by Iranian actions during the attacks themselves. Nor would it have much, if any, ability to follow up with repeat strikes to hit facilities where the initial attack failed to destroy the target. Overall, an Israeli strike would be even less likely to meaningfully set back the Iranian nuclear program than would an American air campaign.[11]

An Israeli Attack on Iran versus U.S. Interests

An Israeli attack on Iran would directly affect key American strategic interests. If Israel were to overfly Iraq, both the Iranians and the vast majority of people around the world would see the strike as abetted, if not authorized, by the United States. Even if Israel were to use another route, many Iranians would still see the attack as American supported or even American orchestrated. After all, the aircraft in any strike would be American produced, supplied, and funded F-15s and F-16s, and much of the ordnance would be American made. In fact, $3 billion dollars in U.S.

assistance annually sustains the IDF's conventional superiority in the region.

Iran would almost certainly retaliate against Israel and may choose to retaliate against the United States as well. To demonstrate its retaliatory prowess, Iran has already fired salvos of test missiles (some of which are capable of striking Israel), and Iranian leaders have warned that they would respond to an attack by either Israel or the United States with attacks against Tel Aviv, U.S. ships and facilities in the Persian Gulf, and other targets. If Iran wanted to retaliate in less risky ways, it could respond indirectly by encouraging Hizballah attacks against Israel and Shi'i militia attacks against U.S. forces in Iraq. Fears of a wider Middle Eastern war could play havoc with the oil market, at least in the short term, and probably would not help American initiatives to stabilize Iraq, resolve the Arab-Israeli conflict, or foster an independent democracy in Lebanon. Further, Iran would be able to argue that it was the victim of aggression and might renounce its Non-Proliferation Treaty commitments. And since even a successful Israeli raid would only delay Iran's nuclear program—and probably by even less than a small-scale American strike—the United States would still have to have a strategy to deal with the basic problem after an Israeli attack, but in an even more complicated diplomatic context.

The Israelis are well aware of the risks and downsides of an attack on Iran's nuclear facilities, especially the possible cost in American lives if Tehran retaliates against the United States. Given these risks, Jerusalem may focus on strengthening sanctions in the near term, but the Israelis may feel compelled to act if they judge that the current administration's diplomatic push has failed. Israeli commentators note that the chances of securing Russian support for tough sanctions have diminished considerably since the 2008 war in Georgia. Russia has a stronger interest in keeping good ties with Iran, another power in the Caucasus, and less interest in appeasing American and European concerns about Iran. Since Israel is a strong supporter of Georgia, Russia may also feel it should pay Israel back by moving closer to Tehran.

U.S. Options and Decision Points

Given the stakes for the United States, the president should make a decision about a potential Israeli military attack against Iranian nuclear facilities. There are four options. The first option is for the United States to give Israel a "green light," permitting Israel to transit American-controlled airspace over Iraq. In this case, the United States would coordinate with Israel beforehand on how to manage the consequences of an attack, including Iranian retaliation and the regional and international political fallout. The option's principal virtue is that if Israel effects a military solution to the Iranian nuclear threat, the United States would benefit from the attack without taking the risks of using its own forces.

The downsides are more numerous simply because no one, least of all Iran, would believe the United States had *nothing* to do with an Israeli attack, especially if the United States allowed Israel to fly over Iraq. As discussed above, one of the most significant consequences of the "green light" scenario could be Iranian retaliation against American targets, which could then lead to a broader conflict between the United States and Iran. Unless the United States is prepared to take draconian measures immediately afterward to distance itself from Israel, such as a complete cutoff of all military assistance and economic aid, Tehran may well blame Washington as much as Jerusalem for the air attack on its territory. However, for the United States to attempt to distance itself from Israel under these circumstances would, of course, amount to a betrayal of the Israelis, since Washington's "green light" would have encouraged them to undertake the attack. In addition, in the aftermath of the approach that allows Israel use of Iraqi airspace, it would be more difficult for the United States to argue that Iran should still abide by its Non-Proliferation Treaty obligations. The United States would have been party to the operation in spirit, if not in fact, and thus have little credibility in trying to persuade Iran that it should not embark on a crash attempt to build a nuclear weapon.

The second option is for the United States to give Israel a "yellow light," encouraging Israel to mount the attack, but not permit it to use Iraqi airspace. The virtues of this scenario would be the same as with the "green light," with the added benefit that the diplomatic fallout for the United States might be mitigated since it could claim it had no advance warning, or that it did and even tried to prevent the attack by closing off Iraq's airspace. The drawback to this option is that many, especially Iran, might still believe that the United States was complicit in the operation, thus making U.S. troops in the region vulnerable to retaliatory strikes by Iran.

A third option would be for the United States to give Israel a "red light," actively discouraging an Israeli attack, either because Washington had decided that it could carry out the attack more effectively and with fewer political complications on its own, or because it determines that the likely costs of a military attack by either the United States or Israel outweigh the potential benefits. The rationale for saying no will determine the pluses and minuses of the red light option. If Washington discourages an Israeli attack because it plans to execute its own invasion or airstrikes, then this approach would accrue all of the benefits and liabilities associated with those options (as discussed in the previous two chapters). If Washington decides not to launch a military operation and, for the same reasons, decides that it would be as bad or worse for Israel to do so, then the United States avoids the risk of Iranian retaliation and the diplomatic liabilities of an attack. The downsides of this rationale for saying no include a difficult argument with Israel over the issue, perhaps played out in the public domain, which could benefit Iran by giving it a propaganda coup against Israel. In addition, Israel could very well carry out the operation even if Washington signaled a "red light," in which case U.S. forces in the region could be in harm's way from Iranian retaliation without Washington having had the benefit of knowing the time and scope of the Israeli attack.

A fourth option is for the president to avoid making a clear decision—giving no light—which could lead to an Israeli attack without any American input. In other words, doing nothing could amount to a decision to let Israel go forward on its own. The outcome of this would be essentially the same as any of the previous options but with additional downsides. The reason for this is that if Israel chose to fly over Iraqi airspace, the president would have to decide whether to order the planes intercepted and turned back or look the other way and allow the planes to proceed. Intercepting the Israeli planes would be akin to a "red light" decision, but worse. Israel, and many of its supporters in the United States, would react bitterly, and there is the possibility of Israeli and American planes even shooting at each other. The alternative decision, allowing the planes to proceed over Iraq's airspace, would be akin to the "green light" option, but worse in that the United States would have had no advanced warning of the strike. As such, American forces in the region would have little time to prepare for a possible Iranian counterstrike. Finally, should Israel decide to proceed with the attack on its own without overflying Iraqi airspace, the consequences would be the same as the "yellow light" scenario, but worse in that the United States would have had no warning of the timing and scope of the attack.

Requirements

In one sense, the requirements of the Israeli airstrike option are minimal. If the United States concludes that this option is worth pursuing, it merely requires a high-level conversation between Washington and Jerusalem. Again, the principal virtue of this option is that it would result in airstrikes against the Iranian nuclear program and could mitigate the political, diplomatic, and even military burdens on the United States. It may also result in a strike against the Iranian nuclear program much sooner than the United States could be able to do, although the punch might be much weaker than what the United States could deliver.

Even in this case, however, the United States is unlikely to get off easily. First, the Israelis may want U.S. help with a variety of things. Israel may be more willing to bear the risks of Iranian retaliation and international opprobrium than the United States is, but it is not invulnerable and may request certain commitments from the United States before it is ready to strike. For instance, the Israelis may want to hold off until they have a peace deal with Syria in hand (assuming that Jerusalem believes that one is within reach), which would help them mitigate blowback from Hizballah and potentially Hamas. Consequently, they might want Washington to push hard in mediating between Jerusalem and Damascus. In addition, the Israelis might request additional military equipment—deep-penetrating munitions to make the attack more effective, more F-15s or F-16s (or F-22s), or the latest defensive systems to help them defend themselves against Iranian retaliation. (And, of course, all of these requests would also greatly extend the time frame for an Israeli strike.)

Second, as noted earlier, the United States would need to prepare for the possibility of Iranian retaliation as well, especially if the Israeli warplanes overflew Jordan and Iraq. Washington would have to be ready to make a major counterterrorism effort to protect the U.S. homeland as well as American diplomatic and military personnel overseas. In both Iraq and Afghanistan, the United States would need to prepare to withstand a wave of Iranian inspired (and armed) attacks against U.S. forces there.

Requirements of the Red Light Option: Enhancing Jerusalem's Security

If the current administration concludes that an Israeli strike against Iran would harm U.S. interests and therefore that Jerusalem must be persuaded not to attack—not just in the immediate future but over the long term as well—then the requirements for Washington change considerably and, in some ways, become far more involved. There is precedent for the United States persuading Israel not to use force against a military threat. In the 1991 Gulf War, President George H.W. Bush pressed Prime Minister Yitzhak Shamir not to attack Iraqi Scud missile launchers that were targeting Israel. Most important, Bush refused to give the Israelis the IFF (identification friend or foe) codes and approval to enter Iraqi airspace, thus indicating that Israeli aircraft would be flying in harm's way. Israel's preferred option of a limited ground force incursion into western Iraq was also rejected. In turn, the United States committed to stepping up its own attacks on Iraqi Scuds, although with little or no effect.[12]

With regard to Iran, the most important element of an American effort to dissuade Israel from launching an attack of its own would be a discussion between Washington and Jerusalem on how to ensure that Tehran does not threaten Israel with nuclear weapons if U.S. diplomatic and military efforts eventually fail to prevent Iran from acquiring them. Ultimately, the United States probably would not be willing or able to prevent an Israeli attack against Iranian nuclear facilities if Jerusalem decides that it could do so successfully and believes that it has no other choice. However, if Israeli leaders are uncertain about the effectiveness and consequences of a military raid, joint planning with the United States on how to contain and deter a nuclear-armed Iran could influence their decision. For example, if Jerusalem were confident that formal U.S. nuclear assurances could be extended to Israel, it might be more inclined to calculate that the risks of living with a nuclear-armed Iran were more manageable. Therefore, in addition to coordinating on day-to-day diplomatic efforts, the U.S. administration should offer to begin a very quiet policy planning exercise with Israel to consider options if diplomacy with Iran fails.

Specifically, Washington should take another look at the pluses and minuses of extending an explicit American nuclear guarantee to Israel. At the Camp David summit in 2000, Israeli Prime Minister Ehud Barak suggested a U.S.-Israeli mutual defense treaty be signed to provide Israel with a nuclear guarantee against Iran. The idea died when the Israeli-Palestinian peace process collapsed, but it is worth reconsidering.

Of course, Israeli capabilities ought to be enough on their own. Estimates of the size of Israel's arsenal by outsiders (Israelis are prohibited by law from doing so) suggest it is formidable. The International Institute for Strategic Studies estimated in 2008 that Israel has the sixth-largest nuclear arsenal in the world, just behind the five original nuclear powers but ahead of India and Pakistan. The Israelis probably have around 100 nuclear devices and can deliver them by aircraft (F-15Is), surface-to-surface missiles (Jericho), and submarine-launched cruise missiles.[13]

Such an arsenal should suffice to deter Iran, but an American nuclear guarantee would provide the Israelis an extra measure of reassurance. If the United States guarantees Israel a nuclear umbrella, then Iran would know that no matter what damage it may inflict on Israel, the United States would be able to retaliate with overwhelming force. This deterrent is strengthened by the fact that Iran would have no delivery system capable of quickly striking back at the U.S. homeland.[14] It would be the target of both whatever residual capability Israel retained and the vast American nuclear arsenal.

The United States could provide Jerusalem with further reassurance. Already the United States has been deeply involved in building Israel's defense against an Iranian missile strike. For almost two decades, the Pentagon has been working closely with Israel to perfect the Arrow anti-tactical ballistic missile system. The two countries have shared extensive technology for anti-tactical ballistic missile systems, including the integration of Israel into the most advanced American early warning radar systems to provide the earliest possible alert of an incoming attack. This defensive cooperation should be continued and enhanced.

The United States could also look at other ways of bolstering the Israel Defense Forces. The F-15I will remain an adequate long-range strike platform for the immediate future, but it is worth examining whether to provide the F-22 Raptor aircraft to the IDF as an even more sophisticated attack system that would be able to ensure Israel's deterrence capability far into the future. Prime Minister Barak raised this issue with President Clinton at the Camp David summit in 2000, and it should be reconsidered.

Finally, the current administration could try to go one step further and develop a multinational nuclear deterrent for Israel by proposing Israeli membership in the North Atlantic Treaty Organization. Under Article 5 of the NATO treaty, an attack on any member is an attack on the whole. As a NATO member, Israel would automatically enjoy the same nuclear umbrella as the existing 26 members. Israel is already a member of NATO's Mediterranean dialogue and participates in limited military exercises with several

NATO partners aside from the United States, including notably both Greece and Turkey.

Getting Israel into NATO would be a very hard sell, however, as many of the European allies believe Israel has done too little to bring about peace with its Arab neighbors, and they would probably condition support for Israeli membership on concrete and public moves toward a final peace agreement. European public opinion is increasingly wary of increasing NATO's membership, and many would find Israel an unattractive ally that could commit Europeans to fighting Arabs.

Finally, all the options for expanding Israel's deterrent through new treaty obligations, either bilateral or via NATO, would face substantial opposition from those in Israel who argue that such commitments weaken Israel's ability to act unilaterally. A mutual defense alliance does not require advance agreement before one party uses force, but it certainly increases the political imperative not to surprise your treaty partners with independent action.

Pros and Cons

The following are the advantages and disadvantages of the Israel approach.

Advantages

—As noted, the most salient advantage this option has over that of an American air campaign is the possibility that Israel alone would be blamed for the attack. If this proves true, then the United States might not have to deal with Iranian retaliation or the diplomatic backlash that would accompany an American military operation against Iran. It could allow Washington to have its cake (delay Iran's acquisition of a nuclear weapon) and eat it, too (avoid undermining many other U.S. regional diplomatic initiatives).

—Israeli forces might be able to execute the attack much sooner and with much less prior notice and preparation than American military forces could.

—It would presumably be easier to convince Israel to mount the attack than it would be to generate domestic political support for another war in the Middle East (let alone the diplomatic support from a region that is extremely wary of new American military adventures). At least some important Israelis want to conduct such an attack and would welcome Washington's encouragement. Other Israelis are less enthusiastic but feel it may be necessary if they believe they have no choice, and they, too, would be far more willing to conduct an attack if they believed that the United States was firmly behind it.

Disadvantages

—An Israeli airstrike against Iran entails many—potentially all—of the same disadvantages as an American air campaign against Iran but has few of its advantages. Its one advantage, the possibility that Israel would bear the entire burden for the strike, in terms of international opprobrium and Iranian retaliation, is highly uncertain and would depend on the circumstances of the strike and a variety of unpredictable perceptions. If the United States is seen as ultimately (or jointly) responsible for the attack, there would be no advantage from the American perspective.

In particular, an Israeli military strike would be weaker than even a limited American air campaign and so would have a lower likelihood of seriously delaying Iran's acquisition of a nuclear weapons capability. Thus, when assessing the American cost-benefit analysis of this option, the benefit is unquestionably less than it would be if the United States mounted the attack itself, while any reduction in cost would be extremely difficult to assess—and could be marginal or nonexistent.

Toppling Tehran

Regime Change

For some Americans, neither the diplomatic nor the airstrike options offer a persuasive approach to Iran. They have little confidence that the Iranians can be persuaded—either with big incentives and disincentives, or with just the big incentives—and fear that airstrikes would fail to disarm Iran and instead would further entrench the clerical regime. Instead, they believe that only taking action to bring about the fall of the Islamic Republic can protect America's vital interests in the Middle East. These Americans see the regime itself, and not merely its behavior, as the real threat to U.S. security. They believe that the regime simply will never live up to any agreements, and even if somehow it did, it would find other ways to undermine U.S. interests because the regime and the United States are fundamentally incompatible. Consequently, Americans who fall into this camp tend to dislike both the diplomatic and airstrike options because none of them offer any reasonable prospect of ousting the regime. They might favor an invasion, but after Iraq and Afghanistan, they tend to believe either that the costs are not worth it or that the American people will not go for it. So for them, the only reasonable way to handle Iran is to pursue some form of covert action intended to bring about the end of the Islamic Republic.

The clerical regime in Iran is brutal and corrupt, and its leaders oppose U.S. interests throughout the Middle East. Thus it is not surprising that some Americans have examined the regime for cracks that could be widened to bring about its downfall. The surprising ascendance of a reform movement with the 1997 election of Muhammad Khatami made a change in regime seem possible, even imminent: not only did Khatami's widespread support suggest considerable disenchantment with the clerical regime, but his election indicated that peaceful means might lead to its replacement under the leadership of a man calling for a "dialogue of civilizations." Over ten years later, however, Khatami's conservative opponents have consolidated power. While many Iranians are cynical toward or even hostile to the regime, the reform movement is in disarray.

The reform movement, however, is not the only means for changing the regime, and in theory the United States has several options if it seeks a new Iranian government. In the past, the United States engineered a coup to restore a government of its liking there, and in recent years, Washington has supported programs designed to bolster a democratic movement in Iran. Prominent voices have also called for helping Iranian oppositionists overthrow the regime and for using Iran's minority groups to undermine the government.

There are several ways in which the United States could change the regime or undermine it: supporting a popular revolution, stirring up Iran's ethnic groups, or promoting a coup. In practice, these options could be pursued simultaneously and overlap in some of their elements, but it is worth considering each separately to understand their nature and requirements. That is the task of the next three chapters.

CHAPTER SIX

THE VELVET REVOLUTION

Supporting a Popular Uprising

Because the Iranian regime is widely disliked by many Iranians, the most obvious and palatable method of bringing about its demise would be to help foster a popular revolution along the lines of the "velvet revolutions" that toppled many communist governments in Eastern Europe beginning in 1989. For many proponents of regime change, it seems self-evident that the United States should encourage the Iranian people to take power in their own name, and that this would be the most legitimate method of regime change. After all, what Iranian or foreigner could object to helping the Iranian people fulfill their own desires?

Moreover, Iran's own history would seem to suggest that such an event is plausible. During the 1906 Constitutional Movement, during the late 1930s, arguably during the 1950s, and again during the 1978 Iranian Revolution, coalitions of intellectuals, students, peasants, *bazaari* merchants, Marxists, constitutionalists, and clerics mobilized against an unpopular regime. In both 1906 and 1978, the revolutionaries secured the support of much of the populace and, in so doing, prevailed. There is evidence that the Islamic regime has antagonized many (perhaps all) of these same factions to the point where they again might be willing to support a change if they feel that it could succeed. This is the foundational belief of those Americans who support regime change, and their hope is that the United States can provide whatever the Iranian people need to believe that another revolution is feasible.

Of course, popular revolutions are incredibly complex and rare events. There is little scholarly consensus on what causes a popular revolution, or even the conditions that facilitate them. Even factors often associated with revolutions, such as military defeat, neglect of the military, economic crises, and splits within the elite have all been regular events across the world and throughout history, but only a very few have resulted in a popular revolution. Consequently, all of the literature on how best to promote a popular revolution—in Iran or anywhere else—is highly speculative. Nevertheless, it is the one policy option that holds out the prospect that the United States might eliminate all of the problems it faces from Iran, do so at a bearable cost, and do so in a manner that is acceptable to the Iranian people and most of the rest of the world.

GOAL

The true objective of this policy option is to overthrow the clerical regime in Tehran and see it replaced, hopefully, by one whose views would be more compatible with U.S. interests in the region. The policy does, in its own way, seek a change in Iranian behavior, but by eliminating the government that is responsible for that behavior without the use of American military forces. Indeed, inherent in this option is the assumption that the current Iranian regime is uniquely problematic for the United States—that a successor would not attempt to acquire a nuclear weapons capability nor seek to overturn the regional status quo by stoking instability. It is worth noting that if a future democratic Iranian regime did continue these policies, that might prove more of a problem for the United States than their pursuit by what is clearly an autocratic regime.

While the ultimate goal is to remove the regime, working with the internal opposition also could be a form of coercive pressure on the Iranian regime, giving the United States leverage on other issues. Iran under the Shah, for example, backed a Kurdish insurgency in Iraq and helped make the rebels quite potent. The Shah then abruptly sold out the Kurds in exchange for Iraqi concessions on demarcating the Iran-Iraq border. In theory, the United States could create coercive leverage by threatening the regime with instability or even overthrow and, after having done so, use this leverage to force concessions on other issues such as Iran's nuclear program or support for militants in Iraq.

This mix of goals can be seen as a spectrum: if the policies achieve relatively limited gains, they can be expanded to try to achieve ambitious results. As Scott Carpenter, who served as a U.S. deputy assistant secretary of state and focused on democracy promotion, contends, "If the U.S. plays its hand effectively, we can weaken the tyrant of Tehran substantially—and ideally empower his own people to effect peaceful change."[1]

TIME FRAME

Because popular revolutions are so rare and unpredictable, and because the Iranian regime vigilantly guards against any popular revolt, it is impossible to know how long it would take for the United States to promote a revolution in Tehran. It may be that, as many proponents contend, the Iranian people are desperate to overthrow the regime and the emphatic commitment of the United States to the cause would be sufficient to trigger the Iranian people to move against their government. But this claim has been made many times in the past, both about Iran and other countries, and has only occasionally proven true. Moreover, even if the people were willing, they may not be able; they may need help organizing and finding leaders, or they may need to wait until the regime suffers some major setback that provides an opportunity to act. In short, it could take years to decades to engineer a popular revolution in Iran, and any American administration that adopts this option should do so understanding that it could happen very quickly (in a matter of months), very slowly (in a matter of years or decades), or not at all.

OVERVIEW OF THE POLICY

Popular revolutions, especially *successful* popular revolutions, are so complex and uncommon that it is difficult to outline a specific course of action that would have a high likelihood of sparking one. Many outside observers, however, are nonetheless optimistic that some form of "people power" could topple the clerical regime. They point to the following favorable factors:

—The regime is unpopular with many Iranians due to graft and economic mismanagement;

—The regime's religious legitimacy has declined considerably, and many senior clerics now reject the *velayat-e faqih* system; and

—Reformers have at times done well in elections, and while the current elected leadership is extremely conservative, it won power in part by excluding more liberal rivals from the process and because turnout was often low.[2]

In addition, these observers note that some Iranians opposed to the clerical regime are pro-American, and even those who are more skeptical of the United States are not as aggressively hostile as the current clerical regime, which is one of the most anti-American governments in the world. Iran is one of the rare Muslim countries where much of the population wants closer ties to the United States, so promoting a democratic change might make more sense there than it would in a country like Saudi Arabia, where popular hostility to the United States is high. This suggests that at least a few of those willing or desirous of moving against the current regime might look to the United States for support in their effort.

Beyond this, however, it is often difficult to be specific about how a popular revolution might start, let alone be carried through to completion, especially when considered in the context of a fragmented and opaque Iranian political system. It could begin with more pragmatic leaders recognizing the problems and illegitimacy of the current system and trying to reform it to the point where the system itself breaks under the weight of the contradictions and tensions that emerge (for example, the process by which Gorbachev's *perestroika* and *glasnost* led to the collapse of the Soviet Union). Alternatively, it could take the form of widespread popular demonstrations and unrest that eventually discredit the government and lead it to exit the scene. Past examples range from the bloody overthrow of the Ceausescu government in Romania to the more peaceful removal of the Marcos regime from power in the Philippines.

The United States could play multiple roles in facilitating a revolution. By funding and helping organize domestic rivals of the regime, the United States could create an alternative leadership to seize power. As Raymond Tanter of the Iran Policy Committee argues, students and other groups "need covert backing for their demonstrations. They need fax machines. They need Internet access, funds to duplicate materials, and funds to keep vigilantes from beating them up."[3] Beyond this, U.S.-backed media outlets could highlight regime shortcomings and make otherwise obscure critics more prominent. The United States already supports Persian-language satellite television (Voice of America Persian) and radio (Radio Farda) that bring unfiltered news to Iranians (in recent years, these have taken the lion's share of overt U.S. funding for promoting democracy in Iran).[4] U.S. economic pressure (and perhaps military pressure as well) can discredit the regime, making the population hungry for a rival leadership.

To a limited extent, the Congress and the Bush administration took steps to support regime change by encouraging democracy in Iran. Under the Iran Freedom Support Act of 2006 (and subsequent renewals), the United States is authorized to provide financial and political aid to organizations promoting democracy in Iran, and has spent tens of millions of dollars to this end.[5] This legislation noted that promoting antiregime media and backing civil society and human rights organizations were appropriate uses of the funding, but it stipulated that the funds were not to be used to support the use of force or for entities that are designated as foreign terrorist organizations. The press has also reported a host of covert programs designed to promote regime change or bolster antiregime officials.

REQUIREMENTS

In one sense, encouraging a popular revolution in Iran might require very little—perhaps even nothing at all—from the United States. Very few true popular revolutions have been successfully abetted, let alone caused, by an external power. Rather, most are propelled by forces indigenous to the country. Even in the case of the velvet revolutions that followed the end of the Cold War, it is hard to find one that the United States directly caused. Certainly, there were some that the United States probably helped by encouraging them and pledging assistance once they got going, but it is impossible to know whether such revolutions would have succeeded or failed without that support—and many others succeeded or failed based on factors wholly unrelated to external assistance.

However, if the United States were determined to try to *cause* a revolution, this could be a very tall order because of the limited knowledge about how these phenomena begin and succeed. At the very least, it is clear that if the United States were going to have any chance at instigating a revolution, it would have to find effective and popular Iranian oppositionists with whom to work. A popular revolution certainly requires homegrown leaders, even if they are brought in by sealed train, as Lenin supposedly was by Wilhelmine

Germany. In addition, the United States would need to ensure that its support does more good than harm. It is also necessary that Iran's existing security services, which have proven themselves quite capable, either are unable to act or choose not to. Finally, all of this, in turn, requires excellent intelligence and, for some options, considerable funding.

Finding the Right Proxies

One of the hardest tasks in fomenting a revolution, or even just unrest, is finding the right local partners. Resisting an authoritarian regime like Tehran's is a dangerous game: failure can mean not only arrest or execution for the rebels, but also severe punishment for their families. In addition, a regime has huge advantages in organization and unity in general: its forces work together (for the most part), magnifying their strength. The opposition, in contrast, often begins as disorganized idealists and has difficulty communicating effectively. A quick look at some of the more plausible candidates for a revolution illustrates the difficulty of finding the proper local channels for effecting a revolution.

THE REFORMISTS. Iran's reform movement would appear to be the most obvious vehicle for popular revolution. There is considerable evidence that many within the reform movement during the 1990s explicitly sought to topple the Islamic regime and replace it with a secular democracy. Unfortunately, the reformist movement rose and fell with the fortunes of former president Muhammad Khatami, who proved unwilling to lead the revolution that so many of his followers seemed to want. The tremendous disappointment of his presidency caused a fragmentation of the movement he led, and today the reformist parties are divided and weak. Many former reformists have abandoned the formal reformist parties for others that are considered more effective. The reformists are suppressed, harassed, and often barred from office by the regime. Although many Iranians still share the same ideals (and probably goals) as the reformists, the parties and their leaders no longer have the ability to mobilize the populace the way they once did.

Moreover, although some reformists clearly sought a full-scale revolution, it is not clear that all did. Many probably only sought specific changes—an end to corruption, greater transparency and accountability, a weakening of the powerful unelected government entities that ultimately rule the Islamic Republic, more competent economic management, and an end to the stringent social codes that still govern Iranian life. Certainly, these would represent dramatic changes in the nature of Iranian governance, but they are not necessarily incompatible with the continuation of the Islamic Republic.

INTELLECTUALS. The questioning of the underlying legitimacy of a regime by intellectuals is often and correctly seen as a serious threat: having the regime discredited among key "opinion shapers" is a critical precondition for its collapse. Iran has a significant intellectual class, consisting not only of academics and reformist journalists but also, and perhaps more important, dissident clerics. Time and again these voices have criticized the regime, with some going so far as to question the legitimacy of the velayat-e faqih system itself. These criticisms appeared to reach a high point under the presidency of Khatami in the late 1990s.

Dissident clerics are a particularly important part of the elite opposition. Their criticisms speak directly to regime legitimacy, which rests on religious credentials. Not surprisingly, the regime has tried to use both formal and informal means to sideline these people. In addition, these clerics are limited in part by their own message: because they push for the clergy to be more apolitical, their own political involvement tends to be limited.

Since the peak of reform in the late 1990s, intellectuals in Iran, both clerical and lay, have suffered tremendous repression. Many have been beaten or threatened with force. Others have been imprisoned on trumped-up charges, have lost their jobs, or even have been killed or driven into exile. Less directly, but probably more effectively, major media outlets have denied them airtime, and the regime monitors them and prevents them from speaking to large groups. Dissent does get out, but because of this censorship and intimidation, it is less effective than it would otherwise be. Even indirect contacts with foreign organizations, particularly ones linked to U.S. democracy promotion efforts such as the National Endowment for Democracy, are grounds for severe punishment.

STUDENT, LABOR, AND CIVIL SOCIETY ORGANIZATIONS. Students and workers are often the shock troops of revolutionary movements. Students typically are willing to take considerable risks and, in so doing, expose holes in the regime's coercive apparatus or create divisions within the existing elite. In the 1990s, students in particular were enthusiastic about Khatami and the promise of reform. Indeed, during the summers of 1999 and 2003,

thousands of students at Tehran University attempted to start just such a revolution, as their forebears had in the revolution of 1978. But this time
around, none of Iran's other popular factions was willing to join them.
Workers too have demonstrated from time to time against regime policies.

As with the intellectuals, the regime has cracked down, often brutally, on
the activities of students, workers, and members of civil society organizations. Student movements are almost certainly heavily penetrated by regime
intelligence services, and the activists are often not allowed to register for
classes. The regime frequently resorts to mass arrests to prevent protests
from happening, but when dissidents are able to stage effective rallies, the
demonstrators are often beaten, and counterdemonstrations (often consisting of pro-regime vigilantes) are swiftly organized to keep unrest in check.
For example, participants in at least one rally for women's rights were called
in advance and warned not to go: those who went anyway faced vigilantes,
who beat some demonstrators, and police, who arrested others.[6] If this were
not enough, the main student organization, *Daftar-e Takhim-e Vahdat*
(Office for Consolidation of Unity), is riven with personality disputes and
schisms over strategy and tactics.

REZA PAHLAVI. Another name pointed to as a potential leader of Iran is
Reza Pahlavi, the son of the last shah. In the United States, Pahlavi has
emerged as a leading critic of the clerical regime, calling for it to be con-
fronted politically and economically. Pahlavi has referred to himself as "a
catalyst" to help bring about regime change and a democratic and constitutional government (including perhaps a constitutional monarchy) rather
than a return to the absolutist monarchy of his father.[7] While Iranian
expatriate-sponsored media have broadcast interviews of Pahlavi into the
Islamic Republic, Pahlavi lacks an organized following within the country.
However, although some Iranians, particularly younger ones with no mem-
ory of his father's regime, appear to evince some nostalgia for the monarchy,
there is no serious monarchist movement in Iran itself.

LESS THAN THE SUM OF ITS PARTS. Although the above list of candidates is impressive, many of the individuals rarely work together, and some
offer little or could even discredit a broader movement. Akbar Ganji, an
Iranian journalist whose articles exposed regime murders and who was
imprisoned for six years as punishment, has said of the Iranian opposition,

"It's not organized. . . . And we still don't have a leader."[8] Many of these peo-ple, like Pahlavi, have little in common with the intellectuals and students who make up the core of the reform movement. So far, no charismatic leader has emerged to unite the different organizations and inspire other Iranians to take up the banner of change.

Money

A significant program to promote democracy in Iran would require far more money than Washington has currently allocated. If the United States is to go beyond its current modest effort to promote democracy, it would have to spend tens of millions of dollars a year, if not more. This requirement would grow if the programs are successful: more people would have to be supported, and they would require more equipment to communicate and travel. In addition, the United States would have to accept the reality of waste and fraud. Some of the money would be siphoned off by schemers, while other money would go to back figures who turn out to have little support.

Excellent Intelligence

Meddling in the internal politics of another country requires excellent intelligence if the efforts are to succeed. Indeed, a lack of intelligence can even lead a program to backfire, as the regime manipulates it to its advan-tage. To support democratic oppositionists, the United States needs to help them organize and be sure that their message is getting across. In addition, Washington needs to support leaders who are effective and who cannot be co-opted by the regime. Without this information, the United States may back the wrong people or be beguiled by figures who are secretly controlled by Iranian intelligence.

Unfortunately, it appears that this level of detailed intelligence on Iran is thus far lacking. Because the United States lacks an embassy on the ground or the ability to dispatch personnel to Iran on a regular basis, information on the country's incredibly complex politics is often negligible. Much of the information the United States requires involves an understanding of Iran's indigenous political forces, which are extraordinarily difficult for outsiders to comprehend, let alone recognize the shifting alliances among them in any-thing like real time. Consequently, strengthening this degree of intelligence collection in Iran would require the U.S. intelligence community—which has already made Iran a priority for decades—to intensify its efforts.

Military Intervention

One of the few elements that scholars do believe is a constant in success-ful popular revolutions is that the regime must lose the will or the ability to employ violence effectively to crush the revolution.[9] It seems unlikely that the Islamic regime will lose the will to crush internal threats to its rule. It is widely rumored among Iranians that Iran's current leaders believe that the *only* reason that they succeeded in overthrowing the Shah in 1978 was because he lost his nerve and refused to let the army crush the revolution (as many of his generals wanted)—and they have no intention of falling as he did. Since 1979, the regime has been ruthless in cracking down on the slight-est hint of domestic unrest. Indeed, this has always been its first priority—for instance, retaining most of its combat power in Kurdistan to crush a Kurdish revolt even after the Iraqi invasion of 1980, when Iran had virtually nothing to stop Saddam Husayn's tanks as they drove into oil-rich Khuzestan.[10]

Consequently, if the United States ever succeeds in sparking a revolt against the clerical regime, Washington may have to consider whether to provide it with some form of military support to prevent Tehran from crush-ing it. In 1991, after the Persian Gulf War, the United States called on the people of Iraq to overthrow Saddam Husayn, and hundreds of thousands (maybe even a few millions) of Iraqis, mostly Shi'ah and Kurds, heeded the call and rose up against Saddam. Washington then decided not to assist them, either by continuing its military operations against the remnants of Saddam's forces or by providing weapons, air support, and other assistance to the rebels. Infamously, what remained of Saddam's Republican Guard then systematically butchered as many as 100,000 Shi'i and Kurdish rebels and broke the nascent revolution. If the policy proposed here succeeds in producing large-scale revolts against the Iranian regime, but nothing else has intervened to weaken the Iranian military (particularly the regime's most loyal services like the Revolutionary Guard, *Ansar-e Hizballah* [Followers of the Party of God], and the *Basij* [militia]), then the United States may need to be ready to intervene in some form to prevent the revolutionaries from being slaughtered in similar fashion.

This requirement means that a popular revolution in Iran does not seem to fit the model of the "velvet revolutions" that occurred elsewhere. The point is that the Iranian regime may not be willing to go gently into that good night; instead, and unlike so many Eastern European regimes, it may choose to fight to the death. In those circumstances, if there is not external military assistance to the revolutionaries, they might not just fail but be massacred.

Consequently, if the United States is to pursue this policy, Washington must take this possibility into consideration. It adds some very important requirements to the list: either the policy must include ways to weaken the Iranian military or weaken the willingness of the regime's leaders to call on the military, or else the United States must be ready to intervene to defeat it.

PROS AND CONS

The following are the advantages and disadvantages of supporting a popular uprising.

Advantages:

—At least on paper, more than any other option, regime change offers the greatest potential benefits for the least cost. If it is successful, regime change could alter Iran from one of America's biggest enemies to a potential friend while at the same time changing an oppressive regime to a democratic one (in some variations), or at least one that is probably more friendly. In addition, this change could occur at a fraction of the cost of overthrowing the regime by mounting an invasion.

—Even if triggering a popular revolution proves impossible, supporting Iranian opposition groups could still weaken and distract the regime and possibly limit its ability to make mischief elsewhere.

—Even if a revolution does not occur during the tenure of the current administration, a steady, low-profile effort to bolster democracy in Iran may pay dividends in years or decades to come.

—Some elements of the policy, such as trying to increase intelligence penetration of Iran's military and security services, should be implemented even if Washington chooses not to adopt the whole approach. Many of these programs can be continued with much less fanfare and, if anything, become more effective in the long term for other policy options.

—By adopting regime change as its policy, the United States can demonstrate a commitment to its democratic ideals that has been sadly lacking in past decades, a situation that has greatly damaged the status of the United States in the Muslim world. Claims of double standards in democracy and

"Arab exceptionalism"—by which Middle Easterners mean that the United States promotes democracy everywhere else in the world except the Middle East, where it is comfortable with autocracies that guarantee the oil flow—are key elements of the anti-Americanism that dominates the Middle Eastern street. If the Iranian regime continues to foment instability across the Middle East, and the United States and the international community are unwilling to stop it, at the very least, the United States would always be able to say that it never enabled or appeased that trend. Washington may not succeed in stopping Tehran, but it would not have been complicit in assisting it.

Disadvantages:

—The biggest challenge to regime change would be its feasibility. For all its many shortcomings, the Iranian government is well entrenched. As Suzanne Maloney notes, "The Islamic Republic has survived every calamity short of the plague: war, isolation, instability, terrorist attacks, leadership transition, drought and epic earthquakes."[11] The regime is absolutely paranoid about the slightest hint of internal revolt and has successfully repressed, co-opted, or isolated potential sources of resistance.

—As a result, the regime has made it extremely difficult for opposition movements to survive, let alone thrive and gain popular support. Ultimately, those oppositionists who are most organized have at best marginal prospects, and many are risky bets.

—The results of regime change may be less to Washington's liking than expected. As Richard Haass points out, ousting a regime is hard enough, but replacing a regime with a government that serves U.S. interests and governs well is far harder yet.[12]

—Even democratic regime change would not necessarily bring to power a pro-American government. Despite the desire on the part of many Iranians for closer relations with the United States, U.S. policies in the region remain unpopular with most Iranians, and past U.S. meddling and current U.S. efforts to isolate Iran also may be viewed with hostility. That said, most alternatives to the current regime would probably be less supportive of terrorism and, in general, less reflexively anti-American in their policies. Iran would still be likely to try to maintain a strong position in Iraq (where its geopolitical interests are overwhelming), and may continue to pursue its nuclear program (support for a nuclear program is robust among most Iranian elites). However, it is possible that new leaders might be more open to cooperating with Washington on these issues and generally would be more sensitive to international opinion and economic pressures than the current regime.

—U.S. support may backfire. In the past, and especially since the 1978 revolution, American backing has typically been the kiss of death for internal Iranian opposition groups (for instance, very modest U.S. efforts to support regime change in the 1990s helped discredit reformers in Iran). So many Iranians instinctively bristle at American meddling in their country's affairs that even groups favorably disposed to the United States typically refuse to accept any American support for fear of being discredited among the people as foreign lackeys, and being arrested and charged with treason by the government. As such, many leading reformers in Iran have spoken out *against* U.S. funding for democracy promotion or other efforts to encourage regime change in Iran. Today, as Abbas Milani of Stanford University notes, "Anyone who wants American money in Iran is going to be tainted in the eyes of Iranians."[13] Not surprisingly, the State Department has often found it difficult to spend the money it has allocated to promote democracy.[14] It is thus possible that an aggressive U.S. regime change policy may lead to a *weaker* democratic movement.

—Greater efforts to promote democracy and work with opposition figures may prompt the regime to crack down harder. Increased (and very high-profile) U.S. funding for democracy promotion in Iran in the past five years led to a crackdown on Iranians involved in Track II dialogue and on those trying to develop civil society organizations. The attention given to the Bush administration's program to promote democracy in Iran suggests the problems with this approach. Although the overall amount of money is a fraction of what a sustained democracy program would require, the Iranian government has proven exceptionally paranoid about it. Iranian intelligence officials regularly bring up this appropriation when they interrogate activists.[15] As a result, many Iranians are wary of activities that could even indirectly be linked to the United States.[16] As Fariba Davoodi Mohajer, who has campaigned for women's rights in Iran, contends, U.S. support for civil society "becomes a ready tool for the Iranian government to use against totally independent activists. It's been very counterproductive."[17]

—Should efforts take off and a mass movement develop, the clerical regime is unlikely to go without a fight. The regime might resort to a brutal crackdown that leads to the death and imprisonment of thousands. Its rhetoric and actions against the reform movement in the past indicate that it believes violence is legitimate and that it does not need to have the support of the Iranian people for its actions, as long as it can justify them according to the regime's ruling Islamic credo. It appears more likely than not that loyal military units would fire into crowds, and the regime would not hesitate to carry out mass trials to stay in power.

Regardless of the policy's ultimate outcome, Iran is likely to retaliate almost immediately against the United States just for having supported reformers and other oppositionists. Tehran is exceptionally sensitive to the security of the regime, and its current leaders are loyal to their vision of the legacy of the Islamic Revolution. If the United States directly threatened its power with a massive campaign, Tehran would likely take several steps. First, it would step up its support for guerrilla and terrorist groups. Iraq would be a particularly likely venue given Iran's extensive paramilitary and intelligence presence there, as well as the availability of many U.S. targets. Afghanistan, too, would be a likely theater for an Iranian response. Attacks elsewhere in the Middle East and Europe would also be quite possible. Second, because U.S. efforts to promote regime change would affirm Iran's paranoia about its own security, Tehran would reinforce its already high commitment to its nuclear program. Third, Iran might step up its military buildup, though even a significant investment would have only a marginal impact on the U.S.-Iran conventional military balance.

CHAPTER SEVEN

INSPIRING AN INSURGENCY

Supporting Iranian Minority and Opposition Groups

A s much as many Americans might like to help the Iranian peo-ple rise up and take their destiny in their own hands, the evidence suggests that its likelihood is low—and that American assistance could well make it less likely rather than more. Conse-quently, some who favor fomenting regime change in Iran argue that it is utopian to hold out hope for a velvet revolution; instead, they contend that the United States should turn to Iranian opposi-tion groups that already exist, that already have demonstrated a desire to fight the regime, and who appear willing to accept U.S. assistance. The hope behind this course of action is that these var-ious opposition groups could transform themselves into more potent movements that might be able to overturn the regime.

For instance, the United States could opt to work primarily with various unhappy Iranian ethnic groups (Kurds, Baluch, Arabs, and so on) who have fought the regime at various periods since the rev-olution. A coalition of ethnic opposition movements, particularly if combined with dissident Persians, would pose a serious threat to regime stability. In addition, the unrest the groups themselves cre-ate could weaken the regime at home. At the least, the regime would have to divert resources to putting down the rebellions. At most, the unrest might discredit the regime over time, weakening its position vis-à-vis its rivals.

The United States could also attempt to promote external Iranian opposition groups, providing them with the support to turn themselves into full-fledged insurgencies and even helping them militarily defeat the forces of the clerical regime. The United States could work with groups like the Iraq-based National Council of Resistance of Iran (NCRI) and its military wing, the *Mujahedin-e Khalq* (MEK), helping the thousands of its members who, under Saddam Husayn's regime, were armed and had conducted guerrilla and terrorist operations against the clerical regime. Although the NCRI is supposedly disarmed today, that could quickly be changed.

GOAL

Supporting an insurgency could have two different potential goals, with one effectively a fallback position of the other. Like supporting a popular revolution, one goal of supporting an insurgency would be to try to overthrow the Iranian regime altogether, in the expectation that doing so would alleviate America's problems with Iran.

However, even if U.S. support for an insurgency failed to produce the overthrow of the regime, it could still place Tehran under considerable pressure, which might either prevent the regime from making mischief abroad or persuade it to make concessions on issues of importance to the United States (such as its nuclear program and support to Hamas, Hizballah, and the Taliban). Indeed, Washington might decide that this second objective is a more compelling rationale for supporting an insurgency than the (much less likely) goal of actually overthrowing the regime.

TIME FRAME

Insurgencies take a long time to succeed, when they succeed at all. It takes time for insurgents to identify leaders and recruit personnel, establish bases and gather equipment, and learn tactics and proficiency with weapons. It takes even longer to win popular support, erode the morale of the government's armed forces, and then undermine the government's legitimacy. There are often crippling setbacks along the way, during which even an ultimately successful insurgency may need to spend months or years regrouping and rebuilding.

For all of these reasons, insurgencies typically take decades to overthrow a government. Over the past century, successful *counter*insurgency campaigns lasted an average of about nine years, and these were typically only mounted against insurgencies that had demonstrated the capability to threaten the government's grip on power, either in a region or the nation as a whole, and thus were already fairly advanced. The Afghan *mujahideen*—one of the most successful insurgencies of recent times—took ten years to evict the Soviets from Afghanistan. The Viet Cong and the Chinese Communists each took more than twice as long to succeed in their respective conflicts. Fidel Castro's guerrilla war took less than six years to overthrow the Batista regime in Cuba, but this victory came against a badly disorganized regime defended by demoralized and disaffected troops. It would be difficult to replicate Castro's rapid success against a well-entrenched Iranian regime that can still muster numerous fanatical defenders.

Consequently, if the goal of this policy is to actually overthrow the Iranian regime, doing so would take many years, if not several decades. It is clearly not a quick fix to Washington's near-term problems with Iran. However, there are two exceptions to the rule that insurgencies take a long time to reach their goal.

First, if the goal of an insurgency is merely to put pressure on the regime, the goal could be met much more quickly than the time span outlined above. History has shown that depending on the state of the insurgency when a foreign power decided to back it, pressure was produced on the targeted regime in as little as a few years or even months. When the Shah of Iran, the United States, and Israel began to back Iraqi Kurds against Baghdad, it took only a few years for the Ba'thist regime to move against them—and only a matter of months of unsuccessful military campaigning to convince Saddam Husayn to cut a deal with the Shah to persuade him to cut his ties to the Kurds.

Second, even if the goal remains to overthrow the regime, an insurgency can be greatly assisted by outside conventional military assistance. A good example of this was the U.S. air support and special forces personnel deployed to help Afghanistan's Northern Alliance during Operation Enduring Freedom in 2001. The Northern Alliance was a competent military force, but it had no chance of overthrowing the Taliban until the United States decided to provide direct military assistance after the 9/11 attacks. When the United States did so, the Taliban regime cracked in a matter of weeks as the Northern Alliance took control of the country.

OVERVIEW OF THE POLICY

The core concept lying at the heart of this option would be for the United States to identify one or more Iranian opposition groups and support them as it did other insurgencies in Afghanistan, Nicaragua, Kurdistan, Angola, and dozens of other locales since the Second World War. The United States would provide arms, money, training, and organizational assistance to help the groups develop and extend their reach. U.S. media and propaganda outlets could highlight group grievances and showcase rival leaders. The United States would help the groups identify a base in a neighboring country, secure the host nation's support for the groups, and help them develop an infrastructure to support operations in Iran.

A key question that the United States would have to address would be the extent of its direct *military* support to the groups. The Central Intelligence Agency (CIA) could take care of most of the supplies and training for these groups, as it has for decades all over the world. However, Washington would need to decide whether to provide the groups with direct military assistance under three scenarios:

—As general support to allow the groups a much greater chance of success and a much more rapid pace of victory. As noted above, massive external conventional military assistance can greatly assist an insurgency. Again, U.S. support to the Northern Alliance against the Taliban regime in Afghanistan in 2001 is a good example.

—To prevent a massacre of the insurgents. Not all insurgencies succeed, and some fail disastrously. In Iraq in 1991 when the Shi'ah and Kurds revolted against Saddam Husayn, and in Cuba at the Bay of Pigs 30 years before, American-backed insurgents called for American military aid when they were on the brink of disaster. In both cases, the United States turned its back on them, and they were slaughtered. The United States should decide well ahead of time whether it would commit military forces to prevent a massacre. If it is prepared to respond, it should have the necessary forces in place near Iran so that they are available if needed.

—To protect neighboring countries providing sanctuary to the insurgents. Any insurgency against the Iranian regime would need a safe haven and conduit for arms and other supplies through one or more of Iran's neighbors. The clerical regime may decide to retaliate against those neighboring states to try to force them to desist, and the United States may be called upon to protect them. During the Vietnam War, Viet Cong fighters had their sanctuary in North Vietnam, and many Americans wanted to invade the North to force it to halt this practice. The U.S. military famously did mount a protracted and unsuccessful coercive air campaign against the North to try to persuade it to end such support. However, the United States chose not to launch an invasion, in part for fear that China and Russia would come to Hanoi's defense.

It seems unlikely that any American administration would be willing to provide the kind of military support envisioned in the first of these scenarios. Operation Enduring Freedom in Afghanistan was closer to an invasion than an insurgency, and mounting a similar campaign against Iran would give up all of the advantages of an insurgency in terms of plausible deniability, thereby undercutting the willingness of neighboring states to support it. Unfortunately, the second situation is a very real possibility that the United States has faced on other occasions. The third situation could also occur, and so Washington would have to be ready to come to the defense of the neighboring states supporting the guerrillas, or else face the prospect of losing their support in the bid to overthrow the regime.

Requirements

The United States should expect to provide an array of assistance to insurgents, depending on their military skill and their degree of popular support. The more competent and popular the insurgents are, the less they would need American aid. Still, U.S. training could greatly augment the effectiveness of their existing forces, and arms and funding could improve their equipment and help them recruit. Direct U.S. military support could help them conduct effective operations and defeat larger Iranian military forces.

Consequently, the United States would have to expect to invest a fair amount of money, weaponry, and other resources in the insurgencies it chose to back. However, especially when compared to the cost of conventional military operations, insurgencies are a bargain. For instance, the entire program to support the Afghan mujahideen against the Soviet occupation from 1979 to 1989 cost the United States only $600 million a year, compared to the $21 billion a year the country has spent on average in Afghanistan since 2001.[1]

Nevertheless, mounting an insurgency against Tehran, especially one that might threaten the regime's survival, would be a difficult undertaking, and there are at least two major requirements: finding an insurgent group that could mount such a challenge and finding a neighboring state willing to act as the conduit (and safe haven) for the group.

Finding a Proxy

The first—and potentially most problematic—requirement to implement this option is to identify a potential insurgent group that is willing and able to play this role with American assistance. The best candidate for such a role would be a broad-based opposition group with cohesiveness, some history of armed resistance, a clear leadership, and widespread popular support. Unfortunately, none of the current candidates can claim to meet all of those criteria. Consequently, the United States would have to opt either for ethnic groups that possess the cohesiveness, leadership, and popular support from a segment of Iranian society, or for the MEK—which arguably has the leadership and cohesiveness but has little popular support at present.

POTENTIAL ETHNIC PROXIES. Although Persians dominate Iran, they represent only half of the population. At least to some outside observers, Iran appears rife with ethnic unrest, and these cleavages could become the means by which the United States could try to mobilize one or more insurgencies against the Islamic regime. Tehran has often been harsh in its crackdowns on minority groups, many of which are concentrated away from the capital and thus are hidden from media attention. Iran's Arab and Baluch populations both are poor and suffer from discrimination. As a result, Arab separatists in the southwestern province of Khuzestan have conducted a number of terrorist bombings in the regional capital of Ahvaz in recent years. In addition, Iran's Kurdish population is large and, after the 1979 revolution, sustained a bloody rebellion that lasted several years and led to the deaths of thousands of Kurds. The anger and strife continue to this day: in 2005, after Iranian police killed a Kurdish leader, 20 Kurds died in demonstrations.

Despite the harsh crackdowns, the Iranian regime is weak in parts of the country. In Kurdish and Baluchi areas in particular, the government has never established comprehensive governance. Instead, several groups have strong tribal ties and, in the case of the Kurds, a cohesive sense of identity that is not tied to the regime. The groups have used smuggling to strengthen themselves, bringing in weapons, to the point where many are now well-armed. Geography and terrain have helped these groups resist Tehran, as large parts of Iran are rugged and thus good guerrilla country.

Although these groups are more organized than students and workers and, in the Kurdish case, represent a sizeable entity, their ability to mobilize beyond their communities is limited. Persians tend to be highly nationalistic and would have to be expected to unite over any perceived attempt to fragment the country. Nor are there strong ties among the non-Persian groups, and in the past, these divisions have allowed them to be contained and defeated piecemeal. Some large ethnic groups also have no desire to oppose the regime. For instance, Iran's Azeri population, which represents roughly a quarter of the country's overall population, is well integrated (Supreme Leader Khamene'i is of Azeri origin) and has worked closely with Persian elites.

As the above discussion suggests, the Kurds are the most likely proxy given their size, cohesive identity, and ambitions. The Kurds, however, are divided internally, and many of their leaders have been co-opted by the state, while those who have not are often subject to brutal intimidation. Iranian intelligence aggressively targets Kurdish leaders abroad, whether in Iraq or Europe—even to the point of assassination. The Kurds are also justifiably suspicious of outside promises, having been used and discarded in the past. Finally, stirring Kurdish separatism in Iran would not play well in either Baghdad or Ankara, two key American allies whose aid would be needed for any insurgent campaign against Iran.

NATIONAL COUNCIL OF RESISTANCE/MUJAHEDIN-E KHALQ. Perhaps the most prominent (and certainly the most controversial) opposition group that has attracted attention as a potential U.S. proxy is the NCRI (National Council of Resistance of Iran), the political movement established by the MEK (Mujahedin-e Khalq). Critics believe the group to be undemocratic and unpopular, and indeed anti-American. In contrast, the group's champions contend that the movement's long-standing opposition to the Iranian regime and record of successful attacks on and intelligence-gathering operations against the regime make it worthy of U.S. support. They also argue that the group is no longer anti-American and question the merit of earlier accusations. Raymond Tanter, one of the group's supporters in the United States, contends that the MEK and the NCRI are allies for regime change in Tehran and also act as a useful proxy for gathering intelligence.[2] The MEK's greatest intelligence coup was the provision of intelligence in 2002 that led to the discovery of a secret site in Iran for enriching uranium.

Despite its defenders' claims, the MEK remains on the U.S. government list of foreign terrorist organizations. In the 1970s, the group killed three U.S. officers and three civilian contractors in Iran.[3] During the 1979–1980 hostage crisis, the group praised the decision to take American hostages and Elaine Sciolino reported that while group leaders publicly condemned the 9/11 attacks, within the group celebrations were widespread.[4] Undeniably, the group has conducted terrorist attacks—often excused by the MEK's advocates because they are directed against the Iranian government. For example, in 1981 the group bombed the headquarters of the Islamic Republic Party, which was then the clerical leadership's main political organization, killing an estimated 70 senior officials. More recently, the group has claimed credit for over a dozen mortar attacks, assassinations, and other assaults on Iranian civilian and military targets between 1998 and 2001. At the very least, to work more closely with the group (at least in an overt manner), Washington would need to remove it from the list of foreign terrorist organizations.

The group itself also appears to be undemocratic and enjoys little popularity in Iran itself. It has no political base in the country, although it appears to have an operational presence. In particular, its active participation on Saddam Husayn's side during the bitter Iran-Iraq War made the group widely loathed. In addition, many aspects of the group are cultish, and its leaders, Massoud and Maryam Rajavi, are revered to the point of obsession. As Iran scholar Ervand Abrahamian claims, "It is a mystical cult. . . . If Massoud Rajavi got up tomorrow and said the world was flat, his members would accept it."[5]

Despite its limited popularity (but perhaps because of its successful use of terrorism), the Iranian regime is exceptionally sensitive to the MEK and is vigilant in guarding against it. During the early years of the revolution, the regime rooted out members throughout Iran and massacred demonstrators who marched in the group's name. Abroad, the regime monitors the group's activities carefully, tries to disrupt its bases, and at times has assassinated its members.

Finding a Conduit and Safe Haven

Of equal importance (and potential difficulty) will be finding a neighboring country willing to serve as the conduit for U.S. aid to the insurgent group, as well as to provide a safe haven where the group can train, plan, organize, heal, and resupply. This was the role that Pakistan played when the United States provided aid to the Afghan mujahideen in the 1980s, and the Shah's Iran played when the United States provided aid to the Kurds in the 1970s. Without such a partner, it would be far more difficult for the United States to support an insurgency. One thing that the United States would have in its favor when searching for a state to play this role is that many of Iran's neighbors dislike and fear the Islamic Republic.

However, balanced against that are a series of hurdles that the United States would have to overcome. Even those states that loathe and fear Tehran have left no doubt that they do not seek an open conflict with Iran, and supporting an insurgency could provoke Iranian retaliation. Moreover, these states fear Tehran would likely retaliate through its unconventional warfare capabilities by increasing support for insurgents, terrorists, and other opposition groups in any neighboring state that supports the insurgency.

To deal with this, the United States would not only have to reassure the neighboring state, but also potentially provide real aid. The neighboring state may seek American counterterrorism assistance as a way of bracing itself for Iranian unconventional retaliation. It might ask for a more conventional commitment of American military protection to deter Iranian aggression. And, almost certainly, the state would use its fear of Tehran's response to get other things from the United States. For instance, during the 1980s, the Pakistanis demanded stepped-up American arms sales and military training (for a conventional war against India) in return for its help in Afghanistan, despite the fact that no one benefited more from the American aid to the mujahideen than did Pakistan. The United States would have to expect the same or similar from Iran's neighbors, which include Pakistan—an obvious conduit for American support to a Baluchi insurgency.

There is another likely obstacle to securing a neighboring safe haven for ethnic insurgencies against Tehran: many of those ethnic groups span the borders between Iran and the potential sponsoring state, which often has the same problems with that ethnic group as does Tehran. Both the Turks and Iraqis would be logical conduits to support a Kurdish insurgency against Iran, but that is highly unlikely because both Baghdad and Ankara fear Kurdish aspirations for independence and believe that supporting an armed Kurdish bid for independence against Iran (which is inevitably what a Kurdish insurgency would aim for) would galvanize their own Kurdish populations to seek the same.

Pros and Cons

The following are the advantages and disadvantages of supporting an insurgency.

Advantages

—This approach has some potential to overturn the regime and bring to power another government more amenable to the United States.

—While an insurgency is typically less dangerous to the regime than a popular revolution (if only because insurgencies often take longer and follow a more predictable course), an insurgency is often easier to instigate and support from abroad. Unlike the option of trying to promote a popular revolution, supporting one or more insurgencies against the regime would rely on groups that are already organized, are committed to opposing the regime with force, and have some history of having done so. Moreover, at least some of these groups have indicated a willingness to accept support from the United States.

—Even if this policy failed to overthrow the regime, supporting one or more insurgencies would put pressure on Tehran. It would divert the regime's attention and resources, possibly limiting its ability to make mischief elsewhere in the region. It also might make Iran more amenable to compromise on issues of importance to the United States in return for Washington's agreement to cease its support to the various insurgent groups.

—This option requires relatively few resources. Insurgencies are famously cheap to support, hence Iran's ability to support them in the Palestinian territories, Lebanon, Iraq, and Afghanistan simultaneously.

—The United States has considerable experience supporting insurgencies and has enjoyed a number of successes in doing so over the years.

—Properly executed, covert support to an insurgency would provide the United States with "plausible deniability." As a result, the diplomatic and political backlash would likely be much less than if the United States were to mount a direct military action.

Disadvantages

—It would be difficult to find or build an insurgency with a high likelihood of success. The existing candidates are weak and divided, and the Iranian regime is very strong relative to the potential internal and external challengers.

—Supporting one or more insurgency groups is much less likely than a popular revolution to produce actual regime change in Iran. The Kurds, the Baluch, the Arabs of Khuzestan—none of these groups is likely to trigger a nationwide movement to topple the regime. Indeed, they are more likely to rally Iran's majority Persian community (54 percent of the population) around the regime. This is not to say that an insurgency could not accomplish meaningful results, only that it would be difficult for an insurgency to produce true regime change—let alone do so in time to prevent the regime from acquiring a nuclear weapons capability.

—A "successful" insurgency is more likely to allow the group waging it to achieve more limited goals, such as secession. Successful cases of secession have a historical tendency to trigger additional bids for secession among other neighboring groups.[6] In the case of Iran, that could easily include the Iraqi and Turkish Kurds, or a variety of Caucasian or Central Asian groups, which would then provoke civil conflict in those countries.

—An "unsuccessful" but well-supported insurgency could easily produce a civil war instead, with the insurgency unable to secede or topple the government but, because of its foreign backing, able to keep on fighting. Civil war itself has a tendency to produce dangerous forms of spillover that can destabilize neighboring states.[7] Again, since many of Iran's neighbors are important allies of the United States, this could be potentially harmful to American interests.

—Iran would likely fight back, and the United States would be engaging Iran in the dimension of warfare at which it is most adept. Iran's greatest military strength lies in the realm of "unconventional warfare"—insurgencies, terrorism, and other forms of low-intensity conflict. While the United States also has formidable capabilities in this arena (capabilities greatly improved by its experience in Iraq and Afghanistan), the U.S. advantage here is not as overwhelming as it is at the conventional level. Doubtless, the Iranians would respond with terrorist attacks, as well as ramping up their support to the Taliban and anti-American groups in Iraq. They might also encourage Hamas and Hizballah to be more aggressive toward Israel. As best we can tell, the 1996 Khobar Towers blast was an Iranian response to an $18 million increase in the U.S. covert action budget against Iran in 1994–1995. Although that covert action program posed little threat to Tehran at the time (and another $18 million was a paltry sum for the United States), the Iranians apparently saw it as a declaration of covert war and may have destroyed the Khobar Towers complex (killing 19 American servicemen) as a way of warning the United States of the consequences of such a campaign. Washington would have to assume that Tehran would react in similar fashion if the United States were to launch a far more determined effort than in the past.

—If the United States commits to supporting an insurgent group, whether it is galvanized by ethnic, ideological, or political forces, it may have to make some very tough choices at some point regarding how far it is willing to support that group. In particular, what if the regime offers the United States major concessions in return for an American agreement to stop supporting the insurgency? If Washington agrees, the insurgents will likely be slaughtered without the American aid, but how could Washington refuse if the Iranians offer the United States something that would meet its ultimate objectives concerning Iran? In 1974–1975, the United States agreed to help Iran support Kurdish insurgents fighting the Ba'thist regime in Iraq. But in 1975, Saddam Husayn gave in to all the Shah's demands on territorial issues in return for Iran pulling the plug on the Kurds (and since U.S. support was provided via Iran, that terminated U.S. assistance as well). The Shah agreed and the Kurds were massacred. Alternatively, the United States could find itself in a Bay of Pigs–like situation: the regime might crush the insurgency despite American support, and then Washington would have to decide whether to intervene militarily to prevent a complete rout. Either situation would present Washington with a Hobson's choice: the United States would lose no matter which course it took.

The only nonethnic opposition group that is organized, armed, and committed to fighting the regime is the MEK. However, as noted, the MEK has badly alienated the Iranian population by its behavior over the years, and American support to the MEK might simply antagonize Iranians toward the United States without meaningfully advancing U.S. interests. At the very least, if the United States commits itself to this course of action, Washington should insist that the MEK reform itself and demonstrate that it has rebuilt some degree of popularity in Iran before taking up its cause.

CHAPTER EIGHT

THE COUP

Supporting a Military Move against the Regime

Because the evidence suggests that it would be hard to move the Iranian people to revolution—even though this would be the best way to effect real regime change—and because supporting an insurgency seems unlikely to achieve regime change quickly, if at all, some Americans have explored the possibility of encouraging a military coup. A nation's armed forces always have an intrinsic capability to depose the government, even if a strongly ingrained professional ethos makes it highly unlikely that they would do so. The Iranian armed forces certainly have a much greater ability to unseat the current regime than any potential Iranian insurgent group. Moreover, coups are typically more successful and easier to instigate and assist from abroad than popular revolutions. Consequently, a military coup has advantages where both the popular revolution and insurgency options have disadvantages.

Unfortunately, the notion of engineering a military coup in Iran has its own disadvantages as well, and these are considerable. The Iranian regime is well aware of the potential for a coup and has thoroughly politicized its various armed forces to minimize the chances. It has two complete militaries—the Iranian Armed Forces (*Artesh*) and the Islamic Revolutionary Guard Corps (*Sepah-e Pasdaran-e Enqilab-e Eslami*)—which compete for the regime's favor and are used to watch and balance each other. Beyond that, Iran has a pervasive intelligence and security apparatus that monitors all of its military personnel carefully for any signs of disloyalty or foreign contact that could be tip-offs of a future coup attempt. Moreover, the United States has no official presence in Iran, and the diplomats of U.S. allies in the country are closely watched by the Iranian security services, making it difficult to contact Iranian military personnel to determine whether any might be interested in moving against the regime. Indeed, for that reason, the United States has historically found the loyalty of the Iranian armed forces difficult to judge. If the president were to order the CIA to pursue this option, it is not clear where the folks at Langley would even start.

GOAL

The ultimate goal of a policy of supporting a military coup against Tehran would be to try to replace the Islamic Republic with another government more amenable to American interests in the Middle East and Central Asia. In this sense, this policy option is considerably closer to the idea of instigating a popular revolution than it is to supporting an insurgency. Moreover, like fomenting a popular revolution, supporting a coup in Iran would be difficult to use as a means of pressuring the regime to make compromises. It is the nature of coups that if the regime has any inkling that one is afoot, it will likely be able to crush it. Consequently, it is hard for an external power to use the threat of a coup as a form of pressure.[1]

TIME FRAME

The timing of a coup is difficult to gauge for two different reasons. First, it is impossible to know how long it would take to make contact with would-be coup plotters. As noted above, the United States does not have a diplomatic presence in Iran, and it is hard for Americans to travel the country easily— let alone to meet with members of the Iranian armed forces. There may well be officers who would like to stage a coup, but U.S. agents may never come in contact with them. Alternatively, it may be that there are not any, and the United States would have to hope that some might change their minds some time soon (or else find a way to persuade them to do so). If there is no one ready to move against the regime, it is impossible to predict when someone might be. And even if there are officers ready to do so, it is impossible to predict if and when the United States would be able to find them.

If this hurdle can be overcome, it then becomes difficult to gauge when the coup would actually happen. Inevitably, the timing of a coup is almost entirely determined by the plotters themselves, as they are in the best position to know when they will be ready and when the regime would be vulnerable. It is extremely difficult for an outside power to order up a coup on a specific date—although the outside power can certainly have input into that decision, especially if it is to provide direct support of some kind before, during, or after the coup itself. Typically, coups take some time to prepare as the cabal will want to recruit supporters, conduct reconnaissance, and plan the operation and its possible contingencies. A cabal that waits too long typically is exposed and rounded up by the regime. Plotters that do not take enough time to prepare often fail in the execution and are killed or arrested by the regime. The problem is that there is no mathematical formula to determine how much recruitment, reconnaissance, and planning is just right. Thus, even after the coup plotters have been identified and contacted, it may take weeks, months, or even years for them to pull the trigger.

Overview of the Policy

Mounting a coup is hard work, especially in a state as paranoid about foreign influence and meddling as Iran is. The United States would first have to make contact with members of Iran's military (and likely its security services as well). This by itself is very difficult. Because of Iranian hypersensitivity to Americans, the United States would likely have to rely on "cutouts"—third party nationals working on behalf of the United States—which invariably introduces considerable complexity. Then the United States would have to use those contacts to try to identify Iranian military personnel who were both willing and able to stage a coup, which would be more difficult still; it would be hard enough for Americans to make contact with Iranian military officers, let alone make contact with those specific individuals willing to risk their lives and their families in a coup attempt. Of course, it is possible that if Washington makes very clear that it is trying to support a coup in Iran, the coup plotters will reach out to the United States. But this is very rare: history shows that coup plotters willing to expose themselves to another national government are usually discovered and killed; furthermore, most of those coming to the United States to ask for help overthrowing this or that government tend to be poseurs or even counterintelligence agents of the targeted government.

In truth, the most successful coup plots are those that do not require much, if any, outside assistance because they then have the least risk of exposure. Since plotters must be secretive in order to prevent the government from preempting the coup, they should be small in number. To succeed, once a coup is launched, it requires that the plotters seize power rapidly. They must then either quickly win the support of potential rivals or neutralize them, often by consolidating control before any opposition can organize. Military and security forces whose leaders are not part of the plot must already be sympathetic, or if they are not, their leaders must be co-opted or arrested in order to prevent them from reversing the coup.

Although many coups are homegrown, one obvious historic model of a foreign-assisted coup in Iran is Operation Ajax, the 1953 coup d'état that overthrew the government of Prime Minister Mohammed Mossadeq and reinstated the rule of Shah Reza Pahlavi. To carry out the coup, the CIA and British intelligence supported General Fazlollah Zahedi, providing him and his followers with money and propaganda, as well as helping organize their activities.[2]

To engineer a coup today, the United States could play multiple roles. Intelligence officials could identify military and security service officers to recruit and help them communicate securely. U.S. money could suborn potentially disloyal officers. During the coup itself, U.S. clandestine media could broadcast misinformation to confuse regime loyalists and try to bolster popular support for the plotters. In addition, U.S. electronic warfare can be used to disrupt the regime's communications and thus paralyze its response.

As with supporting an insurgency, a critical question that Washington would have to decide beforehand is whether the United States would be willing to provide direct military assistance to the coup plotters—either to save them from annihilation or to deliver the coup de grace if it seemed they were doing well but needed something to put them over the top. Because military forces would need to be in place beforehand, this could not be decided on the fly, during the coup. Of course, readying forces around Iran could tip off the regime, which creates one potential disincentive. Another is that military support could undermine the legitimacy of the coup plotters if they appeared to be foreign puppets rather than homegrown nationalists. Moreover, direct military support could involve the United States in a war with Iran if the coup attempt fails, raising all of the liabilities of the various military options. On the other hand, because Iranian security is so formidable, a coup plot might need some outside assistance to succeed.

REQUIREMENTS

The key to this policy option is knowing whom to support and how. This requires a thorough understanding of Iran's military and security forces, not just in terms of their weaponry, organization, and doctrine, but the much more subtle areas of personal and institutional relationships (which determine who might support a coup by any given officer or group of officers), personal histories (which can indicate who holds a grievance against the regime), and standard operating procedures (deviation from which will tip off the regime).

Ultimately, understanding Iran's military and security forces in this way is vital for two distinct reasons. First, members of the military are best positioned to carry out a coup and topple the regime. Second, other forms of resistance are likely to falter if the military and security forces firmly back the regime.

Iran's military, however, has been effectively "coup proofed" by the clerical regime.[3] After the revolution, the new leadership saw the military as the bastion of the Shah's rule. Several aborted coups in the early years of the revolution also increased suspicion of the military as an institution. In response, the regime shot or dismissed many officers, while others fled into exile. After this purge, the regime exercised tremendous control over the leaders of the regular armed forces, vetting them carefully for loyalty and monitoring their activities. In addition, the regime created a parallel military—the Islamic Revolutionary Guard Corps (IRGC)—with a dual mission of fighting internal as well as external foes of the revolution. Today, key facilities and areas are guarded by IRGC forces, not by the regular military. IRGC members, in particular, are a crucial component of the younger conservatives who form the bastion of the current order. Given this recent history and the competition from the IRGC, the regular military is, if anything, even more a pillar of the regime. As dissent appeared to increase in the 1990s with several demonstrations, security forces wavered when confronting unrest. Since then, the clerical leadership reorganized the military and law enforcement services to ensure their loyalty in the event of popular unrest. Special units have been created with leaders carefully vetted for their loyalty.

What all of this means is that the critical requirement of this option is superb intelligence on the Iranian armed forces.

Excellent Intelligence

As explained in Chapter 6 with regard to fomenting a popular revolution, successful meddling in the internal affairs of another country requires excellent intelligence if the efforts are to succeed. Indeed, a lack of intelligence can even lead a covert action program to backfire, as the regime manipulates it to its advantage. For a coup, the United States would need a sense of the loyalties of different unit commanders, knowledge of the key points of communication that must be seized or neutralized, and an understanding of regime counterintelligence measures, among other factors. Without this information, the United States may back the wrong people or be beguiled by figures who are secretly controlled by Iranian intelligence.

Iran also has multiple centers of power, which would make a coup far harder to pull off than in 1953. In addition to parallel militaries, Iran's economic and political institutions overlap in their areas of responsibility. This multiplicity makes it difficult to strike a quick and decisive blow to seize power. Knowing which centers are the most important would greatly aid this effort.

As explained earlier, it appears that the necessary level of detailed intelligence on Iran is simply not there. Because the United States has no embassy and has few Iran experts within government ranks, information on the country's incredibly complex politics is often inadequate or inaccurate. Much of the information the United States requires involves an understanding of Iran's remote areas (for example, Baluchistan) or is difficult to obtain comprehensively, such as the loyalty of various unit commanders. Consequently, any plan to aid a coup would first require a major effort to build up American intelligence on Iran, which would itself be time consuming and difficult given the inherent nature of Iranian society and the paranoia of the regime.

PROS AND CONS

The following are the advantages and disadvantages of supporting a military coup.

Advantages

—Because the Iranian military has power of its own, a coup d'état would conceivably require the least support from the United States. Washington could mostly leave it to the Iranian cabal to summon the power to topple the regime, and in theory, it should be capable of doing so. Based on the history of other coups, both in Iran and elsewhere, the United States might only have to provide some money, communications assistance, and some specialized gear.

—Even a failed coup plot might make the regime fearful—and in so doing, make it more willing to cooperate—or simply cause it to focus internally, lessening its mischief making abroad.

—In theory, if the coup plotters succeeded, they would feel grateful to the United States, and so there would be some reasonable expectation of a better relationship between a new government in Tehran and Washington.

Disadvantages

—Because of Iranian security measures, there is a high likelihood that the regime would uncover the coup plot and kill all of the participants to discourage anyone else contemplating such a step. This would end up strengthening the regime—the opposite of what the United States had hoped to achieve.

—Attempting to foment a coup would require a much more intimate understanding of the Iranian officer corps than the United States currently possesses, and it would be difficult to improve this quickly given Iranian security measures. Indeed, if ordered to implement this option today, it is not clear that the U.S. intelligence community would even know where to start.

—There is little evidence to suggest widespread disaffection against the regime among the security services, or that there are numbers of officers willing to move against it. If anything, based on the very limited information that the outside world has about the Iranian military, it appears that the Iranian Armed Forces and the Islamic Revolutionary Guard Corps compete for the regime's favor.

—A military coup backed by the United States could play very badly among the Iranian people at large. It might appear to be "1953 redux" and trigger a backlash against both the new government and the United States.

—Moreover, it seems unlikely that a military coup would bring a democratic government to power. The United States might be replacing an unfriendly autocracy with a friendly one, but this would hardly endear it to the region or the rest of the world, and one lesson that the United States has learned from the Iranian revolution (among other events) is that supporting autocrats tends to undermine American interests over the long term.

If the Iranians became aware of American efforts to instigate a coup plot, they would likely retaliate against the United States, potentially in all the ways and against all of the locations discussed in association with previous options.

Part IV

Deterring Tehran

Containment

It seems fitting that discussion of the Containment option would come last in this survey of U.S. policy options toward Iran, because Containment is always America's last policy choice. When a state proves too hostile for Engagement or a diplomatic compromise, when it is too strong to be invaded or otherwise attacked, and when it is too repressive to be overthrown, only then does the United States opt to contain it as best it can.

To a great extent, Containment has been the default U.S. policy toward Iran since the Islamic Revolution because Washington failed with the other options—at least to the extent it tried them. Carter, Reagan, Bush 41, and Clinton all attempted to engage Iran and failed. Carter, Bush 41, Clinton, and Bush 43 held out the prospect of a diplomatic compromise of one sort or another without any luck either. Clinton and Bush 43 also tried to aid Iranian oppositionists in the hope of bringing reform to Tehran. No American administration has ever employed military force against Iran as a deliberate policy, although the Reagan administration deployed the U.S. Navy to the Persian Gulf in 1987–88, at the height of the Iran-Iraq War, to escort Kuwaiti oil tankers. This resulted in several skirmishes between U.S. and Iranian forces, but in the final analysis, these were all provoked by Tehran.

Amid all of these different efforts to engage, negotiate with, and even redirect the Iranian regime, the constant in U.S. policy toward Iran over the past 30 years has been Containment. Throughout this period, none of the other policy options gained any purchase with the Iranian regime, although, in truth, they were often applied in a ham-fisted or half-hearted manner. As such, the United States and its allies did as much as they could to limit Iran's ability to support violent extremist groups, subvert friendly governments, develop weapons of mass destruction (WMDs), and otherwise undermine the Middle Eastern status quo. The long list of unilateral sanctions applied by the United States against Iran from 1979 onwards was a critical element of that policy (although it was also meant to try to change Tehran's behavior). So, too, were U.S. efforts to discourage arms sales, trade, and investment with Iran by other countries. Except for those moments when Washington was attempting to engage the Iranian regime, the United States typically was trying to isolate it—diplomatically, economically, militarily, and in every other way conceivable.

The success of Containment during this period was uneven. Iran today seems a more powerful and disruptive force in the international relations of the Middle East than it has been since the early days of the revolution. Given that Containment sought to achieve the opposite, these results alone suggest that Containment failed. But as always with Iran, there is more to it than that. First, Iran's apparent strength across the region is more a product of American mistakes than its own actual puissance or cleverness. The United States eliminated Iran's two most threatening neighbors—Saddam Husayn in Iraq and the Taliban in Afghanistan—and left power vacuums that allowed the Iranians to assert considerable influence where they previously had little. Similarly, American missteps in Lebanon, Syria, and elsewhere, as well as in dealing with the Palestinians, have diminished the power and freedom of action of the United States (and its allies) and handed Iran apparent victories at little cost.

Second, Iran's "strength" is mostly a façade. Iran's armed forces remain relatively weak, with little ability to project power beyond Iran's borders or thwart an Israeli or American military operation. Because of this, Iran is fortunate that it simply does not face any real conventional military threats other than those from the United States and Israel.

But its luck does not extend much further. Politically, the Islamic regime seems less and less popular, and increasing numbers of internal fissures appear each year. Additionally, its economy is a disaster. With inflation and unemployment soaring, non-oil imports and currency reserves evaporating, worker productivity and oil exports declining, and a government unwilling to take the drastic steps necessary to get out of its current predicament, Iran's future seems dark. Since economics underpins all other aspects of national power over the long term, this does not bode well for Iran's role in the region either. The Iranian regime could survive for decades more, but its eventual demise seems increasingly likely, and in the near term, political fractiousness contributes to its difficulty in taking decisive action abroad.

Although Iran's own failings and mistakes have been the most important reason for its internal decline, Containment also played a role. It is difficult to ascertain exactly how much the sanctions were responsible for Iran's economic decay, but they played a part, and many Iranians believe that they continue to play a major role.[1] The sanctions limited Iran's ability to build up its military strength, to become a major economic player, or employ its vast oil and natural gas reserves in the diplomatic realm, and to garner allies willing and able to help it achieve its goals. In short, Containment may not have achieved its maximal objectives, but it seems to have achieved more than its minimal goals.

For all of these reasons, a policy of Containment toward Iran is present in the debate like the proverbial elephant in the living room. Some analysts and experts have suggested that the United States should simply adopt a strengthened form of Containment as its policy toward Iran. Many others leave it as the unspoken but well understood fallback option—that if their preferred policy fails or is not adopted, the United States would be left with no choice but to fall back on Containment. Although we do see Containment as a viable fallback position for the United States, this section examines it by asking the question, "If the United States were to decide to eschew all of the alternatives and pursue a deliberate policy of Containment toward Iran, what would that entail?"

CHAPTER NINE

ACCEPTING THE UNACCEPTABLE

Containment

As in the past, Containment may become the U.S. policy of last resort toward Iran. If Washington is once again unable to persuade Tehran to give up its nuclear program and its other problematic behaviors, if it is unable or unwilling to try to overthrow the regime, if it chooses not to invade or if it chooses not to use airstrikes or to encourage the Israelis to do so, then it may find itself dusting off and applying a policy of Containment toward Iran.[1] Indeed, there seems to be an implicit assumption in many of the arguments made by Americans about Iran policy that if one of the diplomatic or regime change options cannot be made to work soon, then Washington will have no choice but to adopt either containment or one of the military options.

THE THREAT OF A NUCLEAR IRAN

Of course, what is implicit in the admission that the United States may have to resort to Containment or one of the military options if all else fails is that these two approaches are disastrously (and perhaps equally) bad alternatives. The drawbacks of the various military options have already been discussed in Chapters 3 through 5, and they are certainly significant. In the case of Containment, the reason that this option is considered so unpalatable is that it would mean accepting an Iranian nuclear weapons capability and possibly an Iranian nuclear arsenal. Containment makes no effort to prevent Iran from acquiring the capability but instead simply attempts to prevent Iran from causing trouble beyond its borders—both directly and indirectly—by trying to keep Iran weak and, well, contained. Consequently, a critical element in concluding whether to pursue Containment is determining the level of risk that the United States and its allies would face from an Iran armed with nuclear weapons.

Unfortunately, this is an unknowable judgment call. There is no formula, no foolproof information that could provide an objective, definitive answer. Therefore, policymakers will have to make their own judgment about the extent of the threat.

In pondering this issue, policymakers should consider at least six potential threats to the United States that stem from Iran's possession of nuclear weapons:

—*Would the Iranians use them?* The first and most obvious threat is the possibility that if Iran acquires nuclear weapons, it would use them. In military parades, Iran has draped Shahab-3 missiles with banners reading "Israel must be wiped off the pages of history"; the headquarters of Iran's Basij mobilization forces have a huge banner (in both English and Farsi) over the entrance quoting President Ahmadinejad's infamous remark that "Israel should be wiped out of the face of the world"; and Ahmadinejad and other Iranian leaders have said any number of things indicating that they would like to see the end of the Jewish state.[2] The Saudi oil fields, American bases in the Persian Gulf region, and a variety of other high-value targets are also all within range of Iranian ballistic missiles and hence vulnerable to attack if Iran were willing to employ nuclear weapons.

—*Would they give nuclear weapons to terrorists?* Iran has a long history of supporting violent extremist groups that employ terrorism—Hizballah in Lebanon (and elsewhere around the world), Hamas and Palestinian Islamic Jihad in Palestine, Jaysh al-Mahdi and even al-Qa'ida in Iraq, the Taliban in Afghanistan, the PKK (Kurdistan Workers Party) in Turkey, and numerous others.[3] Virtually all of these groups—not coincidentally—attack American allies, and a number have killed Americans with the knowledge, encouragement, and even occasional guidance of Tehran. Therefore, some Americans fear that while Tehran itself might not use nuclear weapons for fear of retaliation, it would be willing to give them to terrorists in hope of achieving the regime's aims while maintaining plausible deniability.

—*Unconstrained asymmetric warfare.* A far more common concern about Iran's acquisition of nuclear weapons is that once Tehran has a nuclear weapons capability, it would become even more aggressive, believing that it is effectively immune to any military retaliation by any other state (including the United States). This was essentially how Pakistan responded once it detonated nuclear weapons in 1998, leading to the 1999 Kargil crisis in which India and Pakistan nearly came to blows over Islamabad's outrageous terrorist campaign against India over Kashmir.

—*Israeli preemption.* The Israelis share all of the above fears, although there is a range of opinion about the threat. Nevertheless, if Israel believed that the United States and the rest of the international community were not going to try to prevent Iran from acquiring a nuclear capability and were simply going to accept it and try to contain a nuclear-armed Iran, Jerusalem might decide that it had to act unilaterally to preclude any of the above risks. Although Israeli leaders seem to be well aware of the drawbacks of an Israeli airstrike against the Iranian nuclear sites (as described in Chapter 5), one cannot assume that they will not calculate that the payoff could be worth the cost.

—*Proliferation.* Few of Iran's neighbors would be happy to see it acquire nuclear weapons or even the capability to produce such weapons. Other states might decide that they need the same to ensure their ability to deter Tehran on their own, without having to rely on any other country to do so for them. Saudi Arabia and the United Arab Emirates have already made ominous noises suggesting that they would respond in this fashion, and given their oil wealth, this is a realistic prospect. Turkey, Egypt, and other countries might decide to go down the same path. A half-dozen or more nuclear arsenals in the Middle East have the potential to spark new crises in the region, and to make all Middle Eastern crises far more dangerous than they already are.

—*The death knell of the NPT.* Because so many of its neighbors do see Iran as a threat, at least some may attempt to acquire nuclear weapons of their own to balance or deter Iran. This trend will get a further boost from the fact that Iran's acquisition of a nuclear weapons capability will probably be the nails in the coffin of the global nonproliferation regime and the Non-Proliferation Treaty. After all, Iran is widely seen as a rogue, and all the great powers, including Russia and China, have explicitly stated that it cannot be allowed to acquire that capability. If Iran nevertheless does so, and does so without paying an exorbitant price, other countries will rightly calculate that they will face even fewer international penalties for doing the same.

The last four of these potential problems arising from Iran's acquisition of a nuclear weapons capability are not merely judgments but potentially also challenges for U.S. diplomacy and military policy as part of the Containment option, and so they are treated later in this chapter. The first two, however, are simply questions of judgment that must be addressed before the United States adopts the Containment policy. If it seems likely (or even just reasonably probable) that Iran would use nuclear weapons or give them to terrorist groups once it gets them, then an option that employs containment would be a foolish policy. There is no way that the United States could prevent Tehran from doing either once the Iranians achieved the capability; the most Washington could do would be to crush the Iranians for having done so after the fact. So if Americans believe that there is a significant risk that Iran would use a nuclear weapon unprovoked or give one to terrorists, that judgment needs to be reached before acquiescing to an Iranian nuclear weapons capability. And it should drive Washington in the direction of adopting one (or more) of the other options to try to preclude this eventuality.

Ultimately, a judgment on these issues rests on the simple question, "Can Iran be deterred?" After all, it is not enough to simply assert that a nation is aggressive, is anti-American, and supports violent extremist groups, even violent extremists who attack the United States. The same could have been said about the Soviet Union under Stalin and Khrushchev, Castro's Cuba, and North Korea throughout its existence, yet the United States found them deterrable. In turn, this question rests on an assessment of whether the Iranian regime is so reckless and heedless of the potential consequences (either because it is indifferent to such costs or has shown a propensity to miscalculate the likelihood of paying them) that it would take actions like these that would risk massive retaliation from the United States, Israel, or another nuclear-armed country.

Unfortunately, it is hard to arrive at such an assessment objectively or definitively. On the one hand, Iranian leaders have consistently shown prudence and a relatively low threshold for suicidal risk. In 1988, Ayatollah Khomeini agreed to end the Iran-Iraq War long before any Iranian population centers were threatened with conquest by Iraqi (or American) forces. In 1996–1997, when Iranian support for terrorist groups and terrorist actions in Lebanon, Saudi Arabia, Bahrain, and Germany had created the risk of conventional attack by the United States and/or multilateral sanctions, Iran reined in its asymmetric warfare operations. Similarly, in Iraq in 2007–2008, when Iranian-backed Shi'i militias began to lose heavily, the Iranians refrained from escalating their support, probably in part out of concern that doing so would provoke direct American military action against them. Likewise, although Iran has had WMDs (chemical warfare agents and probably biological warfare agents as well) since 1988 and has supported various terrorist groups since 1979, it has never sought to mix the two—almost certainly because Tehran believes that in the event of a terrorist attack with WMDs, the targeted nation (and/or its allies) would dispense with the niceties of "plausible deniability" and strike with overwhelming force against whomever provided these weapons.[4]

Nevertheless, there is other evidence to the contrary. Ahmadinejad's outrageous threats tend to belie any sense of prudence in Tehran, although it is worth noting that he is not Iran's ultimate decisionmaker on national security issues and that Ayatollah Khamene'i, who is the decisionmaker, has made speeches specifically meant to undercut Ahmadinejad's more bellicose rhetoric. Still, other Iranian leaders have made statements that are almost as outrageous as Ahmadinejad's. For instance, in 2002 former president Ali Akbar Hashemi Rafsanjani explained that "Israel is much smaller than Iran in land mass, and therefore far more vulnerable to nuclear attack." He went on to point out that a nuclear attack on Israel would obliterate the state, but the Israeli retaliation would only cause "damage" to the much larger Muslim world.[5] Iran's support for terrorist attacks on U.S. assets—such as the Marine barracks blast in Beirut in 1983, Khobar Towers in 1996, and the many explosively formed projectiles dispatched to Iraqi militias and the Taliban in Afghanistan since 2005—all count as aggressive, lethal attacks on Americans that certainly ran some risk of U.S. retaliation.[6]

Thus, even if the evidence tends to suggest that Iran is prudent and averse to suffering catastrophic damage (and therefore deterrable), it is impossible to be certain. But there was no guarantee that deterrence would work with the Soviet Union either; that, too, was a risk that the United States chose to run because the cost of the alternatives (particularly a military "rollback" of the Soviet Union) were so horrific that the risk of deterrence failing still seemed like the safer bet by comparison. Containment of Iran only makes sense if the leadership of the United States reaches the same conclusion about the risks and costs when it comes to Iran.

GOAL

The goal of a Containment strategy toward Iran is to prevent Tehran from harming American interests in the Middle East and Central Asia, preferably while minimizing the costs to the United States. It is intended to prevent Iran from supporting violent extremist groups, subverting friendly governments, or otherwise destabilizing the region. Militarily, it would aim to deter any overt Iranian aggression or use of WMDs. Diplomatically, it would seek to prevent Iran from developing allies or proxies abroad. Economically, it would attempt to keep Iran as weak as possible to ease the military and diplomatic burdens.

Ultimately, this goal puts Containment in a very different category from all of the other policy options. It does not seek to change the Iranian regime's policies, except that by preventing Iran from doing much damage, Containment may eventually convince Tehran to give up the fight. It does not seek to eliminate the Iranian nuclear program and assumes that Iran's possession of a nuclear weapons capability is inevitable. It does not seek to overthrow the Iranian regime, except that by preventing Tehran from achieving its more grandiose ambitions and by maintaining punishing sanctions, Containment may foment popular resentment and hasten the end of the regime.

TIME FRAME

Containment has the easiest time frame of all. The United States could adopt it immediately, and in theory, it could last for the life of the regime—as long as it does not fail catastrophically, with Iran lashing out in some way that proved extremely harmful to American interests and thus necessitating the adoption of another, probably far more aggressive option against Tehran, such as airstrikes or an invasion.

OVERVIEW OF THE POLICY

In some ways, Containment may also be the easiest policy option toward Iran to conceptualize, both because it is effectively what the United States has pursued for most of the past 30 years and because it would be roughly congruent with how the United States contained the Soviet Union during the Cold War, and has contained a host of other antipathetic regimes such as Cuba and North Korea. As with Containment of the Soviet Union, a policy of Containment toward Iran would attempt to keep it as weak as possible and prevent it from making gains abroad, in the expectation that the regime's dysfunctions would ultimately bring about its demise.

However, because the nature of Iranian power, influence, and aggression differs fundamentally from that of the former Soviet Union, so, too, would the nature of its containment. With the Soviet Union, "containment" was a literal description of Washington's goal in seeking to prevent Moscow from using its conventional military might to conquer countries that bordered the Soviet bloc and integrate them into it. Iran has little conventional military power and instead has tried to rely on subversion, support to insurgencies and terrorists, and the abetting of revolutions and coups in nearby countries, hoping to bring to power governments friendly to Tehran. Consequently, in the case of Iran, "containment" would be more figurative than literal. It would attempt to prevent Iran from doing what it would like (rather than attempting to change either the Iranian regime or its behavior) and ensure that Iran would not make gains anywhere it sought to.

A Containment policy toward Iran would consist of five broad categories of activity against the Islamic Republic, intended to keep it weak and prevent it from creating problems elsewhere in the Middle East and Central Asia:

—*Military.* Because of the nature of Iranian power, the military dimension of Containment is important but not as critical as it was in containing the Soviet Union, whose principal means of international influence was its conventional military might. The United States would have to ensure that Iran was not able to use its armed forces to intimidate or conquer other countries, something that would not be difficult given the small size of the Iranian military. The U.S. armed forces may also need to be in a position to retaliate against the Iranians should they take actions that crossed an American "red line."

—*Strategic.* The policy option of Containment makes no effort to prevent Iran from acquiring nuclear weapons, and so it implicitly assumes that Iran may well acquire at least a weapons *capability* at some point in time. Once this becomes the case, the United States would have to deter Iran from using the weapons or from taking aggressive actions that would threaten U.S. vital interests.

—*Economic.* The United States would seek to keep Iran economically weak to prevent it from generating the military capacity or buying the diplomatic support to undermine the containment regime.

—*Diplomatic.* The United States would have to maintain a confederation of countries, starting with Iran's neighbors and the other great powers, to help Washington contain Iran. This could entail contributing military forces to prevent Iranian moves, but it would more likely focus on keeping pressure on the Iranian economy, combating Iranian subversion and support for violent extremists, and otherwise blocking Tehran's own moves.

—*Counterterrorism.* Since Containment makes no provision to eliminate the Iranian regime—or even much of an effort to keep the regime preoccupied with its domestic problems—the United States would have to expect Iran to ratchet up its support for violent extremist groups to try break out of the Containment "box," possibly by overthrowing one or more of the governments cooperating with the United States against it. To deal with that, the United States would need to organize a coordinated counterterrorism and counterintelligence effort to prevent Iranian agents from doing much damage.

REQUIREMENTS

If the course of action envisioned by a policy of Containment is relatively straightforward, the requirements of that policy are quite the opposite. When it comes to Containment, it is the requirements that are daunting. They span the range of foreign policy endeavors, entail complex interactions, and require considerable international support.

Sanctions

As already described, a key feature of Containment would be strong sanctions against Iran to keep it weak and to hinder its ability to take actions harmful to American interests. This is not quite a requirement because it is possible to imagine containing Iran without any sanctions whatsoever. During the Cold War, the Soviet bloc was simply too big and resource rich to be effectively sanctioned, and yet the United States and its allies kept it more or less contained for 45 years. Still, the Coordinating Committee for Multilateral Export Controls (the Western sanctions regime against the Soviet bloc) was helpful in denying the Soviets and their allies technology and hard currency, which left them weaker and hence easier to block. Similarly, there is no question that crippling sanctions against Iran would be extremely useful and would greatly ease the burden of Containment. Moreover, Iran has nothing like the resources of the Communist bloc, and given the weakness of its economy, defense industries, technological base, and conventional forces, effective sanctions against Iran could prove devastating, making the job of containing it infinitely easier.

Consequently, the most useful sanctions to help the Containment option would include:

—A ban on military sales to Iran, to keep its conventional and nuclear forces weak and small;

—A ban on high-technology sales to Iran, both to hinder its indigenous military development and cause stagnation in its economic base;

—Restrictions on trade and investment, to exacerbate the country's economic problems and thereby stoke domestic dissent at home—thus making it harder for Iran to act aggressively abroad—and to further undermine the economic basis of Iranian military and diplomatic strength;

—Restrictions on the travel of Iranian personnel abroad, preferably accompanied by similar constraints on Iranian air lines, to hinder the ability of Iranian intelligence personnel to wage asymmetric warfare;

—Restrictions on the transfer of hard currency to Iran, which the regime needs for arms and technology purchases, intelligence operations, and support of violent extremist groups; and

—Restrictions on the purchase and sale of Iranian oil and natural gas, not to choke them off altogether but to impose a surcharge on them to diminish the amount of revenue the Iranian state derives from them.

Since the United States already has sanctions covering every one of these activities, the real challenge for American diplomacy in pursuit of a Containment option toward Iran would be to convince as many other countries as possible—particularly Iran's major trading partners in Europe, Russia, China, East Asia, and India—to follow suit.

Conventional Military Requirements

Given the weakness of Iranian conventional forces, especially compared to the strength of the American military, this should not be an overly onerous requirement. The United States has typically found that a relatively small naval presence in the Persian Gulf—one carrier, a half-dozen surface combatants, a couple of submarines, and some minesweepers and other specialized craft—coupled with about a wing of strike and support aircraft deployed ashore has been more than adequate to deal with most potential Iranian scenarios. In times of crisis, and especially if Iran ever attempted to close the Strait of Hormuz, more forces would be needed. Depending on the scenario, reinforcements might include another aircraft carrier or two, and/or another one to two wings of strike and support aircraft ashore, along with twice as many subs and surface combatants, and perhaps as many as a dozen minesweepers. Such a force ought to be able to obliterate Iranian air and naval defenses in the Strait of Hormuz, clear any mines, and even raze Iranian military installations along its littoral (if that were desired) in a matter of weeks, or even days.

Given the weakness of Iranian ground forces, it seems unlikely that Tehran would attempt to attack any of its neighbors, especially those most important to American interests. Turkey is a member of NATO, and the Iranians have shown no inclination to provoke the entire Atlantic alliance against them. As long as the United States has 30,000–60,000 troops in Afghanistan and maintains some military personnel in Iraq (even as advisers, trainers, logistical support personnel, and the like), it is equally hard to imagine Iran invading either of those countries. If the regime embarked on a major program to build up its ground and air forces, the United States might want to commensurately support those of Iraq and Turkey—or might want to look into basing American ground forces (or merely their equipment) at prepositioned sites near Iran's borders. However, Iran would require at least five—perhaps as many as ten—years to acquire the ability to threaten either Turkey or American forces in the region. Currently, Pakistan is a mess, but its ground and air forces are probably at least as capable as those of Iran, and it possesses nuclear weapons, which are likely to deter any large-scale Iranian aggression.

At present—and therefore, for the foreseeable future—the only real geographically weak link in the conventional military containment of Iran lies to its north. As weak as Iran is, the states of the Caucasus and Central Asia are weaker still. If Tehran chose, Iran's armed forces probably could do some real damage there. However, the United States has few vital interests in either region, and it is not clear whether Iranian aggression there would benefit Iran or bog it down. Consequently, if the United States felt the need to deter an Iranian attack on these countries, it should look to reestablish bases such as those in Azerbaijan, Kyrgyzstan, and Uzbekistan that it used during the invasion of Afghanistan. Again, if the United States felt it necessary to deter an Iranian conventional military attack on these countries, it might be necessary to build up American forces there—or create an infrastructure to allow the rapid deployment of U.S. forces—because successful "extended deterrence" is often determined by the immediate balance of forces more than the overall correlation of forces.

Strategic Requirements

Because the Containment option assumes that Iran will eventually acquire a nuclear weapons capability and potentially an actual nuclear arsenal, the far more challenging military requirement is dealing with the nuclear threat from Tehran. Historically, different states have responded differently to the acquisition of a nuclear arsenal. Some became more conservative in their foreign relations, but others became more aggressive. There was Soviet bullying under Khrushchev, the Chinese picking a fight with Moscow over their common border in the late 1960s, and Pakistan recklessly escalating its terrorism campaign against India in Kashmir in the late 1990s and early 2000s. This greater aggressiveness has tended to lead to crises with other nuclear powers: the various Berlin crises and the 1962 Cuban Missile Crisis (as well as the 1956 Sinai-Suez crisis) between the United States and Soviet Union, the 1969 Sino-Soviet border clashes, and the Kargil conflict between India and Pakistan in 1999. Iranian foreign policy is already fairly aggressive, and so the United States would have to be prepared that Tehran's acquisition of some sort of nuclear capability would likely exacerbate this preexisting condition.

The lessons of the Cold War offer the best methods to deal with the potential for Iranian aggressiveness and the risk that it could spark a nuclear confrontation. The United States would have to make very clear to Iran what it regards as its vital interests. Washington would have to spell out "red lines" that, if crossed by Iran, would prompt the United States to respond with force—potentially including the use of American nuclear weapons. Where possible and where the interests were most vital, the United States would likely want American troops on the ground, either to defend the interest and so make it unnecessary to escalate to nuclear use, or simply to force Iranian leaders to calculate that any attack could involve combat with American troops, which in turn could provoke American escalation. Finally, the Cold War demonstrated that when two nuclear powers have interests (and military forces protecting those interests) in close proximity, it is important to communicate clearly to avoid mishaps, defuse tense situations, and work out measures that reduce the likelihood of problems between them more generally.

Nevertheless, following this course of action with Tehran could be far more difficult than it was with Moscow. The Iranian political system is far more Byzantine, unpredictable, and prone to misinterpretation of American actions (and words) than the Soviet system was. This places a premium on establishing clear, reliable channels of communication with Tehran. Washington must be able to tell Tehran what it is doing and why, and to warn the Iranians, with the absolute minimum of distortion, when they are threatening an American interest or about to cross a red line. The Swiss channel that the United States has used in the past is inadequate for this requirement because (often well-meaning) Swiss diplomats have at times "interpreted" or "spun" messages passed through them to fit what they believed should happen, typically leading to unpleasant outcomes. Iranian diplomats are often highly professional, intelligent, and competent; they would be good conduits for explaining actions or sending clear signals to the regime. However, even they are at times marginalized or ignored by the senior leadership, making them a good, but imperfect, channel.

Other Diplomatic Requirements

Beyond the diplomatic requirements for an effective sanctions regime as discussed above, the Containment option demands at least two other major diplomatic undertakings. The first is meeting the basing requirements for the forces needed to deter Iranian conventional aggression and to serve as trip wires and enforce red lines. This may be easy if the United States can extend its arrangements with countries like Kuwait, Bahrain, Qatar, and Oman, which actually see advantages in hosting American military bases. However, if the United States sees a need to base forces in Saudi Arabia, the Caucasus, Central Asia, and/or Pakistan—all of which have political reasons to avoid having American troops on their soil—the State Department will have its work cut out for it.

Paradoxically, the fact that the United States would be making no effort to prevent Iran from acquiring nuclear weapons might make some of these states more willing to host American forces as a reassurance against Iranian aggression. However, other countries may reach the exact opposite conclusion. In particular, these countries may (correctly) see the greatest threat from Iran as its support of revolutionaries and insurgents, rather than the possibility it will wage a conventional attack. For them, the presence of American military forces may be more of a problem than a reassurance because it would feed domestic grievances and support oppositionist claims that the national leadership is a puppet of Washington.

The second diplomatic requirement follows from the first: the need to dampen nuclear proliferation in the Middle East and Central Asia. Especially if oil-rich countries like Saudi Arabia and/or the United Arab Emirates opt simply to buy nuclear weapons outright (from the Pakistanis, North Koreans, or who knows who else), the United States could find nuclear arsenals sprouting suddenly all across the region, creating tremendous instability and the potential for nuclear crises amid the world's most important oil-producing region. Obviously, this would be disastrous for U.S. interests in the region and also globally, thanks to the demise of the nonproliferation regime.

Finally, if the United States explicitly adopts the Containment option, it would be sending the signal to Israel that no one else is going to try to prevent Iran from acquiring a nuclear weapons capability. Although the determination of Israeli leaders to prevent Iran from acquiring a nuclear weapon *at any price* has been greatly exaggerated—and many actually believe they probably could deter a nuclear-armed Iran—there is no guarantee that Israel will simply give up. Jerusalem might decide to try its own military option, despite the fact that Israeli leaders recognize it as an unattractive course of action. If Jerusalem concludes that it cannot risk its existence on Iranian rationality and prudence, it may strike, and this could be detrimental to American interests. In particular, it could destroy international support for sanctions, hosting American military bases, and other American diplomatic initiatives in the region.

For all of these reasons, as part of a policy of containment, the United States would want to consider more explicitly extending its nuclear umbrella to Saudi Arabia, the other GCC states, Egypt, Israel, and possibly Iraq.[7] Egypt, Israel, and Saudi Arabia are already major non-NATO allies of the United States, and it is widely expected that the United States would come to their defense with all necessary means. However, any ambiguity might be problematic in the circumstances that would arise from Iran's possession of nuclear weapons, and so it might be necessary to remove it altogether by issuing a blanket declaration that an attack on any of these countries would be regarded as tantamount to an attack on the territory of the United States itself. The GCC should also be afforded the same status, given their importance as oil and gas producers and American allies. Assuming that the United States and Iraq continue to have a close relationship even after the withdrawal of American combat forces, which seems likely given Iraqi demands that the Strategic Framework Agreement include an American guarantee to defend Iraq against foreign threats, Iraq also would fall into this category, if only so as to prevent the resurrection of the atomic arms race between Baghdad and Tehran of the 1970s and 1980s.

Even this momentous step might not do the trick, however. During the Cold War, Germans famously (and perhaps appropriately) worried that the United States would not be willing to risk Boston to defend Bonn. But Washington will have little choice other than to try to make it work as best as possible.

Counterterrorism Requirements

Even more than conventional military defenses, the states of the Middle East and Central Asia would likely look to the United States to help them defend against Iranian-supported subversion, terrorism, and insurgencies if Washington opts for Containment. As noted, Iran simply cannot mount much of a conventional military threat, but it has proven quite skillful at the full spectrum of asymmetric warfare. That is where the other states of the region would face the greatest threat if Iran does become more aggressive once it acquires a nuclear weapons capability. Consequently, the United States would have to make a major effort to improve both the national defenses of these various countries and regionwide integrated programs.

There is an unpleasant Catch-22 inherent in Containment in this area. Specifically, many national governments will be frightened by Iran's ability and presumed greater willingness to stoke internal unrest abroad. As such, they would likely react by clamping down on internal opposition and suspending all political, economic, and social reform programs out of fear that Iran would try to exploit any movements for change. However, in the face of a more assertive Iran looking to more aggressively stoke internal unrest, it would be more important than ever for the governments of the region to press ahead with gradual but comprehensive and determined reform programs to eliminate the underlying sources of popular grievance. The paradox is that the natural inclination of all of these regimes will be to do the exact opposite, and so render themselves potentially more vulnerable over the long term.

Political Requirements

Containment is never an easy sell. Those on the political right will excoriate the policy as strategic suicide because they tend to believe that Iran cannot be deterred. For them, trying to live with a nuclear Iran is impossible and therefore unacceptable. Those on the political left will denounce it with equal vigor as an imperialistic effort to demonize Iran unfairly and to militarize a problem that could be resolved peacefully, through engagement and unilateral gestures. Democracy and human rights activists on both sides will complain (possibly accurately) that the policy abdicates any effort to aid the people of Iran in their struggle against a deeply oppressive regime. If the policy is adopted as Washington's first choice (rather than a fallback option), even the political center will likely fight it in the belief that the United States should have tried one of the other options first.

In short, if the president opts for Containment, he is going to have his work cut out for him at home, as well as abroad. Containment is not the kind of Iran policy that is likely to generate much enthusiasm in any corner of the

American political spectrum. That is another reason why most have tended to consider it a last-ditch, fallback option rather than a first choice.

Pros and Cons

The following are the advantages and disadvantages of the Containment approach.

Advantages

—Given the low odds that any of the other policy options will succeed, the United States may well end up with Containment regardless of what it tries first. Moving immediately to Containment without trying other options first would save the energy and resources that would be spent on those options. In particular, this would mean that the United States would not have to make any painful trade-offs between the requirements of its Iran policy and those of other, equally important policies. For example, opting for Containment might eliminate the need to make any concessions to Russia on everything from missile defense to Bosnia to its treatment of Chechnya, Georgia, Ukraine, and Belarus. It would certainly allow the president to make other issues his priorities and remove Iran as a major drain on American diplomatic capital.

—Containment would imply bearable costs on an annual basis, although those costs would certainly add up over time. The current level of naval and air forces would need to be maintained in the Persian Gulf region, likely with some residual ground presence in Iraq and Afghanistan—all of which was always envisioned by American military and political leaders in any case. There would not need to be any particular military buildup.

—Containment would probably diminish Iran's ability to make mischief in the Middle East and South Asia, possibly to a considerable degree. Over the past 30 years, neither Iran nor the United States has entirely succeeded in achieving its goals with regard to the other, but given the relative power and influence of the two countries in the Middle East and Central Asia today, the United States has done relatively much better. Iran remains weak and poor, and the few allies it has are also weak. Hardly any countries appear ready to embrace Khomeini's Islamic revolution or look to Tehran for advice, support, or permission to act. And internationally, Iran remains a pariah nation, tolerated because of its oil and gas exports, but otherwise shunned. That is not a bad record for Containment, and it suggests that the United States could similarly limit Tehran in the future.

Disadvantages

—Containment assumes that Tehran can be deterred. While there is evidence to support that contention, it is unproven at best, and if it is incorrect, the outcome could be spectacularly horrible. As with containment of the Soviet Union, it rests on the assumption that the other side would not do anything manifestly foolish, but that may not be the case.

—Moreover, in the case of Iran, perverse internal politics have often caused the Islamic Republic to take foreign policy actions that *were* manifestly foolish. An obvious example of this was Iran's holding of the 52 American hostages for 444 days in 1979–1981. This act gravely harmed Iran in a variety of ways—damage that was apparent to any number of Iranian political leaders at the time—but Iran's internal politics trumped these strategic considerations and produced behavior that the rest of the world considered reckless and even irrational.

—Allowing Iran to develop a nuclear weapons capability could well encourage other regional states to develop similar capabilities of their own. Such a nuclear arms race in the Persian Gulf region could be highly dangerous and destabilizing, and it would increase the likelihood of a nuclear crisis (or even a nuclear exchange) by accident or as a result of escalation.

—An American decision to stop trying to prevent Iran from acquiring a nuclear weapons capability and simply rely on policies that use containment and deterrence might cause Israeli leaders to opt for a strike against Iranian nuclear sites, in the belief that they have no alternative. Such a strike could trigger a wider conflict between Israel and Iran that could draw in the United States and other countries.

—Allowing Iran to develop a nuclear weapons capability, despite a publicly avowed consensus among the greater powers that it cannot be allowed to do so, could be the last nail in the coffin of the NPT, eliminating the global nonproliferation norm, with unforeseeable consequences in East Asia, South America, and other parts of the world.

If Iran is seen as no longer on the defensive and more able to go on the offensive—both because Washington had ceased its efforts to coerce Tehran and because Iran someday acquires a nuclear weapons capability—the Arab states will likely become more fearful of Iran. This may lead them to "bandwagon" with Iran, and almost certainly will make them less willing to reform, but at a time when the risk of greater Iranian subversion actually would make it more necessary for them to do so.

CRAFTING AN INTEGRATED IRAN POLICY

Connecting the Options

None of the policy options toward Iran have a high likelihood of succeeding, even as their proponents would define success. None is likely to protect all of America's national interests at low cost and with minimal risks. As should be apparent by this point, all of them are less than ideal solutions to the problems Iran poses. Indeed, one of the reasons that the Iran debate is so contentious and intractable is that there is no obviously right course of action. Instead, policymakers must choose the least bad from among a range of unpalatable alternatives.

What should also be clear is that few, if any, of the options presented in this book constitute an unequivocal, stand-alone policy. At the very least, each will require contingency plans and fallback positions in the event that circumstances change or the approach fails. Even a policy comprised of pure engagement would have to acknowledge that Iran might take action (like mounting a major terrorist attack or testing a nuclear weapon) that could force the United States to abandon this course. Similarly, even if the United States were to commit itself to mounting a full-scale invasion, the need to garner domestic political support (and the hope of securing some international support) would likely require making a diplomatic overture to Iran first.

Other options might be pursued simultaneously with one another—indeed, the Persuasion option includes a tactical version of the Engagement option (which might turn into a strategic version under the right circumstances, thus making Engagement a potential follow-on to Persuasion). Persuasion also allows for the possibility of employing some form of the regime change options as additional sources of pressure on Iran if sanctions alone are considered inadequate. Alternatively, an administration determined to mount a full-court press against Iran short of an invasion might employ all of the regime change options *plus* the Airstrikes option. In other words, there is potentially a great deal of interplay among the options. If Washington policymakers chose to pursue several options simultaneously, or to combine elements of different options, it would have to spend a great deal of time thinking through not only how to make each individual option work, but how to make them work in tandem so that they reinforce one another rather than running at cross-purposes.

Indeed, because the problem of Iran is such a difficult one, any realistic policy toward Iran likely would combine at least two or more options, either in sequence, as contingency plans, or as parallel tracks. A single option approach to the problem of Iran would have much less likelihood of achieving U.S. interests. Consequently, another critical element in forging an effective policy toward Iran is to understand how various policy options can or cannot be integrated.

The Obama administration has already recognized that reality. Although the president himself and many of his top aides, including Secretary of State Clinton and Dennis Ross, her Iran adviser, have all indicated that the core of their policy will be the kind of complex positive and negative incentives embodied by the Persuasion option, they have also made clear that the full policy will incorporate other options in various ways.[1] President Obama has stressed that he hopes for a fully cooperative relationship with Iran. In this he is clearly conveying that he would like to see the tactical engagement envisioned in the Persuasion strategy open up into full strategic engagement as envisioned in the Engagement option, if the Iranians indicate that they are willing and able. In some ways, the administration's offer of a hand of friendship to the Iranians suggests that Washington would be willing to start with the Engagement approach, and will only convert that into the Persuasion approach if the Iranians refuse the offer. Nevertheless, President Obama has steadfastly refused to rule out the military option, which also means that he and his advisers recognize that under certain circumstances, the United States will at least have to consider Airstrikes or even the full-scale Invasion option if the Iranians prove unwilling to compromise.[2] Thus the integrated policy of the Obama administration has a core option but also includes a half-dozen others as contingency or follow-on plans.

THE DOS AND DON'TS OF INTEGRATION

This recognition by the Obama administration is important because Persuasion is the option most easily integrated with other options. To some extent, every other option can become a fallback option for or a compliment to the incentives-based approach of Persuasion. This gives the option a great deal of flexibility and "interoperability" in the sense that it can be married up with many other approaches. It is almost certainly a key reason that the administration opted to make it the centerpiece of its initial Iran policy.

As we have noted several times, inherent in the Persuasion strategy is a form of tactical engagement with Iran meant to facilitate reaching a "deal" in which Washington would give Tehran what it wants on economic, security, and political matters in return for Tehran giving Washington what it needs regarding Iran's nuclear program, support for violent extremist groups, and efforts to destabilize the Middle East. If the Iranians accept that deal (recognizing that it may be an incremental process of piecemeal negotiations rather than a single "grand bargain"), then Persuasion intrinsically envisions a shift to strategic Engagement to fulfill the terms of that deal over the long term.

If the Iranians refuse the deal, Persuasion envisions imposing ever more painful economic sanctions on Iran with the aim of bringing Tehran to accept the deal. It is also at least plausible in theory to try to employ any of the various methods of regime change in conjunction with the sanctions. This was essentially the approach of the Bush 43 administration, which attempted to amplify the pressure on Iran from sanctions by also supporting both democracy movements and reportedly ethnic insurgencies in Iran.[3] Of course, this strategy had not worked before Bush left office, but its proponents could plausibly argue that it did not have enough time to have any impact. It is certainly imaginable that putting the Bush strategy back in place and adding one or more of the regime change options could put much greater pressure on Tehran, and that might increase the likelihood that the regime would agree to compromise.

However, many experts on Iran argue the exact opposite: that the sine qua non of striking a deal with Tehran is convincing the clerical regime that the United States is not seeking its overthrow, and only under those circumstances will Tehran feel secure enough to make compromises. They contend that if Iran feels threatened by the United States, it will be far more inclined to dig in its heels and fight back, thereby undermining the basic premise of Persuasion. There is some evidence to support this contention. For instance, in 1994–1996, when Tehran believed that Washington was ratcheting up its covert action program against the Islamic regime, the Iranians did not signal any greater willingness to compromise but instead lashed out at the United States in whatever manner they could. Tehran was probably behind the Khobar Towers attack that killed 19 American military personnel and conducted aggressive surveillance of American diplomatic and military personnel and installations all across the Middle East, instigated attacks by the Palestinian Islamic Jihad and Hizballah against Israel to subvert the peace process, and attempted to overthrow the government of Bahrain.

In theory, airstrikes also could be employed to exert pressure on Tehran if it refuses an initial deal, although in practice, they could easily prove counterproductive. Airstrikes would likely rally the Iranian people around the worst elements in the regime, at least initially. This, in turn, would make it more likely Iran would retaliate, withdraw from the NPT, and recommit to acquiring nuclear weapons, and/or end any ongoing negotiations with the United States, the United Nations, or other members of the international community.

Nevertheless, if it becomes clear that Iran is not negotiating seriously with the United States but is merely playing for time—or refuses to negotiate altogether—then all three of the military options would take on significantly greater relevance as fallback options for the Persuasion option. If negotiating a deal is simply no longer feasible, the Obama administration will be left with an unpalatable choice between taking military action itself, letting Israel do it, or moving to contain Iran and deter its use of nuclear weapons. If Washington concludes that it does not believe a nuclear Iran can effectively be deterred, or the administration simply does not want to take that risk, the United States might opt for the Airstrikes option or even the Invasion option. The Israelis will have to make a similar decision, itself contingent upon what the United States decides. And while an Israeli airstrike has many potential drawbacks for the United States, in a situation in which Iran has made it clear that it is unwilling to make any compromises, Washington might simply decide that it is not worth expending the political capital to *prevent* Israel from launching a strike if Jerusalem opts to do so.

Furthermore, all of these scenarios could also be raised simply as implicit threats, and those threats might serve as a useful form of pressure on Iran as part of the Persuasion approach in ways that their implementation might not. In other words, the United States could let it be known that if Iran is unwilling to negotiate an end to its problematic behavior, then the United States would have to look hard at all of the other options, and under those circumstances, the military options would look far more attractive than they do at present. The clear implication would be that if Tehran is unwilling to compromise, it may find itself in a war it does not want. Such threats have the merit of being accurate representations of where the U.S. policy debate will likely move if Iran refuses to compromise, and the Obama administration is already signaling as much, including by the president's refusal to take the military options off the table.

Another way that the United States might employ the threat of the military options in support of Persuasion would be to use it to try convince Iran not to break off negotiations or clandestinely cross the nuclear threshold in the midst of them. In this variant, the United States—and possibly Israel as well—might warn Tehran that if it moved to build and field a nuclear arsenal behind the cover of negotiations, the United States would immediately launch preventive airstrikes. Washington might even hint that an invasion was not unimaginable either in these circumstances. In this manner, the threat of the military options would serve as deterrents intended to keep Iran at the bargaining table and prevent the failure of Persuasion despite further Iranian progress in its nuclear program.

Likewise, all of the regime change approaches also will become more attractive if the Iranians refuse to make the compromises offered under the Persuasion approach. Certainly, regime change would be less likely to provoke a diplomatic backlash from regional and European states against the United States in the same way that a military attack on Iran would, making it potentially more palatable. The regime change options might also be employed to keep Iran off balance and on the defensive, and could conceivably produce a new government in Tehran that would at least ameliorate some of the issues between the United States and Iran. While all of the regime change options also have considerable problems to overcome, these loom largest when the diplomatic options appear viable. If at some point the diplomatic options are clearly no longer feasible, then regime change will likely seem more compelling.

The last contingency plan for Persuasion (and every other option) is inevitably the Containment option. As we noted, Containment is the policy the United States traditionally adopts toward a problematic state only when all other approaches have failed (or seem destined to fail). If Iran refuses to compromise and the administration decides not to pursue either regime change or the military option, Containment would be the logical fallback.

Other aspects of Containment might be helpful in pursuing the Persuasion option. In particular, it might also be necessary for the United States to provide the kind of formal nuclear guarantees to Israel and America's Arab allies envisioned as part of Containment to create the necessary time and diplomatic "space" for Persuasion to work. In previous administrations such guarantess were shunned for fear that it would signal a lack of U.S. resolve to curb Iran's nuclear program. However, as Iran's stockpile of enriched uranium grows, its neighbors are naturally becoming more anxious about its intentions. This anxiety is causing them to begin looking seriously at their own options: in Israel's case, a preventive strike; in the Arabs' case, the acquisition of their own nuclear weapons. In other words, the possible unintended consequence of pursuing the Persuasion option is that it could trigger a regional conflagration or a regional nuclear arms race. To forestall such untoward developments, extending deterrence to America's regional allies may actually be an essential and urgent complement to the Persuasion option, one that might well be welcomed by America's regional allies. In these circumstances, it is also conceivable (although not likely) that Saudi Arabia and other GCC states might welcome the kind of American "trip-wire" forces suggested under Containment and that would be an important component of effective deterrence. The idea would be for the United States to "buy time" for Persuasion to work by lulling the fears of our regional allies, all of whom may grow even more alarmed if they see negotiations moving slowly while Iran's nuclear program continues to move quickly.

Similarly, a regional Containment strategy could also be introduced to enhance the likelihood of success for Persuasion. This is because at the same time as Iran considers how to respond to the Obama administration's diplomatic overtures, it is continuing its aggressive efforts to subvert its Arab neighbors and support Hizballah's and Hamas's efforts to block American peacemaking efforts. This has generated a sense of common interest between Israel and its Arab neighbors to counter Iran's meddling in their neighborhoods. There are also signs that Iran's ally Syria is growing increasingly uncomfortable with its position on the wrong side of the Sunni-Shi'ah divide. And as the United States begins its withdrawal from Iraq, Syria and Iran may become rivals for influence in neighboring Baghdad. A containment strategy that sought to limit Iran's influence in the Middle East heartland by working with Israel and the Arabs to resolve the Arab-Israeli conflict in all its dimensions (i.e., seeking Palestinian, Syrian, and Lebanese peace agreements), and by working with Iraq's Arab neighbors to reduce its influence in Baghdad, could do much to concentrate the minds of Iranian leaders. If they began to feel that rather than dominate the region they were at risk of being left behind as a new more peaceful regional order began to emerge, they might be more inclined to take U.S. offers at the negotiating table more seriously.

One of the potential problems with the Persuasion option is that the various clocks are not synchronized. The Iranian clock ticks much more slowly because Tehran has every interest in playing for time while it completes all the necessary elements of its nuclear program. The Israeli and Arab clocks tick much more quickly because they cannot abide Iran achieving a nuclear threshold capability and grow ever more anxious as Iran gets closer to that point. Meanwhile, the American clock for the Persuasion option is ticking at a pace somewhere between these two poles since there is a recognition that time is needed to play out the option but that a dragged-out negotiation will become unsustainable. The challenge for American policymakers will be to synchronize these clocks by making the Iranians feels a greater sense of urgency while enabling the Israelis and Arabs to relax a little more. This is where the elements of the Containment option could become useful complements to Persuasion.

AN ALTERNATIVE EXAMPLE: REGIME CHANGE

Although it is impractical to lay out how each option can be interwoven with every other one, it may be useful for comparative purposes to sketch out how an overarching strategy different from that which the Obama administration has chosen might encompass many different options in a more integrated policy. Instead of adopting Persuasion, the Obama administration might have opted to pursue regime change (it still may if its initial efforts prove fruitless). Regime change is another strategy that could involve most of the other options in various roles.

First, the United States might opt to employ some version of Persuasion to set up regime change. Regime change would seem far more palatable to Americans, Middle Easterners, Europeans, and Asians—and probably even to the Iranian people—if they believe that Iran had been offered a very good deal and turned it down. Indeed, if this is the perception among Iranians, more of them might be willing to oppose the regime. Thus, starting with some effort at Persuasion would be a good way to begin, but if regime change were really Washington's goal, the United States would have to ensure that the Iranians turned down the offered deal, while making sure that the deal looked attractive to others. If the Iran experts are right that Tehran is unlikely to compromise no matter what it is offered as long as it feels threatened, then a clever approach to regime change might be to simultaneously offer a good deal (albeit not one so good that Tehran might overcome its paranoia) while ratcheting up a range of regime change programs that the leadership would perceive as a threat. Arguably, this is what the Bush 43 administration did—although that was certainly not the intention of most members of the administration charged with handling Iran. (Then again, it may have been the intention of others working elsewhere within the administration.)[4]

As far as the regime change options themselves, an American administration might choose to pursue all three of the specific routes—popular revolution, insurgency, and coup—on the grounds that doing so would increase the likelihood that one of them will succeed. Moreover, employing all three simultaneously might create helpful synergies among them. For instance, if the regime becomes bogged down fighting various insurgencies, Iranian military officers might become convinced that the leadership must be replaced and that there is an opportunity to do so. This is effectively what happened in Iraq in 1963 and 1968 when Baghdad was mired in an unsuccessful counterinsurgency struggle against the Kurds. In addition, applying such across-the-board pressure against Tehran would strain the regime's intelligence and security capabilities as well as its decision-making processes, and so might cause the regime to make a mistake that would allow one or another of the approaches to succeed.

A policy determined to overthrow the government of Iran might very well include plans for a full-scale invasion as a contingency for extreme circumstances. Certainly, if various forms of covert and overt support simply failed to produce the desired effect, a president determined to produce regime change in Iran might consider an invasion as the only other way to achieve that end. Moreover, the United States would have to expect Iran to fight back against American regime change operations, as it has in the past. Although the Iranians typically have been careful to avoid crossing American red lines, they certainly could miscalculate, and it is entirely possible that their retaliation for U.S. regime change activities would appear to Americans as having crossed just such a threshold. For example, if Iran retaliated with a major terrorist attack that killed large numbers of people or a terrorist attack involving WMDs—especially on U.S. soil—Washington might decide that an invasion was the only way to deal with such a dangerous Iranian regime. Indeed, for this same reason, efforts to promote regime change in Iran might be intended by the U.S. government as deliberate provocations to try to goad the Iranians into an excessive response that might then justify an American invasion.

In a similar vein, the United States might need to employ airstrikes against a variety of targets in response to Iranian retaliation for regime change programs. In this way, American airstrikes might be a branch of a regime change policy, but it could also be a contingency because it would be difficult to effect regime change in Iran in time to prevent Tehran from acquiring the capability to build one or more nuclear weapons. Consequently, Washington might want to have the option to mount airstrikes against the Iranian nuclear program simply to push that date down the road and thus buy time for regime change to have its desired effect. Finally, as we noted in Part III, all of the regime change options require the United States to consider whether to provide military support (at least in the form of airstrikes) to whichever Iranian oppositionists Washington chooses to encourage. Popular revolutions can only succeed if the government has lost the will or ability to employ its armed forces against the people; insurgencies may need direct military intervention either to stave off a catastrophic defeat, like at the Bay of Pigs, or to bring about final victory, as in Afghanistan in 2001; and coup plotters often need specific units or facilities neutralized to allow them to spring their coup.

Moreover, regime change requires the simultaneous pursuit of Containment.[5] If the United States is trying to overthrow the government of Iran, it will be critical to prevent Iran from making mischief abroad and from growing stronger economically, militarily, and politically. The United States will want to deny Tehran the wherewithal to threaten neighbors that might be providing sanctuary for insurgents or otherwise helping the oppositionists. Thus the sanctions, military deterrence, isolation, and economic warfare envisioned as key components of the Containment option would be invaluable—indeed, indispensible—aids to a regime change policy.

EXPECTING THE UNEXPECTED

As the preceding sections have illustrated, a critical reason that any American strategy toward Iran must integrate a range of different options is the potential for events to occur that would make any of the options infeasible, and so force a change in approach. It is essential to keep in mind this law of unintended consequences when devising a new Iran policy because the interrelated nature of dynamics in the wider Middle East tends to generate sudden and unpredictable developments. Unlikely occurrences happen with surprising frequency, and the complexity of any Iran policy is such that it will depend on a range of developments, all of which will be susceptible to the vicissitudes of fortune.

Any strategy toward Iran is likely to depend on a wide range of developments breaking in particular directions for it to work. Moreover, any strategy toward Iran is likely to require time to have its desired effect. As noted, in theory, an invasion might be implemented within a matter of months, but the reality is that the need to build up domestic political support for such an endeavor—and hopefully blunt antipathy abroad—likely means that even an invasion would require months or even years of political and diplomatic legwork before the ships could sail. Likewise, it would take time for the United States and its allies to formulate a new offer to Iran, propose it, and have Iran accept it. Consequently, recognizing the importance of the element of time also means recognizing the potential for other developments to intervene, and the more time that passes, the more things will happen that will have an impact on U.S. policy toward Iran.

There is a very long list of things that might transpire that would have at least a moderate impact on a new Iran policy. Almost any major development in Iran—for example, the election of a new president, the death of Khamene'i, or economic collapse—would likely have major repercussions for U.S. policy. Not every development in the United States would have the same potential, but there are certainly many that would. Obviously, financial collapse would head that list, but there are others imaginable, such as a change in the makeup of Congress following the 2010 elections. In addition, global events that affected the political, security, or economic fortunes of Saudi Arabia, Israel, Pakistan, or Turkey might also fall into this category. State collapse in Lebanon, Iraq, Afghanistan, or the Palestinian territories would likely have an important impact on the U.S.-Iranian relationship, especially if Tehran were seen as complicit in the fall, or merely moved quickly with its allies and proxies to try to take advantage of the situation. Similarly, because Europe, Russia, Japan, China, India, and other countries beyond the Middle East also have an important role in some of the options, their decisions could make some options more attractive and others less so. The Persuasion option that the Obama administration has chosen relies heavily on the cooperation of all of those countries; thus events that make them more or less willing to participate will affect the ability of the administration to succeed—and this, in turn, could influence its decision to stick with that option or switch to something else.

To illustrate how different events could greatly affect the viability and attractiveness of the various options, imagine that King Abdullah of Saudi Arabia dies within the next one to two years and is succeeded by Prince Nayif ibn Abd al-Aziz, recently named the second deputy prime minister.[6] Although Abdullah is deeply concerned about Iran and its pursuit of a nuclear capability, he has steadfastly pursued a policy of détente with Tehran for more than a decade. Nayif, on the other hand, is widely believed to favor a much tougher policy toward Iran, and he might come to Washington and tell the president that Iranian acquisition of nuclear weapons is simply intolerable for Saudi Arabia. Assume for a minute that Nayif also pledges to support the United States in taking a more aggressive approach than the new Persuasion policy, and asserts that if the United States is unable to do so, then the Saudis will acquire nuclear weapons of their own. This would constitute a fairly dramatic divergence from Abdullah's policy and would significantly change many of the pros, cons, and requirements of the different options. With Saudi Arabia (and the rest of the GCC) behind the United States, Washington might consider airstrikes, regime change, and even an invasion as being both more feasible and less costly than they appear today. Similarly, if the United States believes that it is highly likely that Saudi Arabia will acquire nuclear weapons if Iran crosses the nuclear threshold, both Persuasion and Engagement may look less appealing.

As another important example, if Iran were to detonate a nuclear weapon, this would dramatically alter the calculus of any U.S. administration considering various options toward Iran. Because of the risk of nuclear retaliation, the desirability of an invasion—and even of airstrikes—would become vanishingly small. The United States has never attacked another nuclear-armed state and has done everything it could to avoid doing so. Containment would become more necessary, while Engagement might become far more palatable and popular as an alternative to conflict. The need to try to prevent Iran from acquiring a nuclear capability—a critical criticism of both options—would be gone, and the question would simply be how best to deal with a nuclear Iran. Regime change and Persuasion both would be much trickier, but not necessarily impossible. The United States has maintained covert action programs against other nuclear-armed states. History has demonstrated that the possession of nuclear weapons does not immunize a country from internal problems, including internal revolution, with the Soviet Union and South Africa both being cases in point. The difficulty is likely to lie in the greater reticence of Iran's neighbors to anger a nuclear-armed Iran; but this, too, is not insurmountable, just difficult. As far as Persuasion is concerned, there is evidence of states with actual nuclear arsenals (not just the theoretical capacity to build them) giving up their weapons under the right conditions. The circumstances in which Belarus, Ukraine, Kazakhstan, and South Africa did so are all very different from those that would likely obtain if Iran were to acquire a nuclear arsenal, but they still suggest that it is not impossible that the Iranians might some day relinquish theirs. Moreover, North Korea's situation is much more analogous to that of Iran, and while the current deal has considerable potential pitfalls, and it is not at all clear that the North Koreans will end up disarmed, it also suggests that it might be possible to convince Iran to give up its nuclear program even after it has crossed the nuclear weapon threshold (although it would obviously be much harder than convincing them not to do so in the first place).

One last example of the kind of major development that could fundamentally reorder U.S. thinking about the various Iran options would be the emergence of a charismatic opposition leader in Iran. The clerical regime has assiduously worked to prevent this, using utterly ruthless methods, but the Islamic Republic might slip up and one might rise to prominence and popularity anyway. An Iranian Mandela, Havel, Bolivar, or Walesa—someone who was able to unify the Iranian opposition and generate genuine mass appeal—could also force a transformation in American thinking. First, his or her presence would alter the probability of a popular revolution in Iran, making that regime change option far more feasible than it is at present. (And we do not rule out the possibility that American support for a popular revolution might have enabled the emergence of that leader.) Second, it would be very unpalatable for the United States to betray someone who has galvanized the Iranian people and was organizing a genuine democratic opposition. Not only might this drive the United States to embrace support for a popular revolution as the primary element in Washington's Iran policy, it might similarly convince the U.S. administration to support insurgencies or airstrikes against Iran as a way of putting pressure on the regime and preventing/dissuading it from jailing or killing the charismatic leader. If the regime did so anyway, that might serve as exactly the kind of outrage that would garner both domestic American political support and international diplomatic support for even more aggressive policies toward Tehran, possibly even including an invasion. Alternatively, if this leader were to ask the United States not to stir up ethnic unrest or launch military strikes against the regime because doing so would undermine his efforts, this would just as decisively eliminate those options from consideration.

Of course, there are many other possible developments that could have a similar impact on American thinking. An Israeli airstrike against Iranian nuclear facilities without U.S. approval, a major change in the price of oil, a domestic revolt by one or more of Iran's minorities, the death of Khamene'i, even the resurgence of the Taliban in Afghanistan, could all significantly change the pros and cons, the requirements, and the time frames of various options, making some more attractive and others less.

PRIORITIES AND TRADE-OFFS

A last but crucial consideration that will bear on the integration and salience of different options will be the prominence of Iran policy relative to all of the other pressing matters facing the government of the United States. Most obviously, the Obama administration will have to decide what priority to place on Iran in the midst of the worst economic crisis that the United States has faced in 80 years. Many of the Iran options require commitments that will compete with the needs of economic recovery, at least to some extent, and the administration will have to decide how to prioritize among them. An invasion would demand a major commitment of American military forces and sustaining that military commitment, along with major economic and political assistance, for years. Washington might be loath to commit these kinds of resources to its Iran policy rather than reserving them for domestic economic recovery. Many of the options are also very involved and demanding and, if they are to have a reasonable chance of success, would require considerable time and attention from the president himself—typically the most precious commodity that any administration must allocate. At a moment when the president and his most important advisers may need to spend a considerable amount of time and political capital on the economy or other domestic and foreign priorities, it may be difficult to make these available for Iran policy.

Virtually all of the options require some degree of support from countries in the Middle East at a time when the United States also wants their help to push for a comprehensive Arab-Israeli peace agreement, keep Iraq on the right track, pressure Sudan to end its genocide, bolster Lebanese democracy, draw Syria into a constructive regional role, and support a host of other undertakings. At the same time, the United States also wants these countries to continue to reform their dysfunctional economic, political, and social systems to start addressing the sources of the Middle East's endemic instability. And Washington will probably need the help of the region's oil producers to address the global economic mess. In the past, the regimes of the region have successfully forced the United States to choose among such different interests, and if Washington opts for an Iran policy that they dislike, the United States will be forced to do so again. In that case, Washington would have to decide whether their help for an Iran policy that they dislike is more important than America's other regional ambitions.

Persuasion, the policy that the Obama administration has adopted as the core of its new Iran strategy, will also require the administration to secure the consent of Russia, China, Germany, Japan, and other countries to impose harsh sanctions on Iran—something that few of them favor—if Iran refuses the deal it is offered. All can probably be convinced to do so, but that would require the United States to compromise with them on other issues that will be unpalatable—like energy policy for China and missile defense or U.S. policies toward former Soviet republics for Russia. Again, the Obama administration is going to have to decide which deals it is willing to make to secure international cooperation in implementing harsh sanctions against Iran. And if these countries are unwilling to participate, then it may be necessary to go looking for a different strategy altogether.

WHICH PATH TO PERSIA?

As we warned at the beginning of this study, crafting a new policy toward Iran is a complicated and uncertain challenge. Iran is an extremely complex society, with an opaque and Byzantine political system, and its interactions with the outside world are similarly convoluted. Policymakers must take each of these problems into account and must also allow for American political preferences as well as the potential reactions of several dozen other countries in the Middle East and beyond. It is no wonder that the United States has not yet figured out the solution to the puzzle that is Iran. It is also no wonder that so many American leaders have thrown up their hands in despair and tried to have as little to do with Iran as possible.

But as we also observed at the outset, ignoring Iran is no longer a realistic alternative—not that it ever was. Tehran is acting on a broad range of issues of great concern to the United States. It will not stop doing so just because Americans are baffled by what to do. Nor will other countries refrain from acting even if the United States does. In this study, we have tried to lay out the many different courses of action available to the United States. It is not the purpose of this monograph to argue for one approach over another, in part because no course is unambiguously better than all of the rest. Instead, we have laid out the paths for the policymakers, and it will be up to them to choose which to take. The Obama administration has made its choice, at least for now. Whether this path will lead the United States to a better place is yet to be determined. We can all hope that it will, and there is some reason to believe that it can. But if it does not, the administration will soon find itself right back at the same intersection, with the same choices but less time, fewer resources, and perhaps a weaker will to choose the next path and see if it will lead to the place we seek: a place where Iran is no longer the bane of the United States in the Middle East, and perhaps is even America's friend once again. Given the difficulty of following any of these paths, Americans should be ready to settle for the former, even as they hope for the latter.

Notes

Introduction

1. National Intelligence Council, "National Intelligence Estimate. Iran: Nuclear Intentions and Capabilities," November 2007, http://www.dni.gov/press_releases/20071203_release.pdf, downloaded on February 9, 2009.

2. Said Arjomand, *The Turban for the Crown: The Islamic Revolution in Iran* (Oxford University Press, 1988); William O. Beeman, "Images of the Great Satan: Representations of the United States in the Iranian Revolution," in *Religion and Politics in Iran: Shi'ism from Quietism to Revolution*, ed. Nikki R. Keddie (Yale University Press, 1983), pp. 191–217; Richard Cottam, "Inside Revolutionary Iran," in *Iran's Revolution: The Search for Consensus*, ed. R.K. Ramazani (Indiana University Press, 1990), pp. 3–26; Massoumeh Ebtekar, as told to Fred A. Reed, *Takeover in Tehran: The Inside Story of the 1979 U.S. Embassy Capture* (Vancouver, Canada: Talon Books, 2000), esp. p. 77; Baqer Moin, *Khomeini: Life of the Ayatollah* (London: I.B. Tauris, 1999), esp. p. 220; Robert Snyder, "Explaining the Iranian Revolution's Hostility toward the United States," *Journal of South Asian and Middle Eastern Studies* 17, no. 3 (Spring 1994).

3. On Iranian public opinion, see Terror Free Tomorrow, "Polling Iranian Public Opinion: An Unprecedented Nationwide Survey of Iran," July 2007, http://www.terrorfreetomorrow.org/upimagestft/TFT%20Iran%20Survey%20Report.pdf, downloaded on January 7, 2007; Karim Sadjadpour, "How Relevant Is the Iranian Street?" *Washington Quarterly* 30, no. 1 (Winter 2006–2007): 151–162.

4. Anoushiravan Ehteshami and Mahjoob Zweiri, *Iran and the Rise of its Neoconservatives: The Politics of Tehran's Silent Revolution* (London: I.B. Tau-

ris, 2007); Barbara Slavin, *Bitter Friends, Bosom Enemies: Iran, the U.S., and the Twisted Path to Confrontation* (New York: St. Martin's, 2007).

5. On Iranian politics and the debates over Iranian policy toward the United States, see for instance Ali M. Ansari, *Modern Iran Since 1921: The Pahlavis and After* (London: Longman, 2003); Daniel Brumberg, *Reinventing Khomeini: The Struggle for Reform in Iran* (University of Chicago Press, 2001); Daniel Byman et al., *Iran's Security Policy in the Post-Revolutionary Era* (Santa Monica, CA: RAND, 2001); Elton L. Daniel, *The History of Iran* (Westport, CT: Greenwood Press, 2001); Anoushiravan Ehteshami, *After Khomeini: The Iranian Second Republic* (London: Routledge, 1995); Mark J. Gasiorowski, "The Power Struggle in Iran," *Middle East Policy* 7, no. 4 (October 2000): 22–40; Jerrold D. Green, *Parastatal Economic Organizations and Stability in Iran: The Role of Bonyads* (Santa Monica, CA: RAND, 1997); Nikki R. Keddie, *Modern Iran: Roots and Results of Revolution*, revised and updated edition (Yale University Press, 2003); Nikki R. Keddie and Rudi Matthee, eds., *Iran and the Surrounding World: Interactions in Culture and Cultural Politics* (University of Washington Press, 2002); David Menashri, *Revolution at a Crossroads: Iran's Domestic Politics and Regional Ambitions* (Washington: Washington Institute for Near East Policy, 1997); Mehdi Moslem, *Factional Politics in Post-Khomeini Iran* (Syracuse University Press, 2002); Snyder, "Explaining the Iranian Revolution's Hostility toward the United States"; Ray Takeyh, *Hidden Iran: Paradox and Power in the Islamic Republic* (New York: Times Books, 2006).

6. On Khamene'i's thinking regarding the United States, the best work available is Karim Sadjadpour, "Reading Khamenei: The World View of Iran's Most Powerful Leader," Report, Carnegie Endowment for International Peace, March 2008.

7. In addition to the sources in note 3, above, see also Anthony Cordesman, *Iran and Iraq: The Threat from the Northern Gulf* (Boulder, CO: Westview, 1994); Michael Eisenstadt, *Iranian Military Power: Capabilities and Intentions* (Washington: Washington Institute for Near East Policy, 1997); Michael A. Palmer, *Guardians of the Gulf: A History of America's Expanding Role in the Persian Gulf, 1833–1992* (New York: Free Press, 1992).

8. See, for instance, Martin Indyk, *Innocent Abroad: An Intimate Account of American Peace Diplomacy in the Middle East* (New York: Simon and Schuster, 2009); Kenneth M. Pollack, *The Persian Puzzle: The Conflict between Iran and America* (New York: Random House, 2004), esp. pp. 244–342. Perhaps the most eloquent testimony to the relative lack of interest in devising a proactive strategy toward Iran during the administrations of Bush 41, Clinton, and early Bush 43 can be found in the virtual silence on the topic of Iran in the memoirs of key officials in those various administrations. See, for example, Madeleine Albright, *Madam Secretary* (New York: Miramax Books, 2003); James A. Baker III, *The Politics of Diplomacy* (New York: C.R. Putnam's Sons, 1995); George Bush and Brent Scowcroft, *A World Transformed* (New York: Alfred A. Knopf, 1998); Warren Christopher, *In the Stream of History: Shaping Foreign Policy for a New Era* (Stanford University Press, 1998); Warren Christopher, *Chances of a Lifetime* (New York: Scribner, 2001); Bill Clinton, *My Life* (New York: Alfred A. Knopf, 2004). Also see Condoleezza Rice, "Campaign 2000: Promoting the National Interest," *Foreign Affairs* 79, no. 1 (January–February 2000). This essay by Rice laid out what candidate George W. Bush's foreign policy philosophy would be if elected president. Iran received three short paragraphs, all of which were descriptive, not prescriptive, in nature, and the subject was famously dis-

missed with the remark that "All in all, changes in U.S. policy toward Iran would require changes in Iranian behavior."

9. As one indication of this trend, after James Bill published *The Eagle and the Lion: The Tragedy of American-Iranian Relations* (Yale University Press) in 1988, another major work on U.S.-Iranian relations was not published until 2004. Again, there were numerous journal articles and opinion pieces written on the subject during the interim, but these largely concerned matters of immediate U.S.-Iranian relations rather than efforts to reexamine the relationship as a whole and prescribe a new overarching direction. In 2004 a major task force report was published by the Council on Foreign Relations, again signaling the willingness of the American policy community to try to begin thinking about a new Iran strategy. See Zbigniew Brzezinski and Robert M. Gates, "Iran: Time for a New Approach," Report, Council on Foreign Relations, July 2004.

10. See, for instance, Geneive Abdo and Jonathan Lyons, *Answering Only to God: Faith and Freedom in Twenty-First Century Iran* (New York: Henry Holt, 2003); Jahangir Amuzegar, "Iran's Future: Civil Society or Civil Unrest," *Middle East Policy* 7, no. 1 (October 1999): 86–101; Byman et al., *Iran's Security Policy*; Afshin Molavi, *Persian Pilgrimages: Journeys across Iran* (New York: W.W. Norton, 2002); Elaine Sciolino, *Persian Mirrors: The Elusive Face of Iran* (New York: Free Press, 2000); Suzanne Maloney, "Elections in Iran: A New Majlis and a Mandate for Reform," *Middle East Policy* 7, no. 3 (June 2000): 59–66; Robin Wright, *The Last Great Revolution: Turmoil and Transformation in Iran* (New York: Alfred A. Knopf, 2000).

11. Certainly, there are Americans who believe that some Iranian leaders *are* irrational—in particular, that they subscribe to a millenarian vision of the world in which they must take apocalyptic actions to fulfill God's plan. However, most experts on Iran are doubtful of this prospect or, more important, that such zealotry would guide Iranian actions.

12. National Intelligence Council, "Iran: Nuclear Intentions and Capabilities."

13. Steven R. Hurst, "Mullen: Iran Has Fissile Materials for a Bomb," Associated Press, March 2, 2009.

CHAPTER ONE

1. Interview with President-elect Barack Obama, Meet the Press, NBC, December 7, 2008, available at http://www.msnbc.msn.com/id/28097635, downloaded on January 19, 2009.

2. White House, "Videotaped Remarks by the President in Celebration of Nowruz," March 19, 2009, available at http://www.whitehouse.gov/the_press_office-/VIDEOTAPED-REMARKS-BY-THE-PRESIDENT-IN-CELEBRATION-OF-NOWRUZ/, downloaded on April 6, 2009.

3. One area in which the Bush 43 administration excelled was in finding creative new methods of imposing unilateral sanctions on Iran by targeting its links to international financial networks. There are still ties in this area that the United States could cut and that would inflict real pain on Iran—although they also could spark conflict with other nations. Consequently, though such unilateral actions are possible and would have a real

impact, it is still the case that having European, East Asian, and South Asian countries adopt the kind of sanctions that the U.S. invoked in the 1990s would have a far greater impact on the Iranian economy.

4. See, for example, Robin Wright, "Stuart Levy's War: The Sanctions That Could Coax Iran," *New York Times Sunday Magazine*, October 31, 2008; Laura Secor, "Letter from Tehran: The Rationalist," *New Yorker*, February 9, 2009, esp. pp. 36–38.

5. HEU does have some other esoteric uses, but it is not necessary for Iran's declared purposes. And given the danger of HEU as an explosive, neither the Iranians nor any of their allies could credibly claim that they had a peaceful need for HEU that justified its production.

6. The authors thank George Perkovich both for the general idea and the specific examples.

7 Obama, Meet the Press, December 7, 2008.

8. There is some evidence to suggest that the Obama administration is doing exactly that. See White House, "Videotaped Remarks by the President."

9. Steven Pifer, "Reversing the Decline: An Agenda for U.S.-Russian Relations in 2009," Policy Paper no. 10, Brookings Institution, January 2009.

CHAPTER TWO

1. As we noted in the Introduction, some have referred to the Obama administration's Iran policy as one of "engagement," but this is a misnomer. The Obama administration's policy differs in a number of important ways from a policy of Engagement as it has been described and promoted for nearly a decade. Most important, the administration is already employing a variety of threats against Iran to try to convince Tehran to give up its problematic behavior, and its offer to negotiate directly with the regime is thus limited in time. Both of these elements run directly contrary to the core elements of a policy of pure "Engagement" with Iran. Instead, the Obama administration is pursuing what we have called in this volume a policy of "Persuasion," one that is also often referred to as a policy of "carrots and sticks" (including by the president himself).

2. For the text of the proposal, see France Diplomatie, "Elements of a Revised Proposal to Iran Made by the E3+3," http://www.diplomatie.gouv.fr/en/country-files_156/iran_301/the-iranian-nuclear-question_2724/elements-of-revised-proposal-to-iran_53 14.html, downloaded March 23, 2009.

3. David Menashri, *Post-Revolutionary Politics in Iran* (London: Frank Cass Publishers, 2001), p. 192.

4. "'Islamic New Thinker' Sees Formula for Iran-U.S. Ties," Reuters, May 29, 2001.

5. Karim Sadjadpour, "Reading Khamenei: The World View of Iran's Most Powerful Leader," Report, Carnegie Endowment for International Peace, March 2008, 16. Available at http://www.carnegieendowment.org/files/sadjadpour_iran_final2.pdf.

6. James Dobbins, "How to Talk to Iran," *Washington Post*, July 22, 2007, p. B07.

7. See in particular two pieces of testimony before the House Committee on Oversight and Government Reform, Subcommittee on National Security and Foreign Affairs, November 7, 2007: James Dobbins, "Negotiating with Iran," available at

http://stinet.dtic.mil/cgi-bin/GetTRDoc?AD=ADA474062&Location=U2&doc= GetTR-Doc.pdf; Hillary Mann, "U.S. Diplomacy with Iran: The Limits of Tactical Engagement," available at http://nationalsecurity.oversight.house.gov/documents/20071107175322.pdf.

NOTE TO PART II

1. David E. Sanger, "U.S. Rejected Aid for Israeli Raid on Iranian Nuclear Site," *New York Times*, January 10, 2009.

CHAPTER THREE

1. For experts making this argument, see, for instance, Yair Ettinger, "Former Mossad Chief Downplays Iranian Threat," *Haaretz*, October 18, 2007, available at http://www.haaretz.com/hasen/spages/914171.html; Tim McGirk and Aaron Klein, "Israel's Debate Over an Iran Strike," *Time*, July 24, 2008; Kenneth M. Pollack, *The Persian Puzzle: The Conflict between Iran and America* (New York: Random House, 2004), pp. 382–386; Barry R. Posen, "We Can Live with a Nuclear Iran," *New York Times*, February 27, 2006.

2. During the Tanker War of 1987–1988 (a part of the Iran-Iraq War), U.S. naval forces were deployed to the Persian Gulf to escort Kuwaiti oil tankers that had been attacked by Iranian naval and air forces. Iran responded by mining the Persian Gulf and conducting a number of attacks and aggressive actions against American naval forces, which at times did trigger American military responses.

3. Admiral Mike Mullen, chairman of the Joint Chiefs of Staff, has suggested that they have even moved forward to the point where they have enough low-enriched uranium to make the highly enriched uranium for a bomb. Steven R. Hurst, "Mullen: Iran Has Fissile Materials for a Bomb," Associated Press, March 2, 2009.

4. Bruce Hoffman, "Insurgency and Counterinsurgency in Iraq," RAND Corp., June 2004; Kalev I. Sepp, "Best Practices in Counterinsurgency," *Military Review* 85, no. 3 (May–June 2005): 9; James T. Quinlivan, "The Burden of Victory: The Painful Arithmetic of Stability Operations," *RAND Review*, Summer 2003, available at http://www.rand.org/publications/randreview/issues/summer2003/burden.html. Also, James T. Quinlivan, "Force Requirements in Stability Operations," *Parameters* (Winter 1995): 56–69. Quinlivan has demonstrated that stabilizing a country requires roughly 20 security personnel (troops and police) per 1,000 inhabitants, just as counterinsurgency operations do. In his words, the objective "is not to destroy an enemy but to provide security for residents so that they have enough confidence to manage their daily affairs and to support a government authority of their own." Even in Iraq, this "canonical" figure has proven valid. Iraq's population outside of the Kurdish zone—which was adequately secured by the Kurdish *peshmerga* (fighters) and thus never experienced the same levels of violence as the rest of the country—was roughly 23 million people. This would suggest the need for 460,000 committed security personnel. Although U.S. troops working with small numbers of competent and reliable Iraqi security forces were able to secure large swathes of the pop-

ulation within six to twelve months of the start of the Surge, the change in U.S. strategy and tactics, the end of the Battle of Baghdad, and the onset of the Anbar awakening (all of which occurred in late 2006 and early 2007), they were not able to secure the entire country, and most of southern Iraq—with nearly 40 percent of Iraq's population—lay beyond their control. Only when the total of U.S. and competent Iraqi troops exceeded 450,000–500,000 in early 2008 were these forces able to expand their control to the south without jeopardizing the gains made in the center and west.

CHAPTER FOUR

1. We recognize that a sufficient legal basis for such an attack does not yet exist because the resolutions enacted so far specifically rule out the use of force by other member states to bring Iran into compliance with the Security Council's demands. Consequently, if the U.S. government were to decide to pursue this course of action, it would have to establish a stronger legal basis for its actions *to meet U.S. legal requirements* before it could do so.

2. On the difficulties of coercive air campaigns, see Robert Pape, *Bombing to Win: Air Power and Coercion in War* (Cornell University Press, 1996).

CHAPTER FIVE

1. Lally Weymouth, "A Conversation with Ehud Olmert," *Washington Post*, May 11, 2008, p. B3.

2. Prime Minister Benjamin Netanyahu's Speech at the Knesset Swearing In Ceremony, March 31, 2009, available at http://www.pmo.gov.il/PMOEng/Communication/PMSpeaks/speechnetankness310309.htm.

3. Ephraim Sneh, *Navigating Perilous Waters: An Israeli Strategy for Peace and Security* (London: Curzon, 2005), p. 55.

4. Quoted in David Remnick, "Blood and Sand," *New Yorker*, May 5, 2008, p. 76.

5. Quoted in "Ex-Mossad Chief: Ahmadinejad Is Israel's Greatest Gift," *Haaretz*, August 20, 2008.

6. Shahar Ilan, "Defense Min. to Knesset Panel: Talks Won't Make Iran Nukes Go Away," *Haaretz*, November 6, 2007.

7. That the Iranian dissidents got the information from Israeli intelligence, who fed it to them via a cutout, is according to former IDF chief of staff Moshe Ya'alon. See Adrian Levy and Catherine Scott-Clark, *Deception* (New York: Atlantic, 2007), p. 525.

8. We note that the George W. Bush administration reportedly dissuaded Israel from mounting such a strike in 2008, suggesting that it had concluded that such an operation would be unhelpful to American interests and policies in the region.

9. Israel has three submarines (and is acquiring two more) that could also launch a small number of cruise missiles (American Harpoon anti-ship cruise missiles) against Iranian targets. Once again, the numbers that Israel could launch would be dwarfed by the numbers of (larger and longer range) cruise missiles that the United States could be expected to employ in even a limited air campaign against the Iranian nuclear program.

10. The Jaffee Center for Strategic Studies of Tel Aviv University has claimed this range in its annual volume, *The Middle East Military Balance,* 2003–2004.

11. Some Israeli intelligence officials suspect it would only delay Iran's nuclear program by a year. See "Ahmadinejad Is Israel's Greatest Gift."

12. Scott B. Lasensky, "Friendly Restraint: U.S.-Israel Relations during the Gulf War Crisis of 1990–1991," *Middle East Review of International Affairs,* June 1, 1999. Available at http://www.cfr.org/publication/4870/friendly_restraint.html.

13. See "Israel: Nuclear Monopoly in Danger," in *Nuclear Programmes in the Middle East: In the Shadow of Iran* (London: International Institute for Strategic Studies, 2008).

14. Iran could always retaliate with a terrorist attack, but this would likely take weeks or months to implement.

CHAPTER SIX

1. J. Scott Carpenter, "How We Can Bring Him Down," *New York Daily News,* September 24, 2007.

2. Velayat-e faqih means "rule of the jurisprudent" and is the shorthand term used to describe the philosophical underpinnings of the Iranian regime. Briefly, according to Khomeini's theories about politics, the government should be presided over by the person most learned in Islam and Islamic legal theory, the supreme jurisprudent. This is how Khomeini justified the creation of a theocratic regime in Iran, and his own predominance within it.

3. As quoted in Jeffrey Donovan, "Iran: Pressure Builds on Washington to Promote 'Regime Change,'" Radio Free Europe, June 17, 2003.

4. Eli Lake, "This Pretty Much Kills the Iran Democracy Program," *New York Sun,* November 8, 2007. Lake reports that $49 million of the $75 million authorized in 2006 went to Voice of America Persian and Radio Farda. Lake's article also discusses the allegation that U.S. funding of democracy programs is detrimental for reformers.

5. The act itself authorizes the spending of $75 million, although only $66.1 million was ever appropriated. Some additional monies were added in subsequent years. Only a portion has been spent, in part because the U.S. government did not find suitable recipients.

6. Barbara Slavin, *Bitter Friends, Bosom Enemies: Iran, the U.S., and the Twisted Path to Confrontation* (New York: St. Martin's Press, 2007), p. 158.

7. "Reza Pahlavi Offers Senators Three-Pronged Approach on Iran," PR Newswire, September 14, 2006.

8. Slavin, *Bitter Friends,* p. 155.

9. Theda Skocpol, *States and Social Revolutions: A Comparative Analysis of France, Russia and China* (New York: Cambridge University Press, 1979); Theda Skocpol, *Social Revolutions in the Modern World* (Cambridge University Press, 1994).

10. Ray Takeyh, *Guardians of the Revolution* (Oxford University Press, forthcoming), p. 90.

11. Suzanne Maloney, "Fear and Loathing in Tehran," *National Interest* (September/October 2007).

12. Richard Haass, "Regime Change and Its Limits," *Foreign Affairs* 84, no. 4 (July/August 2005): 66–78.

13. As quoted in Tom Barry, "Iran Freedom and Regime Change Politics," May 19, 2006. Available at http://rightweb.irc-online.org/rw/3277.html. The quote is taken from the *New York Times*.

14. Negar Azimi, "Hard Realities of Soft Power," *New York Times*, June 24, 2007.

15. Robin Wright, "On Guard over U.S. Funds, Pro-Democracy Program Leads Tehran to Scrutinize Activists," *Washington Post*, April 28, 2007.

16. Azimi, "Hard Realities."

17. Wright, "On Guard over U.S. Funds."

CHAPTER SEVEN

1. Amy Belasco, "The Cost of Iraq, Afghanistan, and Other Global War on Terror Operations since 9/11," RL33110, Congressional Research Service, October 15, 2008, pp. 2, 6 and 7; Gilles Kepel, *Jihad* (Cambridge, MA: Belknap, 2002), p. 143.

2. Raymond Tanter, "Iran Building Nuclear-Capable Missiles in Secret Tunnels: Options for the International Community," Iran Policy Committee, November 21, 2005. Available at http://www.iranwatch.org/privateviews/IPC/perspex-ipc-tanter-nuclearcapablemissiles-112105.htm.

3. The MEK claims the individuals responsible were executed by the Shah's regime and thus are no longer part of the movement. See Barbara Slavin, *Bitter Friends, Bosom Enemies: Iran, the U.S., and the Twisted Path to Confrontation* (New York: St. Martin's Press, 2007), p. 168.

4. Elaine Sciolino, "Iranian Opposition Movement's Many Faces," *New York Times*, June 30, 2003.

5. Ibid.

6. Daniel L. Byman and Kenneth M. Pollack, *Things Fall Apart: Containing the Spillover from an Iraqi Civil War* (Washington: Brookings Institution Press, 2007), esp. pp. 35–37.

7. Ibid., pp. 20–45.

CHAPTER EIGHT

1. It is not impossible to do so, just very hard. The foreign power can use a known propensity to support any coup plot against the regime as an indiscriminate threat, which the regime might want to see ended by making concessions to the foreign power. Theoretically, all this is possible, but since it is much easier to snuff out coup plots than to instigate them, in practice, this would be difficult to accomplish.

2. See, among others, Kermit Roosevelt, *Countercoup: The Struggle for the Control of Iran* (New York: McGraw-Hill, 1979); Stephen Kinzer, *All the Shah's Men. An American Coup and the Roots of Middle East Terror* (Hoboken, NJ: John Wiley and Sons, 2003).

3. The term "coup proofing" was invented by James Quinlivan. See James Quinlivan, "Coup Proofing: Its Practice and Consequences in the Middle East," *International Security* 24, no. 2 (Fall 1999): 131–165.

Note to Part IV

1. See, for example, Laura Secor, "Letter from Tehran: The Rationalist," *New Yorker*, February 9, 2009, esp. pp. 36–38.

Chapter Nine

1. As the conclusion discusses, an air campaign against Iran's nuclear sites would likely have to be coupled with a containment strategy—before, during, and especially after the strikes. Containment would be necessary to hinder Iran from reconstituting its nuclear program, prevent it from retaliating against the United States and its allies, and to deal with Iran's support for violent extremist groups and other anti–status quo activities. Moreover, the United States would have to do so in a situation where many of the other options (particularly the diplomatic ones) will likely be impossible because of the political fallout from the strikes.

2. Joshua Teitelbaum, "What Iranian Leaders Really Say about Doing Away with Israel: A Refutation of the Campaign to Excuse Ahmadinejad's Incitement to Genocide," Jerusalem Center for Public Affairs, 2008, available at http://www.jcpa.org/text/ ahmadinejad2-words.pdf, downloaded on February 9, 2009.

3. Daniel Byman, *Deadly Connections: States that Sponsor Terrorism* (Cambridge University Press, 2005), pp. 79–80.

4. For more on all of these points and a more detailed explication on the notion that the Iranian regime is probably deterrable, see Kenneth M. Pollack, *The Persian Puzzle: The Conflict between Iran and America* (New York: Random House, 2004), esp. pp. 275–425.

5. *Jerusalem Report*, March 11, 2002.

6. An explosively formed projectile is a particularly deadly type of improvised explosive design that can penetrate armored vehicles. Many such weapons were provided to various Iraqi militias and insurgents beginning in about 2005, and to the Taliban and other Pashtun groups in Afghanistan beginning in 2008. The United States military has gathered extensive evidence demonstrating that these devices were manufactured in Iran and provided by the Iranian Revolutionary Guard Corps to the Iraqis and Afghans.

7. Turkey presumably would be reassured by its NATO membership and so would not need a similar declaration.

Conclusion

1. In her April 22, 2009, appearance before the House Committee on Foreign Affairs, Secretary Clinton said, "We actually believe that by following the diplomatic path we are on, we gain credibility and influence with a number of nations who would have to participate in order to make the sanctions regime as tight and crippling as we would want it to be. So I think the short answer is, it is our expectation that we will be able to put together such a comprehensive sanctions regime in the event we need it." Hearing of the

House Committee on Foreign Affairs, *New Beginnings: Foreign Policy Priorities In The Obama Administration*, 111th Cong., 1st Sess., April 22, 2009.

2. Following his April 21, 2009, meeting with King Abdullah II of Jordan, President Obama spoke about his administration's policy toward Iran, saying that "tough, direct diplomacy has to be pursued without taking a whole host of other options off the table." The White House, "Remarks by President Obama and King Abdullah of Jordan in Joint Press Availability," April 21, 2009, available at http://www.whitehouse.gov/ the_press_office/Remarks-by-President-Obama-and-King-Abdullah-of-Jordan-in-joint-press-availability/.

3. Seymour M. Hersh, "Preparing the Battlefield," *New Yorker*, July 7, 2008; Joby Warrick, "U.S. Is Said to Expand Covert Operations in Iran: Plan Allows up to $400 Million for Activities Aimed at Destabilizing Government," *Washington Post*, June 30, 2008; Robin Wright, "Stuart Levey's War," *New York Times Sunday Magazine*, October 31, 2008.

4. This kind of "poison pill" stratagem is exactly what some Iranians fear the Obama administration is doing, and what other Iranians claim as a way of justifying rejection of Washington's overtures. These Iranians fear that the United States is not genuine in its pursuit of compromise and cooperation with Tehran, and is simply setting up Iran for much tighter sanctions and/or regime change. Consequently, another hurdle the Obama administration will have to clear to make its preferred policy of Persuasion work will be convincing the Iranians that Washington is sincere and not just looking for an excuse to clobber Tehran, either with much harsher sanctions or regime change. The Obama administration will have to convince at least some key Iranian leaders, probably including Khamene'i, that it is willing to take "yes" for an answer.

5. In theory, Containment might also benefit from the simultaneous pursuit of regime change. Support to Iranian insurgents, oppositionists, and even coup plotters could keep the regime off balance and focused on defending its internal position, which might distract its attention and resources away from offensive operations against the United States and its allies abroad.

6. At present, Nayif's full brother Sultan is first deputy prime minister and crown prince, but he is in extremely poor health and may well die before the king. Thus it is more likely that Abdullah will be succeeded by Nayif than Sultan, although Nayif is not even assured of becoming crown prince once Sultan dies.

About the Authors

Kenneth Pollack is Director of Research at the Saban Center for Middle East Policy at Brookings. He served as Director for Persian Gulf Affairs and Near East and South Asian Affairs at the National Security Council, Senior Research Professor at National Defense University, and Persian Gulf military analyst at the CIA. His latest book is *A Path out of the Desert: A Grand Strategy for America in the Middle East* (Random House). He is also the author of *The Persian Puzzle: The Conflict between Iran and America* (Random House), *The Threatening Storm: The Case for Invading Iraq* (Random House), and *Arabs at War: Military Effectiveness, 1948–1991* (University of Nebraska Press).

Daniel Byman is a Senior Fellow at the Saban Center for Middle East Policy at Brookings. He is Director of the Center for Peace and Security Studies and an Associate Professor in the School of Foreign Service at Georgetown University. He has held positions with the National Commission on Terrorist Attacks on the United States (the "9/11 Commission"), the Joint 9/11 Inquiry and Senate Intelligence Committees, the RAND Corporation, and the U.S. government. He writes widely on issues related to U.S. national security, terrorism, and the Middle East. His latest books are *Deadly*

Connections: State Sponsorship of Terrorism (Cambridge University Press) and *The Five Front War: The Better Way to Fight Global Jihad* (Wiley).

MARTIN INDYK is the Director of the Saban Center for Middle East Policy at Brookings. He served in several senior positions in the U.S. government, most recently as Ambassador to Israel and before that as Assistant Secretary of State for Near East Affairs and as Special Assistant to President Clinton and Senior Director for Near East and South Asian Affairs in the National Security Council. Before entering government service, he served for eight years as founding Executive Director of the Washington Institute for Near East Policy. He has published widely on U.S. policy in the Middle East and the Arab-Israeli peace process. His most recent book, *Innocent Abroad: An Intimate Account of American Peace Diplomacy in the Middle East* (Simon & Schuster), was published in January 2009.

SUZANNE MALONEY is a Senior Fellow at the Saban Center for Middle East Policy at Brookings. She has worked on the State Department's Policy Planning Staff where she provided policy analysis and recommendations on Iran, Iraq, the Gulf States, and broader Middle East issues. Before joining the government, she was the Middle East adviser at ExxonMobil Corporation and served as project director of the Task Force on U.S.-Iran Relations at the Council on Foreign Relations.

MICHAEL O'HANLON is a Senior Fellow in Foreign Policy Studies at the Brookings Institution. He is also Director of Research for the 21st Century Defense Initiative and Senior Author of the Brookings Iraq Index and holds the Sydney Stein Chair at Brookings. A former defense budget analyst who advised members of Congress on military spending, he specializes in Iraq, North Korea, Afghanistan, homeland security, nuclear strategy, the use of military force, and other defense issues. He is the author of *Budgeting for Hard Power* (Brookings) and *The Science of War* (Princeton University Press), both forthcoming this summer.

BRUCE RIEDEL is Senior Fellow for Political Transitions in the Middle East and South Asia at the Saban Center for Middle East Policy at Brookings. He served as Chairman of President Obama's Strategic Review of U.S. Policy toward Afghanistan and Pakistan. In 2006 he retired after 30 years of service at the CIA including postings overseas in the Middle East and Europe. He was a senior adviser on the region to the last four presidents of the United States as a staff member of the National Security Council at the White House. He was also Deputy Assistant Secretary of Defense for the Near East and South Asia at the Pentagon and a senior adviser at the North Atlantic Treaty Organization in Brussels. Riedel was a member of President Clinton's peace team at the Camp David, Wye River, and Shepherdstown summits. He is the author of *The Search for Al Qaeda: Its Leadership, Ideology, and Future* (Brookings).

Index

Abdullah, King, 130, 211

Abrahamian, Ervand, 164

Afghanistan: and Airstrikes option, 123; deployments to, 87; Engagement option in, 77–78; incremental approach in, 68; and Invasion option, 94; Iran's border with, 89; *mujahideen* in, 159, 162, 165; Northern Alliance in, 159–60; reconstruction efforts in, 91; retaliation against U.S in, 156; special forces units in, 96; U.S. failure in, 88; U.S. invasion of, 29, 85, 100, 193; U.S. military presence in, 60, 97–98, 192; weapons from Iran to, 76

Ahmadinejad, Mahmud: and Ayatollah Khomeini, 4; economic policies of, 71; election of, 18; and Hizballah and Hamas military clashes, 18; ideology of, 72, 73; and international community, 34; and Israel, 126, 184; and Khamene'i, 187; and military strike on Iran, 78, 84–85; and negotiations, 74; perceived strength of, 17

Air Force (U.S.), 95–96

Airstrikes option, 85, 103–24; advantages and disadvantages, 120–24; diplomatic requirements for, 118–20; follow-up for, 116–17; goal of, 105–07; and integrated policy approach, 202–03, 204, 209; and intelligence, 108, 113, 121, 122; legal requirements for, 120; military options for, 117–18; and nuclear program, 103–06, 108–14, 116–23, 205; and Persuasion option, 105; policy overview, 108–17; and provocations, 107–08, 118–19, 124; and regime change, 106, 117; retaliation for, 107, 108, 114–16, 117; scaling down of, 112–13; scaling up of, 113–14; time frame for, 107–08

Ajax Operation, 173

Algiers Accord of *1981*, 70

al-Qa'ida, 2, 63, 184

"Arab exceptionalism," 154

Arab-Israeli peace agreement, 7, 14, 58, 61, 75, 129. *See also* Israel

231